09/2.

Adam Oldjum
Salford
1988

THE UNPRINCIPLED SOCIETY

DAVID MARQUAND is one of Britain's most acute political commentators. He was a Labour Member of Parliament from 1966 to 1977, chief adviser in the European Commission from 1977 to 1978, and is currently Professor of Politics and Contemporary History at the University of Salford. He played a leading part in setting up the Social Democratic Party, and has served on its National Committee since its foundation. He is a Fellow of the Royal Historical Society and joint editor of the *Polticial Quarterly*, and has been joint winner of the George Orwell Memorial Prize. His previous books include *Ramsay MacDonald* and *Parliament for Europe*.

THE
UNPRINCIPLED
SOCIETY

New Demands and Old Politics

DAVID MARQUAND

FONTANA PRESS

First published by Jonathan Cape 1988
First issued in Fontana Press 1988

Copyright © David Marquand 1988

Fontana Press in an imprint of Fontana Paperbacks,
a division of the Collins Publishing Group,
8 Grafton Street, London W1X 3LA

Printed and bound in Great Britain by
William Collins Sons & Co. Ltd, Glasgow

CONTENTS

ACKNOWLEDGMENTS

This book is the product of an intellectual journey which has taken a very different direction from the one I expected it to follow when I started, and which I could not have made at all without help from others. I am grateful to the Joseph Rowntree Social Services Trust and to the Hoover Institution at Stanford University for the financial support which enabled me to take leave of absence at crucial stages of it; and to the University of Salford and my friends and colleagues in the Department of Contemporary History and Politics for making it possible for me to take advantage of their generosity. The Policy Studies Institute provided a stimulating and friendly environment in which to start the enquiry. The Hoover Institution's splendid facilities, warm hospitality and robust coffee-hour talk provided equal stimulus, sometimes of a distinctly challenging kind, at a later stage; the fact that I expect most of my fellow talkers to disagree with my conclusions makes my debt to them, and my appreciation of their tolerance, all the greater.

The references and bibliography convey the bare bones of my intellectual debts, but only the bare bones. I should therefore acknowledge how much I have learned from the writings of Samuel H. Beer, James Bulpitt, Brian Lee Crowley, Ronald Dore, Kenneth Dyson, Andrew Gamble, Ghita Ionescu, David Landes, Anthony Lester, Charles Lindblom, Alasdair Macintyre, John Mackintosh, Keith Middlemas, Mary Midgley, Mancur Olson, Harold Perkin, Michael Piore, Charles Sabel, Andrew Shonfield, Trevor Smith and John Zysman. I also owe an enormous debt of gratitude to Vernon Bogdanor, Nicholas Bosanquet, Ronald Dore, Michael Goldsmith, Ghita Ionescu, Rudolf Klein, Bryan Magee, Robert Maclennan, John Pinder, Robert Skidelsky, Trevor Smith and Michael Stewart for reading and commenting on earlier drafts of the manuscript. The errors and infelicities which remain are, in the time-honoured phrase, my own.

I am grateful to Collins/Fontana Books, the OECD, the Oxford University Press and Princeton University Press for permission to reproduce Tables I to VII; to the staffs of the John Rylands Library, the Hoover Institution Library, the London Library and the libraries of the Policy Studies Institute, Salford University and Stanford University for help and advice; to Pat Bellotti and Joan Crawford for help in typing part of the manuscript; and to Jenny Cottom for skilful, enthusiastic and supportive editing.

My debt to my wife, Judith, is of a different order. For much of the time while I was working on this book she was working on a book of her own, approaching some of the same themes from a broader perspective. Not only has she been a constant source of encouragement and support, every chapter bears the impress of her advice and help. I would be happy to think that she has learned half as much from me as I have learned from her.

David Marquand
Buxworth
July 1987

INTRODUCTION

Doctrine and Reality

'It is a commonplace that the characteristic virtue of
Englishmen is their power of sustained practical activity, and
their characteristic vice a reluctance to test the quality of that
activity by reference to principles. They are incurious as to
theory, take fundamentals for granted, and are more interested
in the state of the roads than in their place on the map.'

R.H. Tawney, *The Acquisitive Society*, 1921.[1]

Tawney wrote at a time of upheaval and confusion,
unprecedented in the lives of most of his readers. The First
World War had destroyed the Hohenzollern, Hapsburg,
Ottoman and Romanov empires; the whole mechanism of
international trade was in disarray; a seismic shift was taking
place in British domestic politics, as Labour replaced the
Liberals as the main anti-Conservative party in the state.

Disruptive though they were, however, the changes of that
time were in some ways less disorientating than those of our
own. Since the long post-war boom petered out in the early
1970s, increasingly interdependent national economies have
been weighed down by a world-wide bias towards deflation,
from which no single medium-sized nation state can escape
alone.[2] Big shifts are taking place in the international division
of labour, as the newly industrialising countries of the Third
World become progressively more competitive in stan-
dardised, mass-production manufacturing. International competition is in any case becoming more intense, as communi-
cations become faster and technology transfer easier. Above
all, the 'information revolution' generated by recent advances
in micro-electronics, fibre optics, software engineering, com-
munications and computer technology has begun to re-shape
industrial society, much as the industrial revolution re-shaped

agrarian society in the late-eighteenth and nineteenth centuries.[3]

Doctrine, however, has lagged behind reality. Between them, these changes have overturned the guiding principles of the post-war economic order. Naturally, they have affected different countries in different ways, but almost all industrial societies have faced acute problems of social, political and, above all, intellectual adjustment. Yet, in spite of prolonged searching, no one has discovered a new set of guiding principles to take the place of the old ones. The governments of the industrial world are adrift, unable to steer with the instruments they used in the past, but uncertain what instruments to use instead.

This book looks at the ways in which the upheavals in the world economy have impinged on Britain and on the doctrines over which her politicians dispute, tries to identify the sources of her adjustment problems and explores the implications for the future. But it goes wider than the familiar story of stubborn unemployment, declining manufacturing and lagging competitiveness.[4] Its object is to identify the social and intellectual factors which lie behind the economic record, and to tease out the lessons for the political economy, not to rehearse it yet again. It is based on the assumption that, even in a time of rapid change, behaviour cannot be studied fruitfully in isolation from beliefs and traditions; that people respond to change as they do partly because they think as they do, and that they think what they do partly because they have been brought up to think it. Thus, it is concerned with values and assumptions as much as with policies and actions, and with the legacy of the past as much as with the present and future.

It starts from three related propositions. The first is that, in Britain, doctrine and reality are unusually far apart. From the mid-1940s until the mid-1970s, most of her political class shared a tacit governing philosophy which might be called 'Keynesian social democracy'.[5] It did not cover the whole spectrum of political opinion, of course; nor did it prevent vigorous party conflict. The two great parties often differed fiercely about the details of policy; on a deeper level, their conceptions of political authority and social justice differed even more. They differed, however, within a structure of generally-accepted values and assumptions. For most of the post-war period, most front-benchers in the House of Commons, most senior civil servants, most of the leaders of the most powerful trade unions, most nationalised industry chairmen, most heads of large private-sector companies and most commentators in the quality press shared a common experience and a broadly similar set of aspirations. They were determined to banish the hardships of the pre-war years, and to make sure that the conflicts which those hardships had caused did not return. Thus, both front benches accepted a three-fold commitment to full employment, to the welfare state and to the coexistence of large public and private sectors in the economy — in short, to the settlement which had brought the inter-war conflicts to an end.

The Keynesian social democrats had many achievements to their credit, but they could not cope with the adjustment problems of the 1970s. The post-war consensus collapsed under the Wilson-Callaghan government of 1974–79, amid mounting inflation, swelling balance of payments deficits, unprecedented currency depreciation, rising unemployment, bitter industrial conflicts and what seemed to many to be ebbing governability. The Conservative leadership turned towards a new version of the classical market liberalism of the nineteenth century. Though the Labour leadership stuck to the tacit 'revisionism' of the 1950s and 1960s, large sections of the rank and file turned towards a more inchoate mixture of neo-Marxism and the 'fundamentalist' socialism of the 1920s and 1930s. But these successor-doctrines are no better suited to the world of the late-1970s and 1980s than was the Keynesian social democracy of the post-war period. At the centre of the neo-liberals' moral universe lies the idealised Market of the rising manufacturers of the first Industrial Revolution. At the centre of the neo-socialists' lies the epic struggle between expropriators and expropriated, whose most compelling hymnodist was Marx. Though their intellectual foundations were laid by men of genius, whose insights can still enrich our understanding, neither doctrine addresses the complex, self-reinforcing network of interests, institutions, assumptions and values from which Britain's adjustment problems stem.

The neo-liberal approach to the problems of change and adjustment to change is, at bottom, simple. Adjustment comes through the 'undistorted' competitive market, for the undistorted market automatically rewards those who have the wit and will to adjust, while punishing those who lack them. Governments should therefore leave it to the market to determine how adjustment is to take place. This market-liberal approach contains an important germ of truth. It is true that, in a competitive market, the adaptable will prosper while the unadaptable go under. It is also true that governments cannot indefinitely shield the unadaptable from the consequences of their failure to adapt. But the economic theories underlying the neo-liberal approach cannot encompass the complexities of the adjustment process. They explain − or purport to explain − how resources are most efficiently allocated at a given level of adaptability. They have nothing to say about the cultural, institutional or political factors which help to make some societies − or some groups within a society − more adaptable than others. Yet these factors hold one of the keys to performance in the market. Adaptation depends on innovation; and innovation is not an autonomous force, working in a cultural vacuum. Innovations are sterile unless they are applied, and the men and women who decide whether and how to apply them are shaped by the inherited values, assumptions and institutions of the societies in which they live. These values, assumptions and institutions are not all equally hospitable to innovation, and market forces alone cannot make them so. In the early-nineteenth century, England and Ireland were both parts of the United Kingdom, and governed according to the same market-liberal principles. England had the most productive and innovative economy in the world. Most of Ireland remained poverty-stricken and backward, and her economy fell further behind England's than it had been before.[6]

There is no reason to think that things are different today. Information technology is at one and the same time capital-saving, labour-saving and energy-saving; to societies which exploit it fully, it offers the prospect of enormous gains in productivity and wealth. But the proviso is crucial. It will be exploited fully only if radical changes take place in the pattern of employment, the level of skill, the organisation of industry and the attitudes of managers and workers. Market forces alone cannot ensure that these changes take place, any more than they could ensure that equivalent changes took place in early-nineteenth-century Kerry or Donegal. Still less can they ensure that the gains will spread evenly or fairly. Technological and economic revolutions of this sort bring benefits, but they also have costs; in a market economy, there can be no assurance that those who bear the costs will get the benefits. The children of the handloom weavers whose livelihoods were destroyed by steam-powered textile manufacturing may well have been better off materially than their grandfathers had been before the factories came. In the meantime, the handloom weavers starved. No one is likely to starve as a result of the information revolution, but in the absence of countervailing policies, the poor, the unskilled, the old and the unemployed may well lose more than they gain.[7]

Much the same applies in the international sphere. Only innovative and adaptable societies can take full advantage of technological revolutions; sluggish and unadaptable ones fall behind. Competitive pressures alone cannot force the latter to mend their ways. Late-nineteenth-century Britain is one of the most striking cases in point. Britain had been the pacemaker of the industrial revolution, but in the long upswing of the 1890s and 1900s she fell behind the new pacemakers, who were better adapted to the advanced technologies of the period than she was. Yet she had stuck to market-liberal principles more faithfully than they had done. As the Prussians realised in the nineteenth century, and the Japanese in the twentieth, market-liberalism is a doctrine for those who are already well-equipped for the market. It is no friend to those who need to equip themselves.

The neo-socialist approach is more confused and, in an odd way, more gingerly. At the core of the socialist tradition is the vision of a stable state, in which men will somehow contrive to enjoy the fruits of economic abundance without suffering the pains of economic change. Perhaps because of this inheritance,

neo-socialists are mostly ill-attuned to the problems of adjustment. Their critique of the existing system is directed to
different issues, and their solutions spring from different
preoccupations. In practice, most of them have been more
anxious to shelter from the changes of the last fifteen years than
to adapt to them. All the same, most depict the crisis of the
1970s and 1980s as a crisis of capitalism. If only by implication,
most conclude that it can be resolved only by socialism.
Socialism need not mean state socialism, of course. Many
neo-socialists look forward to a decentralised economy,
socially owned, but based on some form or other of workers'
control.[8] But, as a technique for achieving economic adjustment, what is sometimes called 'market socialism' suffers from
the same disadvantages as market liberalism. Adjustment
would still come through the market; and market forces would
still be powerless, by themselves, to overcome the social and
cultural handicaps which the weak and unadaptable bring
with them to the market.

As the Soviet Union and eastern Europe show, however,
there is no reason to believe that state socialism is a satisfactory
alternative. The market may not always know better than the
state, but it does sometimes know better. In Charles Lindblom's phrase, state direction is a matter of 'strong thumbs, no
fingers'.[9] No better way has been found to mobilise society's
resources for war or for some great collective purpose like the
building of the pyramids or the exploration of space; significantly, even societies in which state intervention is suspect
have relied on it for activities of this sort. By the same token,
however, no one has discovered a more efficient device than the
market for co-ordinating the multifarious private purposes of a
heterogeneous peacetime society.

The second proposition is more complicated. It is that we can
understand the adjustment problems with which these doctrines cannot cope only against the background of two centuries of British history. The British economy was beginning to
lag behind other advanced economies in investment, growth
and competitiveness by the last quarter of the nineteenth
century. Though the curve of relative decline since then has

been jagged and irregular, the forces behind it have been in operation throughout. Britain has had to face the world-wide upheavals of the last fifteen years from the position of a chronic invalid exposed to a snowstorm. If we want to come to grips with her predicament, and close the gap between doctrine and reality, it is not enough to examine her behaviour during the storm. It is also necessary to explain the long years of invalidity which preceded it.

This is, of course, one of the most complex and controversial questions in modern British history. It would be absurd to offer a simple, unicausal answer. All the same, certain themes emerge fairly clearly from the mass of detail which surrounds it. In at least three related respects, twentieth-century Britain has been the prisoner of her nineteenth-century past. She was the first industrial society in history, the pathfinder to the modern world. The values and assumptions of her élites, the doctrines disseminated in her universities and newspapers, the attitudes and patterns of behaviour of her entrepreneurs and workers were stamped indelibly by this experience. But because she was the pathfinder – because she made the passage to industrialism early, at a time when the technology was still primitive, when the skills it required were still rudimentary and when it could still be managed efficiently by the small-scale, fragmented structures of liberal capitalism – the experience taught the wrong lessons.

Britain had become the pathfinder in the first place because she had broken more decisively than any other country in the world with the values and assumptions of what Harold Perkin has called the 'Old Society'.[10] The notions that property has duties as well as rights, that consumers owe producers a just price while producers owe consumers just dealing, that the community is a whole greater than the sum of its parts, that high and low are bound together by a chain of reciprocal obligation, that man is placed on earth by God to serve greater ends than the satisfaction of his own wants – all these were victims of a cultural revolution, which preceded and made possible the industrial revolution. More thoroughly than any other country in Europe, Britain's culture was permeated with the individualism which her intellectuals codified and justified, and to which the astounding growth of her economy gave the sanction of success. To the British, it seemed almost self-evident that industrialism must be the child of individualism, that 'progress' could come only through setting individuals free to pursue their own interests and to make what use they wished of their own property, without reference to society or interference from the state. But although these attitudes suited the conditions of primitive industrialism, they did not suit the sophisticated, science-based and organised industrialism which slowly superseded it. With suitable modifications, the communal ethic of the 'Old Society' has turned out to be better adapted to the capital- and skill-intensive industrialism of the twentieth century than the individualistic ethic of the industrial revolution; and it is in societies where something of the old ethic survived the transition to modernity that sophisticated industrialism has flourished most. Having made one cultural revolution in the seventeenth and eighteenth centuries, however, Britain has been unable to make another in the twentieth. In the age of the industrial laboratory, the chemical plant, and later of the computer, she stuck to the mental furniture of the age of steam.

Much of that furniture was arranged around her extraordinary role in the outside world. Not only was she the first industrial society in history, she was also the first world power in history, the guarantor as well as the midwife of the world-wide trading system which the guns of the Royal Navy had made possible. But she was a world power of a very odd kind. In Andrew Gamble's phrase, she was the 'World Island':[11] the centre of an informal network of trading relationships and capital movements, of which her formal empire was merely a part. This network was permeated with the same individualism that permeated her economy. It was not managed from London, in the interests of the imperial state. In an important sense, it was not managed at all. It depended on the spontaneous, unplanned activities of private entrepreneurs and investors, looking for profit wherever they could find it. They were not agents of some overarching imperial mission; they pursued their own private interests, not the interests of the empire in general or of the mother country in particular. Here too, what had been an asset in the days of Britain's industrial supremacy became a handicap as others overtook her. British entrepreneurs failed to compete with the Germans and Americans in the new technologies of the late-nineteenth and early-twentieth centuries because, in the short term, they could survive and prosper by selling more of their existing products in their traditional markets in Latin America and the colonies. Meanwhile, capital which might have been invested in modernising British industry flowed abroad instead. The same theme sounded repeatedly between the wars and after 1945. This external network, moreover, created a powerful nexus of internal interests with a stake in its survival. Partly because of this, successive governments gave higher priority to the world role, financial or military, than to the home economy. Examples include the return to the gold standard in 1925, the high expenditure on overseas military bases in the 1950s and 1960s and the sacrifice of the National Plan to the $2.80 sterling parity in 1966. And although the long post-script to world power ended with Britain's belated entry into the European Community in the early 1970s, it was plain that her political class found it exceptionally hard to adjust to membership.

The legacy of the nineteenth century does not end there. One reason why British politicians and officials cannot easily adapt to EEC membership is that the 'Westminster Model' of parliamentary government rests on the doctrine – heavily influenced by the utilitarian individualism of Jeremy Bentham and his followers who thought that sovereignty was inherently unlimited and who dismissed the notion of fundamental rights as 'nonsense on stilts'[12] – that the Crown-in-Parliament must be absolutely and inalienably sovereign. An obvious corollary is that British governments cannot share power with other tiers of government, sub-national or supra-national. In its day, the 'Westminster Model' was a remarkable example of successful adaptation. The accommodations and concessions which gave birth to it made possible Britain's peaceful transition to democracy, and the peaceful incorporation of the Labour Movement into the political order. Here too, however, assumptions born of successful adaptation in the past impede adaptation to more recent changes. Not only do we live in an interdependent world, in which absolute national sovereignty is an illusion and transnational power sharing inevitable, we also live in an interdependent society, dense with organised and unorganised groups, whose co-operation in the productive process is essential to the smooth running of the economy. In practice, governments have either to break the power of these groups – a costly and uncertain business, itself inimical to the health of the economy – or to share power with them. Thus, in fact even if not in form, they too have ended the Westminster monopoly of sovereignty. Buttressing the doctrine of absolute parliamentary supremacy, moreover, are the twin assumptions that the courts should not limit the freedom of action of the sovereign Parliament, and that there is in any case no need to limit it since informal restraints and political processes provide adequate safeguards against the abuse of power. Yet, in an increasingly diverse society, in which deference to customary authority is waning, these assumptions have become recipes for mistrust and alienation.

Half a century of social change has, in short, invalidated the doctrines which are supposed to underpin the political order. This, in turn, has undermined public confidence in its equity, and made it more difficult for governments to mobilise consent for the changes without which economic adjustment is impossible.

This leads on to the third proposition: that Britain's adjustment problems have as much to do with politics as with economics, and with tacit political understandings as with political institutions. If we reject market liberalism and state socialism, we are left, in practice, with some variant or other of the mixed economy – of an economy in which resources are largely allocated through the market, but in which public power intervenes on a significant scale to supplement, constrain, manipulate, or direct market forces for public ends. That sentence, however, raises as many questions as it answers. Public intervention implies a public purpose: otherwise, those who do the intervening cannot know what they are trying to achieve. But in a political culture shaped by the assumption that society is made up of separate, atomistic individuals, pursuing only their own private purposes, the notion of a public purpose which is more than the sum of private purposes is apt to seem dangerous, or meaningless, or both.

The result is an intellectual and moral vacuum at the heart of the political economy. Since the war, at the latest, Britain has had a substantial public sector and a large capacity for public intervention. But because the notion of a public purpose is alien to it, her political class has had no philosophy of public intervention or of what might be called the public realm. There are no agreed criteria for determining the ends which public intervention is supposed to serve, and no agreed procedures for deciding what the criteria should be; and the suggestion that there should be seems quaint, if not utopian. So does the suggestion that the public sector should be seen as the instrument of a public good, which the members of the public have agreed in common, and to the pursuit of which they therefore have a common obligation. Yet, without such a philosophy, it is hard to see how a political economy which depends on public intervention can command the support which it needs to function properly. In its absence, the public sector is apt to become a battleground for warring private interests, while its 'outputs' appear increasingly arbitrary and capricious. In good times, no obvious damage need result. Hard choices can be avoided, and predatory interests bought off. In default of active support, the system can make do with passive acquiescence. But in bad times, when passive acquiescence is no longer enough and when all decisions hurt, arbitrary ones are likely to undermine support for the system, at the very point when it is most needed. It would be wrong to suggest that this is a complete summary of the recent history of Britain's political economy, but few would deny that it summarises a good deal of it.

This has obvious implications for the problems we have been discussing. The questions of how to halt the decline in Britain's international competitiveness, of how to devise a satisfactory form of transnational power sharing and of how to respond to the growth of group power and the decay of traditional authority all pose hard choices. Except in the shortest of short terms, the answers cannot be imposed successfully from the top down. Yet none of the doctrines around which post-war British politics have revolved offers anything other than imposed answers, for none of them provides the moral basis for the sense of community and mutual obligation which would make it possible to look for answers in a different way.

By the same token, however, solitary speculation is unlikely to produce a satisfactory alternative. The notion that social problems can be solved by a Wise Man's cerebrations is only slightly less pernicious than the notion that salvation lies in a Great Man's will. The hope that, if only a new Marx or a new Keynes or a new Freud arose among us he would be able to tell us what to do, rests on a dangerous misunderstanding of the relationship between social thought and social change. Usable doctrines do not spring, fully armed, from a theorist's brow. They have to be hammered out in the give and take of a debate, provoked and shaped by the lived experience of particular societies at particular times. Because of this, the debate is unlikely to yield worthwhile results if it takes place in a historical vacuum. Men are made by their histories, and start their journeys to the future from the point where past history has left them. Ahistorical theorising, based on the implicit assumption that the awesome complexity of real-world behaviour can be reduced to simplified models, which apply in all societies at all times, may sometimes yield useful insights into the human condition, but it is a perilous guide to action. One reason why so many discussions of Britain's current political and economic problems lead nowhere is that they are based on over-simplified interpretations of the recent past. Like a beach whose old contours have been partially – but only partially – reshaped by a storm at sea, the political landscape of today still bears the double impress, first of the long hegemony of post-war Keynesian social democracy and secondly of the crises which destroyed it. We cannot hope to pick our way across it unless we understand the nature and origins of those crises and of the governing philosophy which failed to cope with them.

This book is intended as a contribution to the search for a

new governing philosophy which has been the dominant theme in British politics since the post-war consensus broke down. Its object is to help clear the ground of the obstacles which have so far held up the search and, if possible, to point towards a more promising direction. Rather than proposing a new doctrine, it sketches out an approach through which a new doctrine might be sought. Part One shows why such an approach is necessary and why the doctrines we have discussed are all, in different ways, unsatisfactory. In Chapter 1 I examine the origins, assumptions and implications of the Keynesian social democracy of the post-war period, and try to expose its uncertainties and ambiguities. Against that background, the second chapter investigates its failure to come to grips with the political and economic crises of the 1970s, and tries to relate that failure to the weaknesses revealed in Chapter 1. Chapter 3 explores the rival alternatives offered by the neo-liberals and neo-socialists, and attempts to show that, despite the claims made on their behalf, neither has the intellectual or moral resources to solve the problems which undermined the Keynesian social-democratic consensus.

In Part Two I look at the realities with which these doctrines could not cope and which any other doctrine would have to address. Chapter 4 assesses the lessons which more successful mixed economies elsewhere in the industrial world may have for the British version, and argues that the chief lesson is that Britain has failed to evolve an entrepreneurial or developmental state. In different ways, chapters 5, 6 and 7 try to investigate the reasons for this failure. Chapter 5 examines the long relative decline of the British economy, and investigates the failures of successive attempts to halt it. Chapter 6 tries to account for these failures, and argues that their roots are to be found in the 'possessive individualism' of early capitalism. Chapter 7 examines the role of the 'Westminster Model' in frustrating the evolution of a developmental state, and the impact of its growing disarray.

Part Three tries to pull the threads together and, against the background of the analysis in Part Two, suggests an approach through which solutions might be sought.

Part One

DOCTRINES

1

Keynesian Social Democracy

'The Government accept as one of their primary aims and responsibilities the maintenance of a high and stable level of employment after the war.'

White paper, *Employment Policy*, 1944.[1]

'[F]or as far ahead as we can see, it is both possible and desirable to find a solution of our economic difficulties in a mixed system which combines State ownership, regulation or control of certain aspects of economic activity with the drive and initiative of private enterprise . . . '

Harold Macmillan, 1938.[2]

'It is clear to the serious student of modern politics that a mixed economy is what most people of the West would prefer . . . It is neither prudent, nor does it accord with our conception of the future, that all forms of private property should live under perpetual threat.'

Aneurin Bevan, 1952.[3]

In Britain, even more than in most other western countries, the changes now sweeping through the world economy have been reflected in confusion and acrimony in domestic politics. The Keynesian social-democratic consensus of the post-war period has plainly broken down, but no new consensus has replaced it. Though political and economic leaders have groped for new approaches, their gropings have mostly over-simplified recent history and produced more heat than light. The search for a new governing philosophy should begin with an appraisal of the old one: debate about the future is likely to be productive only if it is grounded in understanding of the past.

The consensus prevailed for about thirty years. The dating is bound to be imprecise. If only for reasons of symbolic resonance, however, June 1944, when the wartime coalition published its famous white paper committing its post-war successors to maintain high employment, is a good approximate starting date. October 1976, when James Callaghan told a bemused Labour Party conference that attempts to increase employment by cutting taxes and increasing public spending only worked 'by injecting a bigger dose of inflation into the system', and so did more harm than good,[4] makes an equally resonant concluding one. Of course, no one ever called himself a Keynesian social democrat. There was no self-conscious tradition of Keynesian social democracy with which its adherents could identify, no Keynesian social-democratic myth to stimulate their loyalty. The term is used here as shorthand for a set of commitments, assumptions and expectations, transcending party conflicts and shared by the great majority of the country's political and economic leaders, which provided the framework within which policy decisions were made. But these commitments, assumptions and expectations did not spring from an explicit set of teachings, consciously held. Conservative Keynesian social democrats thought of themselves as Conservatives, belonged to a self-conscious Conservative tradition and appealed to the myths and symbols of that tradition. Labour ones thought of themselves as socialists or as members of the Labour Movement, and appealed to a socialist or Labour tradition. The two big parties had different aims and different values as well as different constituencies; the conflicts between them were about principle as well as about power, place and social interest.

The fact remains that, when they were in government at any rate, their leaders approached the management of the economy and the operation of the social services in a remarkably similar fashion. Though their differences of interest and belief were real and important, what stands out in retrospect is the extent to which their policies overlapped in practice. Keynesian social democracy may be defined as the philosophy of the overlap. Three of its features deserve attention at this stage in the argument. On the most obvious level, it was a philosophy of the mixed economy: the product of a long search for instruments through which governments could intervene in the market without destroying it, and mitigate the hardships of unregulated capitalism without sacrificing consumer choice or entrepreneurial initiative. On a deeper level, it was also a philosophy of the middle way. However strongly its adherents disagreed on other matters, they agreed in repudiating the dichotomies of market versus state; capital versus labour; private enterprise versus public ownership; personal freedom versus social justice. Central to it was the belief that capitalism and socialism were not inherently opposed: that it was possible to combine elements of both in a synthesis more benign than either. Allied to that was the belief that capitalism had, in any case, changed; that the economic system described in the old textbooks of classical political economy no longer existed in the real world; and that it would be necessary to diverge still further from the classical model if the new system were to work.

The third feature was less obvious and more paradoxical. Keynesian social democracy took a new road in economics, but not in politics or ethics. Its adherents rejected the classical market liberalism of the nineteenth century, but they never quite broke with the utilitarian conception of man and society which lay behind it. The full implications will not become clear until a later stage in the argument, but one or two need mentioning at the outset. For utilitarians, the sovereign individual − voter or consumer − chooses his own purposes; and the choosing self is, so to speak, impermeable.[5] All freely-chosen purposes are, in principle, morally equal; and the choice of purpose is a private act, with which politics and government have nothing to do. These assumptions are so deeply embedded in our culture that it is difficult, even now, to shake oneself free of them; and it is not surprising that the Keynesian social democrats of forty years ago mostly took them for granted. Yet they are incompatible with the kind of interventionism which Keynesian social democracy entailed. For the interventionist state has, by definition, to change behaviour; if it did not, it would not need to intervene. In order to change behaviour, it has to influence choices and purposes. It can influence them through a mixture of punishments and rewards − perhaps indirectly, by manipulating the punishments and rewards of the market, perhaps directly by regulation and prohibition. Or it can influence them through persuasion. And in order to persuade, it has to appeal to a civic morality of some kind, on the basis of which some choices and purposes rank higher in the moral scale than others.

Because the Keynesian social democrats were imprisoned in the utilitarian intellectual framework inherited from their nineteenth-century ancestors, they could not develop such a morality. Some of them sensed that an active state needed active citizens, willing to accept their share of the obligations it had assumed on their behalf, but they could not articulate that notion convincingly, or make it resonate in the society around them. Only rewards and punishments were left. Thus, Keynesian social democracy became, for most of the time, a technocratic philosophy rather than a political one: a philosophy of social engineering, rather than of persuasion, negotiation and debate. In Peter Clarke's terminology, its view of government, and of the relationship between government and governed, was 'mechanical', not 'moral', emphasising outward changes of structure and law rather than inner changes of value and belief.[6] By the same token, its adherents were more concerned with the role of the state than with its character, and gave little thought to its relationship with the society in which they wanted it to intervene. In practice, they took the political institutions they had inherited from the nineteenth century for granted, hoping to use them for different ends. Only towards the close of their ascendancy did it occur to them that different ends might require different means.

These attitudes and beliefs bridged the party divide, but it would be wrong to see them as alien growths, appearing from nowhere and imposed on unwilling party politicians by force of circumstance. If we are to understand them — above all, if we are to understand the tacit assumptions on which they were based, and which helped to determine how those who held them behaved in practice — we must look at their sources in the social and intellectual history of the period before the Keynesian social-democratic era. They were, of course, rooted in the main party traditions. Their Conservative adherents could trace them back to Burke and Disraeli, with their emphasis on

the values of community, order and security, and their insistence on the obligations of society's natural leaders to the led.
Liberals, whether with a big or a small 'l', looked back to the
New Liberals of the turn of the century, who had stood classical
nineteenth-century liberalism on its head, justifying state-
provided welfare services and state intervention in the economy
in the name of a new conception of social liberalism. Labour
attitudes were heavily influenced by the legacy of the early
Fabians, with their trust in the capacity and benevolence of the
democratic state and their commitment to slow, piecemeal
change through the ballot box. More important than the party
origins of Keynesian social democracy, however, are its origins
in the academic and political controversies of the inter-war
years, and in the experiences of the wartime coalition.

It was an amalgam of four strands of thought and experience
above all. The most obvious of these was the Keynesian
revolution in economic thought. Keynesianism is a doctrine of
market failure. In the Keynesian system, market forces do not
necessarily produce full employment. On the contrary, there is
an inherent propensity for supply and demand to balance at
something less than full employment. But the failure ends
there. Where the classical economists taught that supply calls
forth demand, Keynes held that demand calls forth supply.
Government's role is therefore confined to the management of
demand. For Keynes, as much as for his classical predecessors,
government intervention in the supply side of the economy was
pointless, or damaging or both. When only 9,000,000 men had
jobs out of 10,000,000 willing and able to work, he wrote in *The
General Theory*: 'there is no evidence that the labour of these
9,000,000 men is misdirected. The complaint against the
present system is not that these 9,000,000 men ought to be
employed on different tasks, but that tasks should be available
for the remaining 1,000,000'. Government intervention was
needed only to establish 'an aggregate volume of output
corresponding to full employment'; that done:

> the classical theory comes into its own again from this point
> onwards. If we suppose the volume of output to be given, *i.e.*
> to be determined by forces outside the classical scheme of

thought, then there is no objection to be raised against the classical analysis of the manner in which private self-interest will determine what in particular is produced, in what proportions the factors of production will be combined to produce it, and how the value of the final product will be distributed between them.[7]

The Keynesian Revolution was, in short, to be a limited revolution: a theoretical 1688, not a 1917. A neat, surgical operation would remove the one fatal flaw from the classical system, and then things would go on as before. Yet there was a gap in the Keynesian synthesis. Keynes did not fully appreciate the enormity of his own achievement, or anticipate its consequences. In his system, the state was to be responsible — in a sense which had never been true before — for the level of demand, and therefore for the level of employment; instead of being the unintended outcome of a myriad disaggregated individual decisions, the unemployment figures would be the products of conscious political choice, and therefore subject to political scrutiny and debate. Keynes knew this, of course, but he did not reckon with its implications. Though the Keynesian state was to have highly sensitive new responsibilities, he had no theory of the state and appears to have seen no need for one. He assumed that, demand management apart, the Keynesian state would behave as the pre-Keynesian state had behaved. The possibility that it could not discharge these new responsibilities successfully without a change in its character — that they would generate new expectations and demands, which could be accommodated and reconciled only by a new kind of state, engaging the public in a process of consultation, negotiation and mutual education — does not seem to have occurred to him. If it had, he would almost certainly have found it abhorrent. As his biographer has pointed out, his approach to government was quintessentially mandarin.[8] He took it for granted that the state would exercise the new powers which his system conferred upon it in the public interest; one reason was that he also took it for granted that the public interest would be defined, in practice, by an enlightened technocracy, immune from public pressure. Just as, in the classical system, outcomes emerge from the automatic operations of the market rather than from the messy processes of persuasion and debate, so, in the Keynesian system, they were to be determined by aseptic technocratic expertise rather than by the crudities of politics.

This leads on to a further gap. As well as vastly extending the role of the state, the Keynesian revolution vastly increased the bargaining power of organised labour. Keynesians knew this too, but they knew it as practical men and women, not as Keynesian economists. For them, the changes in the balance of industrial power which full employment was bound to bring in its train, and the effect of those changes on the expectations and demands of wage earners were, in economists' language, 'exogenous' – they impinged on the system from outside; they were not part of it. Keynesian policy makers were quick to see a connection between full employment and wage restraint. The 1944 white paper warned that wage and price stability was 'a condition vital to the success of employment policy', and that 'the joint efforts of the Government, employers and organised labour' would be necessary to achieve it.[9] In his *Full Employment in a Free Society*, the product of an unofficial enquiry in which he was decisively influenced by a group of younger, largely Keynesian, economists, William Beveridge conceded that a combination of full employment and 'sectional wage bargaining' might produce an inflationary spiral, thereby undermining the very policy of full employment which had made it possible.[10] But although plenty of Keynesians saw these connections, Keynesianism, as a doctrine, had – and logically could have – nothing to say about them.

In principle, at any rate, it could cope with demand inflation: the state could take excessive demand out of the economy just as it could pump needed demand into it. About cost inflation it was bound to be silent. Since there was no Keynesian theory of the state, there could be no Keynesian theory of the relationship between the state and the wage bargainers whose activities might generate cost inflation. Still less could there be a Keynesian theory of distributional conflict, explaining why wage bargainers might behave in an inflationary way or suggesting how to modify the attitudes and values which led them to do so. After all, part of Keynes's object was to save the market economy and the liberal polity. And in a market economy, distributional questions are settled by the market; while in a liberal polity, attitudes and values are freely chosen by the sovereign individual.

Keynes's legacy to the post-war Keynesian social democrats is familiar and unmistakable. The legacy of the second strand — best described as the planning or mixed economy strand — is less obvious, but in some ways even more important. It had similar origins and similar gaps, but a different emphasis. On the surface, Britain's inter-war history was one of ideological polarisation and class conflict. On a deeper level, it was a history of repeated attempts, on both sides of industry and in all political parties, to bridge the ideological and class divides. Business leaders tried to promote 'rationalisation' in industry, sometimes with help from the Bank of England and even from the government. Employers and trade unionists tried to hammer out common responses to the declining competitiveness of the old export trades.[11] Young Conservative politicians campaigned for state intervention in the economy. Young Labour intellectuals tried to reconcile socialist planning with the price mechanism. Where Keynes concentrated on demand, most of these attempts focused at least as strongly — sometimes, much more strongly — on supply. Though they differed a great deal in other ways, almost all of them sprang from the assumption that the invisible hand of competitive capitalism no longer functioned as it was supposed to function: that, whatever may have been the case in the past, it was no longer true that resources were best allocated by market forces alone. Almost all of them arrived at the conclusion that a visible hand,[12] perhaps belonging to the state, perhaps to the large firm or to a group of large firms, perhaps to a new kind of authority, combining public and private power, should supplement the invisible one.

The most impressive attempt of this sort came from the Liberal Party, in the shape of the famous Yellow Book of 1928. Arguing that 'the supposed choice between Individualism and Socialism is largely an obsolete issue', its authors advocated a National Investment Board; an Economic General Staff; a

Council of Industry with members drawn from government, the unions and the employers; profit sharing and wider share ownership; works councils in all undertakings with more than fifty employees; and a degree of public ownership.[13] In similar vein, the Next Five Years Group, a cross-party alliance formed in the mid-1930s, sought to transcend the 'historic controversy' between 'a wholly competitive capitalistic system and one of State ownership, regulation and control' and called for the socialisation of transport, electricity supply, arms manufacture and some forms of insurance as elements in the 'mixed system' of the future.[14]

Thoughtful and iconoclastic members of the two big parties also groped for new approaches. The results differed sharply from party to party, but the similarities were more significant for the future than the differences. A few examples must suffice. In *Industry and the State*, published as far back as 1927, four young Conservative MPs, Oliver Stanley, Robert Boothby, Harold Macmillan and John de V. Loder pointed approvingly to 'a great world movement away from unfettered competition' and argued for more government intervention to promote industrial amalgamation and improve industrial relations.[15] In 1931, Lord Eustace Percy called for a new deliberative body, representing local government, trade and industrial associations, farmers and trade unionists, to 'mobilize the industrial power of the nation'.[16] In *The Middle Way*, published at the end of the decade, Harold Macmillan advocated public ownership of the mines, electricity and the Bank of England; state control of transport and foreign trade; and an elaborate scheme of national and sectoral planning, supervised by a National Economic Council, chaired by a Minister of Economics and representing the employers and trade unions as well as the government, the proposed foreign trade organisation and the Bank of England.[17]

Though they set off from a different starting point, some of the 'New' Fabian intellectuals who tried to devise an economic strategy for the pre-war Labour Party reached a similar destination. In *The Socialist Case*, published in 1937, Douglas Jay advocated a mixture of Keynesian demand management, income redistribution and the nationalisation of natural monopolies, actual monopolies and industries where imperfect competition led to inefficiency.[18] In *The Politics of Democratic Socialism*, three years later, Evan Durbin set out a subtle and complicated case for combining planning with the price mechanism. Thanks to the rise of the trade unions, the expansion of the social services, progressive taxation and depression-induced regulation of output in hard-hit sectors of the economy, Durbin argued, competitive capitalism could no longer function properly. But there was no point in trying to sweep away the restrictions which frustrated it; they were the products of popular pressures, inevitable in a democracy. Only planning could correct the failures of the monopoly-ridden capitalism which had succeeded the competitive capitalism of the past; and planning required a Supreme Economic Authority in charge of an extensive public sector. But the private sector would still be much bigger than the public; and planning would operate through market pricing.[19] Durbin and Jay were egalitarian socialists; their ideal societies would have been very different from Harold Macmillan's. Despite their somewhat larger public sectors, however, the political economies depicted in *The Socialist Case* and *The Politics of Democratic Socialism* were much closer to that of *The Middle Way* than to the command economy favoured by Jay's and Durbin's contemporaries on the left wing of their own party.

There was a gap in the planning strand as well. In the Keynesian system, the state played a limited role, although a crucial one. Treasury mandarins were to manipulate the controls on the economic dashboard; they were not expected to lift the bonnet and dirty their hands in the engine. The planners' state was much more grubby, intruding into hosts of detailed decisions which had previously been left to private individuals. Like Keynes, however, most of the politicians and intellectuals who contributed to the planning strand lacked a theory of the state, or of the relationship between the state and the economic agents in whose activities they thought it should intervene. They did not explore the effects on the state of the new responsibilities which they proposed to give it: the interventionist state of the future was merely the non-interventionist state of the past, writ large. In the 1920s, a lively debate took place in the Labour Movement about the way in which the polity and the economy would relate to each other in a socialist society. Sidney and Beatrice Webb advocated a 'Social Parliament' to look after the economy, alongside the familiar political parliament. G.D.H. Cole and the Guild Socialists wanted a system of functional representation to replace political representation altogether.[20] But this debate found only muted echoes in the other parties, and in any case it soon petered out.

Many saw that an interventionist state would have to be better co-ordinated and more knowledgeable than the existing one; the notion of an 'Economic General Staff' was one of the commonplaces of the case for planning. Few paid much attention to the harder questions of how an interventionist state would be held to account, of how the planners would win consent for their plans and make sure that they were implemented on the ground, or of who should be represented in the planning process and in what way. Like the Fabian pioneers at the turn of the century, the New Fabian interventionists of the 1930s were concerned with the use of state power, not with its nature. Despite notable exceptions, most of them shared the early Fabians' faith in the expert, and the early Fabians' distrust of the voluntarist, decentralist strand in British socialism. For them, as for their political ancestors thirty years before, socialism was state socialism, to be managed by a disinterested élite of public servants. Economic planning was a matter for planners, acting in the interests of the consuming public; consent, representation, implementation and accountability presented no problems.

To be sure, Liberal and Conservative interventionists showed more interest in these matters. The Liberal Yellow Book with its 'Council of Industry', Lord Eustace Percy with his additional deliberative assembly, Harold Macmillan with his 'National Economic Council' — by implication, at any rate, all these linked new forms of state intervention in the economy with new forms of functional representation in the polity. Here too, however, what was not said was as significant for the future as what was said. Though the Liberal and Conservative interventionists were institutionally more innovative than their

Labour contemporaries, they left their proposed institutional innovations in a limbo of good intentions. They did not ask how new forms of functional representation would affect old forms of territorial representation or how the functional structures they advocated would relate to the existing structures of Parliament, Cabinet and Party. Still less did they tackle the really intractable questions of where power and authority would lie, of how conflicts would be resolved or of how consent would be mobilised. They had erected a few tantalising signposts to a new kind of political economy. They had not mapped out the path.

The third strand is more difficult to pin down. It is most easily identified as the welfare strand, or perhaps as the strand of social rights. Its most spectacular documentary monument was the 1942 Beveridge Report; its most impressive legislative achievement, the creation of the National Health Service. Beveridge fired the imaginations of the wartime public with the promise of a single, universal system of state social insurance, buttressing a free national health service, family allowances and a full employment policy – each playing its part in a concerted attack on the 'five giants' of Want, Disease, Idleness, Ignorance and Squalor. Now the Beveridge Report did not come from a clear sky. Beveridge saw himself as a revolutionary, but he recognised that he was proposing a peculiarly British revolution. He fired imaginations because he worked with the grain of what was already there: because he drew out the underlying logic of the existing patchwork of partial systems, and built a universal system upon it.[21] That patchwork was the product of a long process of piecemeal evolution, beginning in the mid-nineteenth-century heyday of *laissez-faire*, through which an inexplicit and imprecise ethic of communal responsibility for common needs had slowly grown up alongside the individualistic ethic of market liberalism. Beveridge achieved what he did because he grasped the implications of this communal ethic more fully than anyone had done before, and pushed it further. Perhaps inevitably, the other side of the coin was that he did not clarify its ambiguities or remove the inconsistencies between it and the individualistic ethic with which it uneasily co-habited.

Like Keynes, Beveridge wanted to reconcile interventionism with liberalism. Like Keynes, he did not see that the kind of interventionism he advocated was incompatible with the liberal view of man and society to which he clung. The Beveridge Revolution had more to do with status and mutual respect than with distribution. It was not designed to redistribute income from rich to poor, but from one point in the individual's life cycle to another. The flat-rate contributions which were fundamental to the insurance system were regressive, not progressive. It is possible that the National Health Service brought more benefits to the middle class, which had not been eligible for free treatment before, than to the working class, which had. As T.H. Marshall pointed out, what made the Revolution revolutionary was its implicit insistence – against the market-liberal teaching that the state and civil society belong in different compartments – that citizenship entails equal social rights, as well as equal legal and political ones. It had produced, Marshall wrote, 'a general enrichment of the concrete substance of civilised life . . . Equalisation is not so much between classes as between individuals within a population *which is now treated for this purpose as though it were one class*'.[22] Marshall's formulation caught the aspirations embodied in the welfare strand better than any other. The rich man and the poor man would collect the same pensions from the same post-office counter, and sit next to each other in the same doctor's waiting room. They would be no less rich or poor for doing so, but they would be that much more full citizens of one community.

Unfortunately, Beveridge and his followers insisted on trying to square the communal notion of social citizenship with individualistic values which ran counter to it. As Marshall implied, the keystone of the system was entitlement. The sick were entitled to medical care; the elderly to old age pensions; mothers to family allowances; the unemployed to unemployment benefits. That was one of the main reasons for the scheme's extraordinary popularity, for it was through entitlement that it conferred equality of status. The trouble was that its entitlements had different bases, embodying conflicting views of how the social rights of citizenship arose. The right to medical care sprang from citizenship pure and simple; all were eligible for it, and it was paid for out of general taxation. The same was true of family allowances. Elsewhere in the system, however, entitlement rested on the fiction of social insurance, inherited from the original Lloyd George legislation of 1911. Benefits were to be paid out to those who had previously paid in contributions. Beveridgean doctrine saw this as the moral lynch-pin of the social security system, protecting the values of thrift and self-respect. It was because the benefits had been earned in this way that they were entitlements, rather than charitable 'doles'; and it was because they were entitlements that they avoided the indignities which 'doles' brought with them. So far as social security benefits were concerned, in other words, citizenship was not a sufficient basis for entitlement after all: the basis was individualistic, not communal. Yet in the case of the Health Service, it was the other way round.

These inconsistencies might not have mattered if the scheme had worked as its authors expected. Unfortunately, it did not; and as A.W. Dilnot, J.A. Kay and C.N. Morris have argued, it almost certainly could not have done.[23] As we have seen, a necessary corollary of the insurance principle was that income would be redistributed from one point in the life cycle to another, rather than from rich to poor. Yet the system was also supposed, in Beveridge's language, to slay the giant of Want. These two objectives could be reconciled only on the assumptions that the system's authors had identified the causes of Want, knew when in the life cycle they would come into effect, and had ensured that it was then that the benefits would be payable. Just as Keynes's system rested on the expertise of the Treasury mandarinate, in short, Beveridge's rested on the expertise of the social investigator. But if his confidence turned out to be misplaced, if the assumptions underlying the system turned out to be invalid, the whole edifice would come crashing down. Beneficiaries who had paid in their contributions, and who had earned their benefits by doing so, might find themselves in poverty after all. The only way to relieve them would be to pay out additional benefits, which had not been earned by any contribution – 'doles' in a new guise. In the event, that is precisely what happened. The giant of Want turned out to be far too protean a creature for Beveridge's net to catch. 'Doles' duly reappeared, only faintly disguised; and the promise of equal citizenship was denied by the very mechanism which had been designed to make it a reality.

The first three strands were held together by the fourth, the strand of wartime experience. It had a double significance. In the first place, the Keynesian strand, the planning strand and the welfare strand all took it for granted that where the market had failed, the state would succeed. They also took it for granted that, to echo the title of one of the best popular statements of the case for intervention, there would be 'freedom under planning'.[24] Between the wars, these were acts of faith. During the war, faith was justified by works. The British state was, by any reckoning, remarkably successful, both by the standards of its own past, and by the standards of the other belligerents. It was successful, moreover, not only in raising armies and waging war, but in the gentler activities which Keynesians, planners and social reformers wanted it to undertake in peace.

Ministers and civil servants turned out to be surprisingly good at managing the economy. No one who looked at the contrast between the fully-employed, highly-mobilised command economy of war and the waste and misery of peacetime unemployment could deny that, in some circumstances, state intervention might be considerably more efficient than the higgle of the market. Successful economic management, moreover, went hand in hand with a highly egalitarian social policy. More important still, the economically competent and socially egalitarian wartime state did not trample on the individual. There were abuses, of course. Civil liberties suffered. But considering that the country was fighting for its life, they did not suffer much. F.A. Hayek's famous 1944 polemic, *The Road to Serfdom*,[25] arguing that economic planning was inherently incompatible with political freedom, could hardly have appeared at a less auspicious time for the case it set out. Economic planning was plainly in operation, and political freedom was plainly intact. No doubt, it was spurious to argue that because planning and state control had been necessary to win the war, they would be equally necessary to win the peace, and that because wartime planning had not infringed freedom, peacetime planning would not infringe it either. A war in which virtually the whole adult population had agreed on the central objective of military victory, and in which all other considerations were subordinate to that objective, had few lessons for the peacetime government of a complex society, which has to trade off divergent objectives against each other. The fact remains that these arguments did much to water the soil in which post-war Keynesian social democracy took root.

That is only part of the story, and not the most important part. As we have seen, the other three strands which contributed to post-war Keynesian social democracy — the Keynesian strand, the planning strand and the welfare strand — were all, in varying ways, technocratic. All assumed that expert and disinterested public servants could manage the economy and society from above; none reckoned with the possibility that an interventionist state might need a different kind of relationship with the citizen, based on a different conception of man and of the relationship between man and society. The wartime strand was a different matter. On the level of central decision making, it is true, the wartime political economy was also highly technocratic. But, on a deeper and more subtle level, technocratic decision making was supported and legitimised by a sense of community and mutual obligation, partly contrived by insistent propaganda on the part of the decision makers, but partly derived from shared experiences and feelings. To use Peter Clarke's terminology again, the wartime state was 'moral' as well as 'mechanical'. It relied on persuasion as well as on authority; and it was able to persuade successfully because wartime patriotism provided a substitute for the civic morality which was lacking in peace.

Part of the reason lay in a more complex difference between the wartime strand and the other strands. Keynes, Beveridge and the inter-war planners were all, in an odd way, distributionally neutral. For Keynes, distribution was a matter for the market. Beveridge had insisted that poverty could be eradicated without redistribution from one section of the community to another. Though socialist planners like Jay and Durbin wanted a more equal distribution of income, they did not link their distributional aims to their economic ones. Egalitarianism was an optional extra for the morally enlightened, not a prerequisite of successful economic management. For all practical purposes, Conservative and Liberal planners had shown no interest in distribution at all. Here too the wartime strand ventured into territory which the others had left alone. Albeit in a confused, unsystematic and sometimes inconsistent way, the wartime coalition saw that a civic morality must be, in part, a distributive morality: that a sense of community and mutual obligation depends, among other things, on a sense of fair shares.[26] Of course, it is dangerous to romanticise. Selfishness, greed and snobbery were doubtless as plentiful in wartime as in other times. All the same, there is plenty of evidence to suggest that a class-divided, socially-fragmented people discovered reserves of solidarity which it had not known it possessed; and that part of the reason was that, in however muddled a fashion, the political nation accepted an ethic of equality of sacrifice. One example must speak for many. There were credit items on the wartime balance sheet, wrote the journalist, H.V. Hodson, in September 1944:

We've given coal-miners a minimum of five pounds a week; we've opened up shipyards that had been derelict; we've made waste-lands fruitful, and cultivated millions of acres that lay idle. Our evacuation exposed hideous sores in the form of children under-nourished and ill-brought-up; I hope we shall be sensible enough to profit by the exposure. Our heavy taxation and our rationing of food has, willy-nilly, achieved some levelling-up of the nation; fewer folk have gone hungry and fewer have gorged themselves; the poor have been a trifle better-off and the rich a little less rich.[27]

That mood did not survive indefinitely. Attempts to evoke it when wartime memories had faded, as when Harold Wilson appealed to the 'Dunkirk spirit' in the early 1960s, fell flat. But the memory of it lingered into the early post-war period, clothing the dry bones of economic theory in emotional flesh, and giving the first Keynesian social-democratic governments a stock of moral capital which enabled them partially to offset the intellectual inconsistencies in their assumptions.

From this disparate ancestry, post-war Keynesian social democracy inherited three overarching commitments. The first, and in practice the most important, was to use the Keynesian economic regulators in a way that would maintain full employment. The second was to retain a substantial publicly-owned sector alongside a still-predominant private sector. The third was to preserve what came to be known as the 'welfare state' — in other words, the half-innovatory, half-conservative mix of social measures foreshadowed in the Beveridge Report and enacted by the post-war Labour government.

Inevitably, these commitments were fuzzy at the edges. The political parties could, and did, differ over their practical implications. For the Labour 'revisionists' of the 1950s, socialism was about equality rather than about ownership.[28] Under their influence, the Labour Party increasingly saw the welfare state as a vehicle for redistribution, and the 'social wage' as an index of social justice. Conservatives emphasised its role as a safety net, providing a base for individual initiative. More notoriously, the two big parties differed over the frontier between the public and private sectors of economy. Steel was nationalised, de-nationalised and then re-nationalised in the space of eighteen years. A shorter battle took place over road haulage, which the Conservatives also de-nationalised in the early 1950s. If we look at what was done rather than at what was said, however, the differences appear marginal. The pattern of welfare spending which Labour had set after the war continued with only minor variations under the Conservative governments of the 1950s; as a percentage of gross domestic product (GDP) the total fell slightly in the first few years of the decade, but by 1961 it was higher than it had been in 1951. A big increase in welfare spending took place in the 1960s, both absolutely and as a proportion of GDP; it began under the

Conservatives and continued under Labour. The momentum of the increase continued in the early 1970s, again under both parties.[29] Much the same was true of public ownership. Steel and road haulage were discordant exceptions, proving a rule of unacknowledged harmony. Apart from them, the Conservatives made no real effort to whittle away the public sector which they had inherited from the Labour Party, while Labour made only fitful and half-hearted efforts to extend it.

Two sets of assumptions underpinned this network of commitments. The first set had to do with the economy. Almost self-evidently, Keynesian social democratic governments assumed that Keynesian demand management worked and would continue to work: that economists schooled in Keynesian techniques knew how to manipulate the economy in such a way as to maintain full employment, and that the economic relationships which enabled them to do this would persist. Anthony Crosland, the leading Labour revisionist of the period, put it most clearly. 'Demand', he wrote confidently in a key passage in *The Future of Socialism*, 'has proved to be malleable, and in a broadly predictable manner'; thus, there was no need to fear that pre-war unemployment would return.[30] But that was only the beginning of the story. Along with that assumption went two less obvious, but equally important, assumptions. One was that governments could maintain full employment solely by manipulating economic variables: that, for practical purposes, they could treat the economy as an autonomous realm, free of influences from other social realms; and that the techniques with which they managed it need not be affected by non-economic factors. The other was that full employment could be reconciled with an acceptable rate of inflation: that if prices rose faster than the authorities thought appropriate, they would have no difficulty in bringing the rate of increase back to a tolerable level, without abandoning the fundamental full-employment commitment: that, in language beloved of contemporary chancellors of the exchequer, any competent macro-economic helmsman could steer between the twin dangers of inflation and unemployment, with only slight touches on the tiller.

This leads on to a bog of more complex assumptions, hard to

penetrate even with the benefits of hindsight. As we have seen, the Keynesian regulators were designed to deal with demand inflation, not with cost inflation. Yet policy makers knew perfectly well that a sellers' market for labour was bound to generate pressures for cost inflation; and they also knew that if these pressures got out of hand, even the most competent macroeconomic helmsman would be unable to avoid both excessive inflation and excessive unemployment at the same time. Plainly, then, the whole system rested on the assumption that this would not happen: that organised labour would not use the bargaining power which full employment had given it in such a way as to make Keynesian economic helmsmanship impossible. Once again, however, that was only the beginning of the story. Given that a sellers' market for labour was bound to generate inflationary pressures, what was to stop the pressures from getting out of hand? Given that full employment gave organised labour the bargaining power to wreck the Keynesian system, what was to stop it from using it? On these questions, as we have seen, Keynes himself was silent, but Keynesian social democrats had to find answers of some sort. In practice, they found two. One was that the pressures would only be little ones; that organised labour, knowing that full employment was in its interests, would not wish to put it in jeopardy by using its bargaining power irresponsibly. The other was that the pressures could, in any event, be held in check by an incomes policy, either agreed with the unions or imposed upon them. Thus, by an irony which Keynes would probably not have appreciated, the apparently technical, social-scientific assumption that Keynesian demand management would work turned out to depend, in practice, on quintessentially political assumptions about the likely behaviour of the unions and the effectiveness of incomes policies.

That was not the only irony. By definition, the inflationary pressures generated by a sellers' market for labour could be contained only if the distributional conflicts which those pressures reflected could also be contained. As Beveridge had pointed out in *Full Employment in a Free Society*, inflation-free full employment was possible only if the trade unions either accepted the existing pattern of income distribution or, at any rate, refrained from using their industrial power to change it. But Keynesian social democracy had no theory of distribution, and therefore no grounds on which to base such hopes. Though the Labour 'revisionists' preached a rather abstract doctrine of equality, they did not make it clear what it would mean in practice or reconcile it with the Labour Movement's long-standing determination to maintain traditional differentials. Their Conservative counterparts favoured an even vaguer notion of equal opportunity, but that notion never became operational either. In practice, Keynesian social-democratic politicians relied on economic growth to resolve the distributional conflicts to which they had no other answer. But they saw growth in the way that they saw full employment, as an essentially economic phenomenon, to be achieved by techniques developed by the economics profession; and the complex social and cultural processes bearing on it eluded them.

The second set of assumptions had to do with the polity. Again self-evidently, Keynesian social democrats took it for granted that the state would be able to act as their governing philosophy said it should act: that its policies would be implemented once it had adopted them: that even adversely affected groups and individuals would do what Keynesian social-democratic legislation required them to do. The last point goes wider than might appear at first sight. Apart from a brief period before the First World War, the fundamentals of Britain's political order had not been called into question for more than a hundred years. The authority of governments and the consent of the governed had rarely been in doubt, and British ministers and officials could hardly credit that they ever would be. As so often, however, the conclusions which they drew from their long history of institutional stability went further than the evidence. Nineteenth-century British governments had enjoyed great authority, but their role had been limited. They had had little difficulty in implementing their policies, but their policies had not impinged much on the public. Even inter-war governments had not intervened in the economy and society on anything like the scale of their Keynesian social-democratic successors. Yet few suspected that what had been true of the limited state of the past might not be true of the intrusive state of the present and future.

Not only did Keynesian social democrats assume that the state would be able to implement its policies; they also assumed that the state that did so would be the familiar British state, operating through the familiar processes of the Westminster Model. Two sets of consequences followed, one concerning the international environment and the other, domestic political arrangements. In the first place, it was taken for granted that the familiar British state would have the familiar attributes of sovereignty: that it would be able to retain the network of external ties which it had inherited from the nineteenth century without jeopardising its freedom to use the instruments which the Keynesian Revolution had given it as it thought fit. Secondly, the old, Whig-Radical doctrine of parliamentary supremacy was also taken for granted, along with the network of assumptions and conventions which had grown up around it. Two aspects of this network deserve attention here. It was almost axiomatic that ministers and ministers alone were responsible for the government's policy decisions, which their officials then carried out: in other words, that the administrative culture which had suited Gladstone and Salisbury would be equally appropriate for the complex mixed economy which Keynesian social democrats were busily bringing into existence. It was also axiomatic that a continuous adversarial struggle between two great parties, bound together in broad, though tacit, agreement on the consensus we have been discussing, was both a necessary and a sufficient condition of democratic accountability. Though this was not often said in so many words, it followed that the real function of the House of Commons was to serve as a cockpit for a continuous, never-ending struggle between two teams of political gladiators, competing for votes at the next election, and that its older roles as a legislature and as a watchdog over the executive had faded into comparative insignificance.

Here too a more complex and less obvious assumption lurked in the background. The formal constitution — the constitution of politicians' speeches, lobby correspondents' reports, television discussion programmes and legal textbooks

— ran in uneasy double harness with a different set of practices, the logic of which pointed in a different direction. Keith Middlemas has shown that a loose, informal, fluctuating system of bargaining and mutual accommodation between the state, the organised employers and organised labour was beginning to take shape as far back as the First World War.[31] It developed further between the wars, and further still during the Second World War. It was a dominating feature of Britain's political economy throughout the period under discussion here. But the most remarkable characteristics of this system of 'corporate bias', as Middlemas calls it, were precisely its looseness and informality: formally, the Westminster Model remained intact. Ministers and officials consulted the leaders of the organised producer groups, brought influence to bear on them and were, in turn, influenced by them. But they usually did so behind closed doors. Parliament, parties and public, for that matter the ordinary members of the producer groups themselves, rarely knew what was said and done in their names. This informal constitution of producer-group pressure and state counter-pressure came into existence because it was necessary: because an interdependent society could not be governed successfully by the rules of the formal constitution, and because the rules therefore had to be broken in spirit even if they were observed in the letter. But it existed *sub rosa*, uncodified, only half-acknowledged, and unjustified by any public philosophy or generally accepted theory. In assuming that interventionist governments could govern through the familiar processes of the Westminster Model, Keynesian social democrats were also assuming that this state of affairs would continue: that there was no need to close the gap between the formal and informal constitutions: that the political economy could be managed indefinitely through a kind of controlled institutional schizophrenia.

With the advantage of hindsight, it is easy to see that this network of commitments and assumptions was unlikely to survive for ever. Yet it lasted for the best part of a generation; and the processes through which it unravelled were slow, complex and confusing. The object of the next chapter is to try to make sense of them.

2

The Collapse of Consensus

'I think that this Government must be finished.'

'Nearly, but not quite yet? Thursday?'

'Yes. I meant in principle, leaving it to the forecasters to put numbers on it.'

Exchange of notes between two Treasury officials, November, 1976.[1]

'I have changed everything.'

Mrs Thatcher, in conversation, 1976.[2]

Under the Keynesian social-democratic governments of the 1950s and 1960s, living standards rose more rapidly than in most previous periods; personal freedoms and opportunities expanded; Britain became a kinder and, on most definitions, a fairer society. Yet the commitments which lay at the heart of their governing philosophy have plainly been abandoned. The Wilson-Callaghan government of 1974–79 reluctantly gave up the commitment to full employment half-way through its term of office. The associated commitment to Keynesian demand management was weakening in the last two years of Labour rule; the Thatcher government repudiated it when it came to power in 1979. Unspoken agreement about the frontier between the public and private sectors has ended too. On the neo-liberal assumption that state enterprises and public services are bound to be less efficient than private ones, the second Thatcher government sold off a significant part of the public sector. It and its predecessor also tried to cut the proportion of GDP going to public expenditure, failing only because increased unemployment generated increases in welfare spending, which offset economies elsewhere. By the mid-1980s, the Labour leadership was edging its way back to the revisionism of the 1950s and 1960s, but the Party was still pledged, on paper, to large extensions of public ownership. Both big parties still proclaim a commitment to something they call the welfare state, but they differ violently over what the something means. The National Health Service is the sole legacy of the welfare strand of Keynesian social democracy which survives in approximately its original form.

Two obvious questions arise. Why has the Keynesian social-democratic consensus fragmented in this way? What light does its fragmentation throw on the present and future of the political economy? It is not difficult to trace the shift of opinion which undermined it. Labour's shift towards neo-socialism began under the Wilson government of 1964–70, and went further in the 1970s. Neo-liberalism began to make headway in the Conservative Party in the 1960s, and made more after the fall of the Heath government in 1974. By the late-1970s, the Conservative leadership was in neo-liberal hands. Though Keynesian social democrats still predominated in the Labour Cabinet, they had lost control of the party outside Parliament. Outside formal politics, the 1960s and early 1970s saw a remarkable renaissance of Marxism. In the 1970s, such writers as F.A. Hayek, Milton Friedman, the Virginia school of public-choice economists and their British popularisers gave a new lease of life to classical, market-liberal doctrines as well. For a long time, Keynesian social democracy remained the orthodoxy of the decision-making establishment, but it gradually lost the sparkle and self-confidence of its post-war heyday. By the end of the decade it was clearly on the defensive intellectually as well as politically.

All this, however, only outlines the chronology of its downfall. The important question is why it fell. It is important for two reasons. Current debates about the present and future of the political economy are also debates about its recent past. Just as the victorious free-traders' interpretation of the crisis which led to the repeal of the Corn Laws in 1846 helped to shape the political agenda of the mid-nineteenth century, so the political agenda of today is, to a large extent, the product of rival neo-liberal and neo-socialist interpretations of the crises which brought Keynesian social democracy to grief in the 1960s and 1970s. If we want to understand these interpretations and make sense of the agenda they have produced, we must try to dig down to the experiences they reflect. By the same token, if we want to tease out the implications for the future, it is not enough to know that successive Keynesian social-democratic governments failed to resolve the crises facing them. We must also try to understand the reasons for their failures. In the last chapter I set the scene for this attempt by bringing out some of the ambiguities and inconsistencies in their assumptions. I will now try to show how and why those assumptions slowly disintegrated.

The story is more complex than it seems at first sight. The thirty-year-long Keynesian social-democratic ascendancy falls naturally into three unequal phases. The first, heroic phase lasted from the end of the war to the late 1940s. In it, the Attlee government nationalised the so-called 'basic industries'; implemented Beveridge's welfare proposals; and, after initial hesitations, gave Keynesian demand management pride of place among the economic instruments of the state. The last point deserves more than a passing mention. The Labour ministers took office with what Sir Alec Cairncross describes as a 'nebulous but exalted' vision of a planned economy.[3] They had inherited a battery of controls from the wartime coalition and they assumed that these could be used to plan for peace. But it soon became clear that wartime controls were too negative and too inflexible to be of much use to peacetime planners. It also became clear that peacetime planning would encounter two formidable sets of obstacles, one deriving from the attitudes and values of the private economic agents whom it would affect, and the other from the character of the administrative machine. Employers suspected it as a cat's-paw for 'socialism'. For their part, the unions, though willing to accept a temporary wage freeze, were bitterly opposed to the permanent wages policy which economic planning logically implied. These attitudes were mirrored in Whitehall. The government's economic advisers were mostly antipathetic to supply-side intervention on grounds of economic principle.

More fatally still, the civil service and parliamentary cultures were unsuited to it, as was the departmental structure.[4] Across the channel, post-war France embarked on an ambitious form of state-led modernisation, promoted by a planning commission almost independent of political control. In post-war Britain, anything of the sort would have required a virtual administrative revolution.

Had ministers known what they wanted and been determined to get it, they might have forced through such a revolution. In retrospect, one of the most striking features of the Attlee government is that they did not and were not. Though they wanted to plan, they did not know what to plan, how to plan it or how to create the machinery to put the plans into effect. So they havered. As wartime shortages eased, they gradually dismantled the wartime controls. At the same time, they tried to establish a form of peacetime planning by consent – setting up an Economic Planning Board, representing both sides of industry; and publishing a four-year plan, called *The Long-Term Programme of the United Kingdom*.[5] But as time went on, the impetus waned. The Economic Planning Board ceased to count, and in practice ministers relied increasingly on the Keynesian manipulation of demand, leaving supply to a mixture of market forces and moral exhortation.[6]

The second phase – the phase of arm's length economic management – lasted from the closing years of the Attlee government in the late 1940s to the middle years of the Macmillan government in the early 1960s. In this phase, governments relied almost entirely on Keynesian demand management, using a mixture of fiscal and monetary instruments for the purpose. When they thought unemployment was too high, they added to demand; when they thought the economy was overheated, they subtracted from it. In orthodox Keynesian fashion, they left supply to respond to market forces. As in the heroic phase, they also stuck firmly to Britain's role as a world power, both military and economic. By the same token, they made no significant changes in the institutional sphere, and took it for granted that the Westminster Model was as suitable for export to newly-independent former colonies as for home consumption.

The Attlee government slipped apologetically into the arm's length phase, without acknowledging, perhaps without fully realising, what it was doing. The Macmillan government ended it in a flush of enthusiasm. It did so for two reasons. The first and simplest was that, although the economy had grown rapidly by previous British standards, arm's length management had coincided with precipitate relative economic decline. Despite full employment, Britain's growth rate averaged 2.7 per cent a year between 1950 and 1960, against a German rate of 7.8 per cent, a French rate of 4.6 per cent and a West European average of 4.4 per cent.[7] (See Table II.) *Pace* Keynes, demand had not, after all, called forth supply – or not, at any rate, enough of it. Technocratic manipulation of the rewards and penalties of the market had maintained full employment, but it had not sufficed to galvanise sluggish economic actors to emulate their foreign counterparts.

The second reason was more complicated. It began to look as though the kind of arm's length management which had prevailed in the 1950s had actually helped to cause the relative decline of the period. For the managers had been responding to two contradictory sets of stimuli. As well as trying to maintain what was then defined as full employment, they had been trying to keep the balance of payments in equilibrium. Unfortunately, they could not achieve both these objectives simultaneously within the framework of the prevailing consensus and with the policy instruments at their disposal. Their attempts to do so trapped them in the notorious stop-go cycle. When employment was full and demand buoyant, costs rose and imports were sucked in. The balance of payments came under strain and sterling under pressure. Since ministers took it for granted that sterling should remain an international trading and reserve currency, and that devaluation was therefore ruled out, the only way to return the balance of payments to equilibrium was to cut home demand. That righted the balance of payments, at the cost of raising unemployment; ministers then proceeded to set the cycle off again by raising the level of demand to bring unemployment down. Whether the stop-go cycle in fact lowered the long-term rate of growth is a moot point. Since more successful economies experienced similar, and in some cases more violent, oscillations, the probability is that it did not. But in the early 1960s it was generally believed to have done so. Growth was low, the argument went, partly because investment was low; investment was low partly because recurrent fluctuations in the level of demand discouraged businessmen from investing.[8]

Because wartime destruction had been so much worse on the continent than in Britain, the gap between Britain's growth rate and those of her more successful continental competitors was slow to impinge on the consciousness of decision- and opinion-makers. By the early 1960s, however, virtually the entire political class had become convinced that the rate of growth was too low, and that something had to be done to raise it. Large sections of it were equally convinced that they knew how to do this. The planning strand in Keynesian social democracy would have to buttress the Keynesian strand. As well as managing demand, government would have to take direct measures to improve supply. In order to encourage the higher private-sector investment without which such measures would be ineffective, the stop-go cycle would have to be evened out. Two key conclusions seemed to follow. In a predominantly privately-owned economy, government could not itself deliver improvements in the supply-side; in practice, its attempts to obtain them would succeed only with the agreement of private economic agents whose activities it could not control. To work, supply-side intervention therefore required a system of industrial consensus-building – what the economist, Christopher Dow, described as 'organized, mutual discussion'[9] – through which the state, organised capital and organised labour would consult together about what needed to be done, and hammer out a common approach to which they would then be committed. The chief cause of the stop-go cycle was that, when demand was buoyant, wage costs rose more quickly in Britain than in competing economies. If the economy were to be run at a consistently high level of demand, an incomes policy would be needed to hold wage costs back.[10]

This was the rationale for the third and final phase of Keynesian social democracy, the phase of what might be called hands-on intervention. It began with the Macmillan government's conversion to indicative economic planning in 1960–62, and died away during the long diminuendo of the Wilson-Callaghan government of 1974–79. In it, governments followed a bewildering variety of policies with a bewildering variety of instruments – often undoing, in one mood, what they had laboriously and painfully done in another. It is not necessary to trace the details of these twists and turns here,[11] but the most salient points need mentioning. Two themes predominated throughout. Keynesian demand management was buttressed by consensual intervention in the supply-side; both were buttressed by controls, sometimes statutory and sometimes voluntary, over the movement of wages and prices.

The Macmillan government began the hands-on phase in 1962, when it set up the National Economic Development Council ('Neddy' for short), on which representatives of both sides of industry sat alongside ministers, to work out an agreed strategy for faster growth. Associated with the main Neddy were a number of 'little Neddies', whose role was to promote greater efficiency in particular industries. The government also imposed a 'pay pause', followed it with a 'guiding light' for future wage increases and established a National Incomes Commission to pronounce on its implications for particular claims and settlements. The 1964–70 Wilson government went further – creating a Department of Economic Affairs to act as an expansionist counterweight to the Treasury; drawing up a National Plan; and setting up a National Board for Prices and Incomes to police an originally voluntary, and subsequently statutory, incomes policy.

Though it was returned to office on a partially neo-liberal ticket, the 1970–74 Heath government followed where its predecessor had led. It began its term of office opposed to formal incomes policies, committed to liberalise the labour market by 'reforming' industrial relations law and anxious to reduce the scale of state intervention in the supply-side of the economy. Only two years later, it passed the 1972 Industry Act giving the secretary of state unprecedented powers of industrial intervention and assistance. It also spent long hours trying to win trade-union consent to a voluntary incomes policy, tacitly conceding, in the process, that trade-union opposition had made its industrial relations legislation unworkable; and it ended by introducing the most ambitious statutory incomes policy of the period. In much the same way, the Wilson-Callaghan government of 1974–79 eschewed the compulsory 'planning agreements' advocated by the left wing of the party in favour of a consensual 'industrial strategy', agreed with the employers as well as with the trade unions. After a year of accelerating inflation, it also launched a quasi-statutory incomes policy, the unstated objectives of which were to restore private-sector profitability and to cut real wages.[12]

Where the arm's length phase had been internationally and institutionally conservative, the hands-on phase also saw belated British entry into the European Community, a slow, grudging withdrawal from Britain's world role and a spate of institutional changes. The Macmillan government applied unsuccessfully to join the EEC; the Heath government joined it; after a cosmetic renegotiation of the original entry terms, the second Wilson government remained in it. The first Wilson government devalued sterling and took the decisive steps towards liquidating Britain's military commitments east of Suez. The 1960s saw the introduction of a new system of public-expenditure planning, a sweeping reform of London government, an abortive attempt to reform the House of Lords, the Fulton Commission's proposals for civil-service reform and the creation of a number of regional economic planning councils. In the 1970s, these were followed, inter alia, by the establishment of a Central Policy Review Staff to strengthen the Cabinet's capacity for collective decision-making, the reorganisation of local government in Scotland and in the rest of England and Wales and unsuccessful attempts to set up devolved assemblies in Scotland and Wales.

Against this background, the ideological polarisation which destroyed the post-war consensus takes on a new significance. Its two most obvious features are that it took place during the hands-on phase of Keynesian social democracy, and that it did so at a time when successive hands-on governments were failing to achieve their stated purposes. Of course, other factors played a part in it as well. In Britain, as in the rest of the western world, the late 1960s and early 1970s saw a shift of mood and aspiration — a growing suspicion of hierarchy, bureaucracy and complexity; a longing for the small-scale and the familiar; a growing demand for wider participation in decision-making; in some quarters, at any rate, a new disdain for the economism of the post-war period and even a new hostility to the pursuit of economic growth.[13] Although this new mood was logically compatible with middle-way political attitudes, it was out of tune with the methods and structures through which post-war British governments put those attitudes into practice. It was correspondingly hard for the politicians of the post-war consensus to adjust to it, and in a confused and nebulous sort of way it too helped to discredit them and the governing philosophy which guided them.

That said, it is hard to believe that the consensus would have collapsed in the way that it did if the consensus politicians had been more successful in doing what they set out to do. Three failures, or sets of failures, stand out. The most obvious one had to do with the competitiveness of British industry and the growth of the economy. The governments of the hands-on phase were all trying, by a mixture of bribery, cajolery, arm-twisting and argument, to raise the level and quality of investment, so as to improve the efficiency of British industry and raise the rate of growth. Despite all their efforts, investment and productivity rose much more slowly than in competing economies. To judge by its falling share of total Organisation for Economic Cooperation and Development (OECD) manufacturing output, and the sharp increase in import penetration, British industry became less competitive rather than more.[14] Meanwhile, faster growth obstinately failed to materialise. One of the first actions of the National Economic Development Council was to publish a so-called 'green book' arguing that it was possible to reach an average growth-rate of 4.0 per cent a year over the period 1961–6.[15] More modestly, the Wilson government's National Plan aimed at an average growth rate of 3.8 per cent a year between 1964 and 1970. In the event, the average annual rate of growth over the government's six-year term was only a little more than 2.0 per cent.

Over the decade as a whole, it was 2.8 per cent — only 0.1 per cent more than in the 1950s. The gap between Britain's growth rate and the West European average actually widened.[16] (See Table II.) In the early 1970s, the Heath government managed, by a lavish, and highly inflationary, exercise in Keynesian pump-priming, to produce a short-lived spurt in the growth-rate, only to see it fall back to its old level before the subsequent general election. As the world-wide post-war boom died away after the 1973 oil shock, growth almost petered out. Between 1973 and 1979, it averaged only 1.3 per cent a year, while unemployment and inflation both rose to levels unprecedented since the war.[17] (See Table I.)

The second set of failures helps to explain the first. Not only did the hands-on governments fail to raise the rate of growth; they also failed to achieve steady growth. One of the most persuasive arguments for the switch to hands-on intervention was that it would cut through the vicious circle of stop-go. Knowing that government had committed itself to maintain a high and stable level of demand, industry would invest more; higher investment would make it more competitive, thus making it easier for government to escape from the balance-of-payments straitjacket which had held growth and investment back in the past. Here too the hopes of the early 1960s were soon belied. The 1963–4 'Maudling boom', with which the Macmillan government ended its term of office, led to a balance of payments deficit of the familiar kind. Within a few weeks of its arrival in office, the incoming Wilson government found itself facing a sterling crisis, of an equally familiar kind. For twenty months it procrastinated, refusing to devalue, but refusing also to do anything more than nibble at deflation. In July 1966, however, it at last brought in a package of defla-tionary measures, unfamiliar only in that they were harsher than any of their predecessors — destroying, in the process, any hope of carrying out the National Plan which it had announced less than a year before. The rest of its term of office was dominated, first by the defence of the old sterling parity and, after the forced devaluation of 1967, by the defence of the new one; so far as macro-economic management was concerned, the result was close to a permanent stop.

The pattern was repeated in the 1970s, but in incomparably more sombre colours. As the Macmillan government had tried to break out of the cycle of low growth and balance-of-payments constraints with the 'Maudling boom', so the Heath government tried to break out with the 'Barber boom'. Unlike any previous government, moreover, it explicitly gave higher priority to the growth rate than to the defence of sterling, floating the pound to signal its determination. Once again, the result was a record balance of payments deficit, this time swollen by the effects of the 1973 oil shock. Faced with this deficit, the 1974 Labour government procrastinated as its predecessor had done ten years earlier. As before, sterling came under pressure; as before, a series of mildly deflationary measures failed to restore confidence. The story ended in 1976, when the dollar value of sterling fell from around $2.00 to around $1.60 in six months, forcing the government to obtain long-term credits from the International Monetary Fund (IMF), at the price of heavy cuts in public expenditure, which made a mockery of the programme on which it had been returned to office.

The third set of failures was closely connected to the other two. Central to the whole hands-on strategy was the proposition that incomes policy held the key to inflation-free growth. Though economists disagree about the long-term impact of the incomes policies of the period, it seems clear that some of them, at any rate, were highly effective in the short term.[18] Effective or ineffective, however, successive policies collapsed in acrimony and recrimination. The unions ignored the Macmillan government's 'guiding light'. In the initial, voluntary, phase of the 1964–70 Wilson government's incomes policy, the rise in earnings was about twice the norm which the union leaders had agreed. For a while, the subsequent statutory policy was remarkably successful. But, in a doomed attempt to win trade-union acquiescence for its 'In Place of Strife' white paper, proposing legislation to control unofficial strikes, the government decided to abandon it, only to abandon the white paper shortly afterwards. For its pains, it spent its last few months of office presiding over a wage explosion of hitherto unprecedented ferocity. In the following decade, the first and second stages of the Heath government's statutory policy were also highly successful. Unfortunately, the mineworkers' refusal to accept the third destroyed the policy and the government with it. Under the voluntary policy embodied in the second Wilson government's social contract with the unions, settlements of 30 per cent became commonplace, while the rate at which prices were rising reached more than 25 per cent. The quasi-statutory policy which the government and the unions agreed together in the inflation-haunted summer of 1975 was perhaps the most successful of the entire period, but it became a 'dead letter' three years later when the unions refused to accept the Callaghan government's 5.0 per cent norm. The government itself lost the next election largely because it seemed helpless in the face of the ensuing rash of unofficial strikes.[19]

By the end of the period, these three sets of failures had been subsumed by a failure of an even more disconcerting kind. The familiar Keynesian levers gradually ceased to function or, to put it more precisely, it gradually became impossible for British chancellors of the exchequer to behave as though they would function. As we have seen, the Keynesian social-democratic commitment to full employment rested, among other things, on the assumption that Britain's international ties would not prevent British governments from using the Keynesian regulators as they wished. That assumption was beginning to look implausible as early as the late 1950s; and after the forced devaluation of 1967, it looked more implausible still. The world-wide 'stagflation' which followed the 1973 oil shock destroyed it altogether. In a country with an open economy and a chronically weak balance of payments, Keynes's doctrine that the cure for unemployment was to raise the level of demand was no longer usable. The government of such a country was no longer master in its own house. Irrespective of its wishes, it could not raise — indeed, as the second Wilson government discovered, it could not even maintain — the level of demand unless other governments did so too. Unilateral reflation, it became clear, was simply not feasible: well before it produced higher employment, it would produce a deteriorating balance of payments and a depreciating currency. These, in turn, would produce higher inflation and yet more currency depreciation.

That was not the only assumption to crumble in these years. Most of the other assumptions underpinning the commitment to full employment had crumbled too. The assumptions that the inflationary pressures generated by a sellers' market for labour could be kept in check, that incomes policies would work and that the unions would not try to use their industrial power to change the existing pattern of income distribution had all become hopelessly implausible. Because of this, so had the crucial assumption that increases in unemployment could be traded off against increases in inflation and vice versa, and that, given reasonable skill on the part of demand managers, neither would reach an intolerable level. Even before the oil shock, unemployment and inflation were both appreciably higher than they had been in the 1950s, and the trade-off between them was less favourable.[20] Thereafter, so far from finding a point at which a tolerable level of unemployment balanced a tolerable level of inflation, governments found themselves trying to cope with intolerable levels of both.

Thus, policy-makers were trapped in an impasse, from which Keynesian social democracy could offer no escape. The result was a crisis of confidence and belief, more disorientating than the economic crisis which had given rise to it. Even in the halcyon years of the 1950s, governments had not been as good at demand management as they would have liked. But they had at least known approximately what objectives they wanted to achieve, and approximately what instruments to use. Now they did not know. The old Keynesian assumptions had collapsed, much as the pre-Keynesian assumptions had collapsed between the wars. There was nothing − nothing of a Keynesian social-democratic parentage at any rate − to put in their place. With a kind of dogged fatalism, Keynesian social-democratic ministers and officials soldiered on, but it was clear that many of the central pillars of their governing philosophy had disappeared.

That is only the beginning of the story. The crisis of confidence had two dimensions, not one. The policy failures of the 1960s and 1970s called the political assumptions of Keynesian social democracy into question as well as the economic ones, and in a fashion which was even more disorientating for the politicians and civil servants who had previously taken them for granted.

As we have seen, Keynesian social democrats had assumed that they could achieve their purposes through the well-tried processes and institutions of the Westminster Model. Their experience of the arm's length phase gave them no reason to question that assumption. In it, governments influenced the economy through what Max Weber called 'legal-rational' procedures. They operated on individual economic agents impersonally and at one remove, through general rules applying to all the agents in a specified category.[21] They changed the environment in which market forces functioned, strengthening certain market stimuli and weakening others, but they left private agents to decide for themselves how to respond to the changes. Because they operated on them at one remove, they did not need the consent of the private agents concerned for the changes to take effect. Treasury statisticians and economists read the tea-leaves which told them how the economy was moving. Ministers raised and lowered taxes and interest rates accordingly. Investors, managers, trade unionists and consumers might or might not adapt their behaviour in the way that ministers had hoped they would, but even if they did not, they could not stop the new taxes or interest rates from coming into force. The government's policies might fail, but failure could not be laid at the door of identifiable groups within society, and ministers did not need to negotiate with such groups before deciding what policies to introduce.

The hands-on phase was a different matter. As before, governments raised and lowered taxes and interest rates and determined global aggregates of demand. But they also tried to influence particular pay settlements, particular price increases, the efficiency of particular industrial sectors, the location of particular factories and the profitability of particular firms. Often, they could do this only through direct, face-to-face negotiation and discussion with the private economic agents whose behaviour they wanted to change, or with the organisations representing them — tacitly conceding that organised groups within society could prevent the elected government from doing what it wanted to do. At least four consequences followed. Because government was trying to do more, and because the things it was trying to do were intrinsically more difficult, it ran a greater risk of failure. Because many of the things it wanted to do could only be accomplished, in practice, by private agents outside its control, it needed, not just the passive acquiescence of these agents, but their positive co-operation. Because it often had to seek their co-operation in a public or semi-public way, rebuffs were likely to be visible and correspondingly damaging to its authority. Because the Westminster Model contained no mechanism for winning the co-operation of private economic agents, or for averting rebuffs, new institutions had to be set up alongside it.

As we have seen, a range of new institutions was duly established. Unfortunately, they did not produce the results for which their creators had hoped. Plainly, the consensual interventionism of the hands-on phase could not work without the agreement of organised labour and capital. Notoriously, labour often refused to agree. The abandonment of the 'In Place of Strife' proposals; the subsequent abandonment of the first Wilson government's statutory incomes policy; the resultant wage explosion of 1969–70; the failure of the 1971 Industrial Relations Act; the failure of the Heath government's statutory incomes policy; the failure of the second Wilson government's social contract with the unions and the galloping inflation of 1974–75; the defeat of the Callaghan government's 5 per cent norm and the 'winter of discontent' — these were all due, largely if not wholly, to trade-union resistance to, or disdain for, policies which the government concerned believed to be essential to the health of the economy. The resistance and disdain, moreover, were public and flagrant; and, as such, profoundly humiliating for the government at the receiving end. Harold Wilson, after his surrender over 'In Place of Strife', and James Callaghan during the 'winter of discontent', looked and sounded like broken men. More important still, their policies were unmistakably broken as well. Though he was made of sterner stuff, and managed not to appear broken, much the same was true of Edward Heath in the struggle over the 1971 Industrial Relations Act and in the closing stages of the 1973–74 mining dispute. In the first case, trade-union resistance effectively emasculated the government's most important piece of legislation. In the second, it threatened to destroy the most important element in the government's economic policy, forcing ministers into a general election which they had not wanted to fight and in which they were defeated.[22]

Yet the 'union question' was merely the peculiarly jagged tip of a much bigger iceberg. It was not only organised labour which prevented successive governments from achieving their purposes: albeit more quietly, less directly and less obviously, capital did so too. It is often forgotten that wage settlements, not wage claims, determine the success or failure of an incomes policy; and settlements have to be made by employers as well as by unions. In any case, incomes policy was only one element in hands-on intervention. Industrial policy was equally funda-mental to it; and, almost by definition, industrial policy required capital's co-operation as much as, perhaps more than, labour's. To be sure, the kind of co-operation which government wanted from capital differed, in a number of ways, from the kind it wanted from labour. Broadly speaking, it was trying to stop labour from doing things which labour had been accustomed to do, and wanted to go on doing. With capital, it was the other way around: governments wanted industrialists to invest more than they had invested in the past and more than they would have invested if they had been left to themselves. But the similarities were at least as significant as the differences. In both cases, government, as the custodian of the general interest of the community, was trying to induce the producer groups to behave in ways which they did not consider to be in their particular interests. As the figures for industrial investment show, it was no more successful with capital than it was with labour.[23]

Thus, one of the central political assumptions of the govern-ing philosophy of the period had turned out to be false. Adversely-affected groups and individuals could not, after all, be relied upon to do what Keynesian social-democratic policies required them to do. Despite all the consensual arrangements of the hands-on phase – the NEDC, the little Neddies, the sector working parties, the high-level negotiations in Downing Street – the producer groups persisted in going their own way. The state depended on them, but it could not bend them to its will; if it tried to impose its will upon them, it was likely to become embroiled in a bruising struggle in which defeat was at least as likely as victory. Worse still, it could not be sure that, if it made concessions in order to reach agreement with them, their own members would allow them to carry out their part of the bargain. To use one of the favourite analogies of the period, it looked less and less like the skilful and authoritative techno-cratic manager which post-war Keynesian social democracy had presupposed, and more and more like a medieval king, struggling unsuccessfully to assert himself against a voracious and untrustworthy baronage.[24]

Failure to win the consent of the producer groups went hand in hand with an even more disturbing failure. In constitutional theory, government spoke for the general interest of consumers and taxpayers, as against the particular interests for which the producer-group leaders spoke. But in the push and pull of will and power in which it and the producer-group leaders were so frequently engaged, constitutional theory gave it little help. What determined the outcomes were, for example, the willing-ness of the general public to put up with the inconvenience of a big public-sector strike: the willingness of rank-and-file trade unionists to obey a strike call: the willingness of ordinary workers not involved in a dispute to cross a picket line: the willingness of a company board to seek export markets instead of selling at home, or to invest in new plant and machinery rather than in property. In these and similar situations, government's chances of having its way depended, in part, on its ability to persuade the general public (including, of course, rank-and-file members of the producer groups whose behaviour it was trying to change) that its policies were right and ought to be carried out, even at the cost of inconvenience to those affected by them. Knowing this, governments repeatedly tried to appeal over the heads of the producer-group leaders to their members and to the public at large. Though this is impossible to prove, it is hard to escape the impression that they became less and less successful at doing so as the hands-on phase continued. The clearest — and the most damaging — case in point was the Heath government's defeat in the first 1974 election. The object of the election was to mobilise public opinion in support of stage three of the incomes policy and against the miners' leaders, some of whom were explicitly trying to destroy it. By implication, at any rate, the voters backed the miners against the government. That was only one example. In much the same way, the second Wilson government's appeals for voluntary restraint failed to stem the tide of inflationary wage demands in the first stage of the social contract from 1974–5, and the Callaghan government failed to halt the 'winter of discontent' in 1978–9. Each time, government tried to mobilise the general public, including rank-and-file trade unionists, in support of what it saw as the public interest. Each time, it failed.

All this was part and parcel of an institutional crisis, which seemed to be feeding on itself. On the most obvious level, the failure of a policy often represented, justly or unjustly, a defeat for an institution — in many cases, for a new institution, which had been set up only a short time before amid a fanfare of trumpets. Thus, the failure of the Macmillan government's incomes policy was a defeat for the National Incomes Commission, the failure of the first Wilson government's incomes policy a defeat for the National Board for Prices and Incomes and the failure of the Heath government's incomes policy a defeat for the Pay Board and the Price Commission. More damagingly, failure sometimes represented a defeat for Parliament or, at any rate, a successful challenge to an Act of Parliament: the failures of the Heath government's Industrial Relations Act and statutory incomes policy are the most obvious cases in point. On one famous occasion — the first Wilson government's abandonment of the 1969 'In Place of Strife' white paper — it resulted from a successful challenge to the government's declared intention to pass an Act of Parliament at some stage in the future. Sometimes no institution or Act of Parliament was involved. On virtually all occasions, however, the policy which failed had carried a heavy investment of political capital, so that its failure dealt a severe, sometimes even crippling, blow to the authority of the government which had initiated it. Each such blow made it more difficult to mobilise consent, and therefore to succeed, in future.

To a growing number of politicians and opinion formers, the moral seemed plain. Hands-on intervention carried excessive political risks. The political economy was full of 'no-go' areas, where government's writ might not run. If it intruded into them, it would probably burn its fingers, and might start a conflagration in which the whole edifice of political authority would be destroyed. Since these were precisely the areas into which hands-on governments did intrude, and since they intruded into them because that was the only way to honour the fundamental commitments which Keynesian social democrats had taken for granted since the war, the obvious implication was that Keynesian social democracy would have to be abandoned.

The truth was less palatable and more complex. Keynesian social-democratic policies were frustrated by Keynesian social-democratic politics. The interventions of the hands-on phase — interventions which had to be carried out if the governments of the period were to honour their fundamental policy commitments — required different political institutions and, on a deeper level, a different approach to politics and government as such. But although Keynesian social democracy had a theory of the economy (indeed, more than one theory), it had no theory of the political economy. In all three of the policy phases described here, the technocratic assumption that the economy could be understood and managed as an autonomous realm, conceptually separate from the polity, remained unquestioned. Lacking a theory of the political economy, Keynesian social-democratic politicians and officials could not come to terms, either with the political implications of their economic policies, or with the economic implications of their political assumptions. In a muddled sort of way, the governments of the hands-on phase sensed that consensual intervention in the supply-side would not work without a different kind of relationship between the state and the producer groups. As the hands-on phase continued, they also sensed that it needed a different kind of relationship with the public at large. Hence, the flurry of institutional changes and the repeated attempts to appeal for public support over the heads of the producer-group leaders. But because they had no coherent theory on which to base them, and therefore could not address the questions of direction and value they raised, their institutional initiatives were unsystematic and half-hearted and their appeals for support, inconsistent and unconvincing.

The conflict between policy and politics was particularly noticeable in three areas. The first and most obvious had to do with the relationship between the state and the organised producer groups. As we have seen, the governments of the hands-on phase recognised that the detailed micro-economic intervention they wanted to practise would not work without consultation and negotiation between the state, the organised employers and organised labour, and set up new institutions for the purpose, reminiscent of the functional bodies which the pioneers of the planning strand in Keynesian social democracy had advocated between the wars. Dismay at the apparent failure of these institutions, and exasperation with the producer groups' inability to 'deliver' their members, were among the most potent sources of the shift of opinion which destroyed the old consensus.[25] On one level, the dismay and exasperation were justified. All too often, the producer groups did fail to deliver, and, for the most part, the new institutions did not live up to the expectations of their founders. But the roots of these failures went much deeper than most politicians and officials were prepared to recognise. The governments which created the new functional institutions were trying to have their cake and eat it. They remained wedded to the traditional Westminster doctrines of parliamentary sovereignty and ministerial responsibility, and tried to tack new approaches and new institutions on to the old approaches and institutions which those doctrines implied. Instead of acknowledging the tension between the territorial representation of individuals embodied in Westminster parliamentarianism and the functional representation of groups implied by bodies like the NEDC and the 'little Neddies', and trying to answer the questions of political

and constitutional principle which it raised, their characteristic tactic was to obfuscate it. Partly because of this, and
partly, no doubt, because they were in any case unwilling to
allow others to share the powers which Westminster parliamentarianism conferred upon them, the roles of the new
functional bodies which they set up were often ambiguous, and
their authority uncertain. The result, to use a phrase of
François Perroux's, was that the British economy in the
hands-on phase was not so much 'concerted' as 'discussed';[26]
since the governments concerned were unwilling to be bound
by the discussions, it is not surprising that the producer groups
should have been equally unwilling.

The second area had to do with distribution. The incomes
policies and industrial interventions of the hands-on phase all
raised complex distributional questions. Were wage controls to
freeze the existing pattern of income distribution or to change
it? If the latter, what changes were they to make? Part of the
point of an industrial policy is to allocate resources differently
from the way in which the market would have allocated them.
How were the costs and benefits to be distributed? Though
they were often cloaked in technical jargon, these questions
were, at bottom, normative, not technical. But none of those
involved − politicians, officials, or producer-group leaders −
had normative criteria to provide the answers; and the familiar
practices and institutions of the Westminster Model provided
no mechanism for negotiating criteria. The result was that
policies oscillated, while consensus was lacking. Because there
was no consensus, the distributional judgments which governments were obliged to make were apt to seem capricious and
unfair. That, in turn, made it easy for powerful groups to
challenge them, and helps to explain why governments found it
so difficult to mobilise the public against the challengers.

The third area concerned the international implications of
domestic economic management. As we have seen, hands-on
intervention was designed, among other things, to cut through
the stop-go cycle of the 1950s. But, as we have also seen, the
stop-go cycle was itself, in part, the product of constraints
which Britain's role in the world imposed on domestic
economic policy. The obvious implication was that hands-on

intervention would not work without changes in that role. But just as it had no theory of the domestic political economy, so Keynesian social democracy had no theory of international political economics; and just as Keynesian social democrats took the Westminster Model for granted, so they took it for granted that Britain should remain, so far as possible, a world financial and military power. In 1966, when the conflict between domestic expansion and international aspirations became acute, the first Wilson government abandoned the National Plan rather than devalue sterling. *Mutatis mutandis,* the same thing happened ten years later when the Callaghan government cut public expenditure in order to obtain credits from the IMF. By now, it is true, Britain was a member state of the European Community; the world role had gone; and the pound had been floated. But participation in the increasingly competitive and interdependent world free-trading system imposed even harsher constraints on domestic economic management in the 1970s than it had in the 1950s. In an open market economy of Britain's size, national economic sovereignty, at any rate over macro-economic policy, was plainly an illusion. But it did not follow that there were no circumstances in which public power could be exerted in the macroeconomic sphere. Two strategies for asserting it still made intellectual sense. One was to accept that the nation-state could no longer exercise the powers which the Keynesian revolution had given it, and to create inter- or supra-national institutions to exercise them instead. The other was to make a reality of national economic sovereignty, by opting out of the world free-trading system. Successive governments of both parties rejected the second, but none seriously contemplated adopting the first.

Either policy or politics had to give. The real significance of the ideological polarisation of the 1970s is that it marked the victory of politics over policy. Faced with a choice between the fundamental policy commitments of the Keynesian social-democratic era and the political assumptions which the Keynesian social democrats had inherited from the past, the political class increasingly opted for the latter. For although the neo-liberals and neo-socialists differed violently from each other, they were in agreement on two crucial points. In the first place, each camp held that consensual intervention in the supply-side, of the sort which the governments of the 1960s and 1970s had all attempted and on which they had all burned their fingers, was in any case pointless and even damaging. Secondly, and more importantly, each offered a way of running the economy − in the case of the neo-liberals, greater reliance on the supposedly impersonal and therefore apolitical forces of the market; in that of most neo-socialists, greater reliance on direction by a centralised state − which would obviate the need for the political changes which industrial and international power-sharing implied. Both purported to offer solutions to the country's economic problems. The real attraction of both was that they offered ways of avoiding the political questions which the hands-on phase of Keynesian social democracy had raised, and to which the inherited assumptions of the political class could provide no answers.

Yet their offers were more ambiguous and less consistent than they appeared at first sight. In the next chapter I explore these ambiguities and inconsistencies.

3

Neo-Liberals and Neo-Socialists

'The middle ground turned out to be like the will-o'-the-wisp, the light which flickers over marshlands by night, beguiling the weary traveller; as he moves towards it, the currents of air he sets up by his movement send it dancing away from him, and he goes on following, stumbling deeper and deeper into the mire.'

Sir Keith Joseph, 1975.[1]

'Social-democratic revisionism . . . was killed, not by the left, but by the bankers.'

Tony Benn, 1982.[2]

The course taken by Britain's political economy in the 1960s and 1970s is difficult to trace, and the sequel is even more confusing. In some ways, the 1979 election marked a clear break with the preceding thirty-five years. As we have seen, the Conservative leadership was now largely neo-liberal in ideology; and the new government followed a broadly neo-liberal path. But in Britain, as in all complex modern societies, the margin of manoeuvre available to any government is extremely narrow. Past commitments, past entitlements and the expectations they generate ensure that profound shifts in public policy take place only slowly. Inevitably, the new regime left much of its Keynesian social-democratic inheritance undisturbed. Equally, Labour's shift towards neo-socialism went nothing like as far as the neo-socialists of the 1970s had hoped, or as their opponents had feared. As in the 1930s, the party went left after one election defeat, only to go right after a second. To depict the political history of the late 1970s and early 1980s as a clear-cut ideological struggle between neo-liberals on the right and neo-socialists on the left would be to caricature an enormously more complex reality.

From our perspective, however, these complexities are of secondary importance. This book is not a political history. Its object is to explore the gap between doctrine and reality in contemporary Britain, and to see whether it can be closed. From this point of view, the survival of a substantial Keynesian social-democratic legislative and administrative legacy in an inhospitable climate is neither here nor there. What matter are the policy failures described in the last chapter, and the search for an alternative governing philosophy which they have provoked. For better or worse, neo-liberalism and neo-socialism are still the chief claimants for that role; and if we are to contribute to the search, it is more important to tease out the underlying assumptions and implications of their claims than to assess their impact on events. Hence, we now follow a different path from the last chapter's, and focus on the logic of neo-liberal and neo-socialist *arguments* rather than on the policies of governments and oppositions.

Neo-liberalism and neo-socialism appeal to different values, look forward to different futures and attract different constituencies. Yet in certain respects, they have more in common than their followers would be happy to realise. In the first place, both camps hold that Keynesian social democracy collapsed because it was bound to collapse. For both, the policy failures of the 1970s proved that it had always been futile to search for a middle way between capitalism and socialism: that even in the days when the search had appeared to be successful, success was sowing the seeds of eventual failure. As we shall see, they arrive at this conclusion by different routes. The important point, however, is that, for both, the whole attempt to transcend the dichotomies of market versus state and personal freedom versus social justice was always and by definition vain. The market is the market, and the state, the state. Attempts to use state intervention to soften the rigours of the market are bound to fail: without the rigours it will not work.[3] For both, moreover, that conclusion is axiomatic — the logical corollary of assumed truths about individual or class behaviour, which are held to apply in all places and at all times. When Sir Keith Joseph declared that the middle ground had turned out to be a 'will-o'-the-wisp' he did not mean that particular mistakes at a particular moment of history had prevented its discovery. He meant that the nature of economic man is such that it had never existed and never could exist. When Tony Benn said that 'the bankers' had killed social-democratic revisionism, he did not mean that the revisionists had been too cowardly or too stupid to survive. He meant that the logic of capitalism is such that revisionism could never have been more than a deceptive flash in the pan. For both, it is therefore a waste of time to examine the record of Keynesian social democracy in detail, to see whether the mistakes made by Keynesian social-democratic governments could have been avoided or what lessons they hold for those who might wish to realise the same values in different ways. The details are irrelevant: the only lesson is that such values cannot be realised at all.

This leads on to a deeper and more complicated similarity. As we have seen, the problems which baffled the Keynesian social-democratic governments of the 1960s and 1970s were quintessentially political. They had to do with the distribution of income and power; with the tensions between short-term private interests and long-term public benefits, and between the realities of group power and the values of liberal individualism; above all, with the mobilisation of consent and the limits of authority. Keynesian social democracy collapsed, not so much because its economic policies were defective, as because political factors which its intellectual ancestors had not foreseen prevented it from coping with a deepening economic crisis. Neo-liberalism and neo-socialism are the legatees of its collapse. But they do not offer solutions to the political problems which it could not solve: they represent parallel escape routes from the tedious, exhausting and some-times bruising search for a political diet capable of sustaining a mixed economy in an advanced industrial society. To be sure, both are political doctrines, whose exponents wish to change the world through political action in democratic systems. Yet both have inherited from their nineteenth-century intellectual ancestors a strange ambivalence about democracy as a method, and even about politics as an activity: and it is in the nature, sources and consequences of that ambivalence that their real significance lies.

In the case of the neo-socialists, it is easy to see where it comes from. The society which Marx expected to follow the overthrow of capitalism was to be stateless as well as classless. In it, there would be no conflicts of interest, and therefore no need for coercion. The 'government of persons' as Engels put it, would give way to the 'administration of things':[4] politics, in any normal sense of the term, would cease to exist. Meanwhile, in the brutal, class-divided, exploitative society of the present, 'bourgeois' democracy was nothing more than camouflage for class oppression. For Marxists, democratic politics, and the give and take of democratic politics, are at best a staging post on the way to the non-political society of the future, and at worst a delusion, diverting the working class from its mission.

The sources of the neo-liberal ambivalence are less obvious. In Britain, after all, the golden age of classical, nineteenth-century market liberalism was also the golden age of parliamentary politics; many (though by no means all) of the early champions of democracy were market liberals as well. On a deeper level, however, the classical market-liberal ideal of the frictionless, 'undistorted' market has more in common with Marx's vision than most Marxists or market liberals would like to admit. In the market-liberal ideal, free men, freely exchanging goods and services without intervention by the state, maximise the general interest by pursuing their own interests; though the state does not wither away, as it does in the Marxist vision, it comes near to doing so. The relationships which matter, which turn the wheels of society and determine how resources shall be allocated, are exchange relationships, not political ones; persuasion, argument and debate, the stuff of democratic politics, do not intrude into the serious business of making a living. The hero, the lynch-pin of the system, is the self-denying, risk-taking, wealth-creating capitalist. The ruler, the statesman, the office-holder, is at best an auxiliary, whose function is to provide the political conditions in which the market can work properly. At worst, he is a parasite. Earlier, as Albert Hirschman has shown, the eighteenth-century apologists for emergent capitalism saw the 'passions' — in particular

the aristocratic 'passion' for the glories of government and
politics — as irrational and destructive, and looked to the
'interests', above all to the inglorious, but supremely rational,
bourgeois interest in gain, to hold them in check.[5] And
although classical, nineteenth-century market liberals did not
see democracy as a sham, many of them saw it as a threat and
others as a risky, even perilous, gamble.[6]

It would be wrong to suggest that the neo-liberals and
neo-socialists of the late-twentieth century share all the attitudes of their nineteenth-century predecessors. Yet strong
traces show through. For neo-liberals, market relationships are
freer, more spontaneous, in a strange way more authentic than
political relationships: market power does not exist, while the
state is, by definition, the realm of power and domination. It is
in the market that men express themselves as they really are; in
politics their preferences are thwarted or twisted.[7] Though
most neo-socialists have softened the old Marxist contempt for
bourgeois democracy, they still take it for granted that there
can be no genuine community of interests, and therefore no
genuine political community, in a capitalist society.

On a deeper level, moreover, neither neo-liberalism nor
neo-socialism can logically accommodate the notion that a
political community is, among other things, a web of reciprocal
duties and rights: that rights imply duties, and that the health
of the community depends as much on its members' willingness to perform duties as on their ability to enjoy rights. Partly
because of all this, both camps share a pervasive, though
sometimes unacknowledged, scepticism about the possibility
of changing attitudes or behaviour through democratic politics. For both, the notion of a common civic morality taming
individual and class appetites, is not merely alien, but absurd.
The polity is and can only be an arena for the pursuit of
interests — of individual interests in the case of the neo-liberals,
and of class interests in the case of the neo-socialists. For both,
these interests are given; the products of prior individual
preference or objective class situation, and therefore not
subject to change by argument or debate. For both, politics as,
among other things, a process of mutual education, in which
the members of a community listen to and learn from each

other, and in doing so re-define their interests, is therefore impossible.[8]

Moreover, the underlying assumptions of both imply that democracy and capitalism are, in the long run, incompatible — or, to put it more precisely, that they can be rendered compatible only by imposing restrictions on the scope of the former so tight as to negate the promise of equal rights which lies at its heart. Naturally, the two creeds explain this incompatibility in different ways. As we shall see, neo-liberals believe that democratic electorates are bound to behave short-sightedly and greedily: that, whereas economic man is inherently rational, political man acts in a way which is destructively irrational, at any rate from the point of view of society as a whole. Though neo-liberals do not always draw it explicitly, the logical conclusion is that unfettered democracy will sooner or later undermine the essential foundations of a market economy which is itself one of the essential foundations of a free society, and that democracy should therefore be restrained so that freedom may flourish. The neo-socialists do not share those values, or the conclusions to which they point, but they offer an uncannily similar analysis. For them, as for the neo-liberals, political man — at any rate, political man under capitalism — is inherently insatiable even if not inherently irrational. So long as the fundamental contradictions of capitalism endure — and, by definition, they will endure so long as capitalism endures — the working class can have no stake in the system. It will not benefit the community by restraining its demands, for there is no genuine community. In a capitalist economy, working-class restraint benefits only the capitalists. Thus, the more mature and confident the working class, the more likely it is to press its demands relentlessly against the limits of supply; and the system will remain legitimate in working-class eyes only to the extent that it accommodates these demands.

The neo-socialist escape route needs only a brief discussion here. To be sure, writers in the Marxist tradition have made important contributions to academic debate on the subjects with which this book is concerned; some of the argument of

Part Two draws on their insights. In an intellectual history of the 1970s and 1980s, they would bulk large: at least as large as writers in any other tradition. But this is not intended to be an intellectual history of the recent past, any more than a political one. It is concerned with ideas as signposts to action: with theories put forward in order to change the world as well as to understand it. And from this point of view, neo-socialism is surprisingly uninteresting.

Two neo-socialist diagnoses repay attention. The first is what might be called the theory of the 'fiscal crisis'.[9] Because the fundamental contradictions of capitalism have not been overcome, the central argument runs — because the means of production are still privately owned, and because as a result society is still divided into antagonistic classes — the capitalist state must perform two complementary, but at the same time antagonistic, functions. It must maintain the conditions in which profitable capital accumulation can be carried on: the 'accumulation function'. It must also maintain sufficient social harmony for the system to survive: the 'legitimisation function'. Both functions burden the national exchequer. The accumulation function does so because in advanced, late-twentieth-century capitalism, the inevitable costs of economic growth — the infrastructure investments needed to make it possible; the welfare programmes needed to ease the social tensions which it brings in its train — are increasingly borne by the state rather than by private capital itself. The legitimisation function does so because the processes of capital accumulation have themselves created an organised and self-conscious working class, with sufficient economic and political power to insist on a substantial social wage as the price of its acquiescence in the system.

In the boom years of the 1950s and 1960s, the exchequer could bear both burdens without difficulty. But, as the rising individual wages won by an increasingly demanding working class cut into profits, and the growth of trade-union power at the work-place made it more difficult for management to raise productivity, the boom petered out. As private capital became less profitable, the state had to spend more on the accumulation function; as rising unemployment alienated the working class, it also had to spend more on the legitimisation function. But, as the economy slowed down, the fiscal dividend disappeared. The result was a fiscal crisis, followed and exacerbated by a social crisis. The growth in public expenditure could be financed only by cutting private consumption, or investment, or both; in the inevitable resistance to such cuts, the class conflicts which made it necessary for the state to perform the legitimisation function in the first place became more intense. This double crisis eroded public support for the system and destroyed the basis on which the Keynesian social-democratic consensus had rested.

The second neo-socialist explanation which repays attention derives from Galbraith rather than Marx. It might be entitled 'the escape of the meso-economy'.[10] In the Keynesian system, the argument runs, the economy has only two dimensions: the 'macro-economy' of global aggregates, which Keynesian theory was designed to master, and the 'micro-economy' of the classical textbooks, which Keynes thought should be left to its own devices. Unfortunately, a third dimension has grown up since he wrote, which his system does not explain and with which it cannot deal. Between the micro-economy of the small firm and the macro-economy which the Keynesian levers are supposed to manipulate, there is a 'meso-economy' (from the Greek *meso*, meaning intermediate) of giant, multi-product, sometimes multi-company and often multinational firms. These giants defy the postulates of all neo-classical theory, Keynesian as well as anti-Keynesian. Through their market power, they have escaped from the control of the sovereign nation state. They can frustrate its monetary policies through their access to credit beyond its boundaries, and its fiscal policies through transfer prices which lower their profits in high-tax countries and raise them in countries where taxes are lower. By the same means, they can also frustrate its attempts to manage the exchange rate. Since their investment horizons are longer than those Keynes presupposed, their investment intentions do not respond to Keynesian pump-priming in the expected way. Thus, the levers of Keynesian demand management have broken on the realities of meso-economic power. Hence, the crisis of the

Keynesian state: a crisis, in essence, of political and institutional under-capacity.

At first sight, the implications of both these arguments are uncompromisingly intransigent. Capitalism is still capitalism: its contradictions are still inescapable: social-democratic reformism is still a blind alley. As so often in the history of the left, however, uncompromising intransigence is first cousin to a curious kind of millenarian defeatism. Unrecognised by supporters or opponents, there was a paradox about the neo-socialist tide which reached its high point in the late 1970s and early 1980s. In spite of the ground it gained and the alarm it provoked – in spite, for that matter, of the theoretical sophistication displayed by many of its exponents – neo-socialism lacked, and still lacks, a strategic doctrine, proceeding from diagnosis to cure. The theory of the fiscal crisis purports to explain the collapse of the Keynesian welfare state; it fails conspicuously to link that explanation to a coherent programme of action. In it, socialism is a kind of *deus ex machina*, which will descend when the balance of class power has reached the right point. Meanwhile, socialists can only wait and keep their powder dry. Despite appearances to the contrary, it is, in practice, a defensive theory, not an offensive one – a theory for a shrinking proletarian ghetto, not for an advancing proletarian army.

This is not quite so true of the theory of the escape of the meso-economy. It provided the intellectual under-pinning for the Labour Left's 'alternative strategy' in the middle 1970s, and has inspired a series of broadly similar proposals since.[11] Yet these proposals – import controls, withdrawal from the European Community, extensions of public ownership – also lack a coherent strategic foundation. For they do not take account of the social realities which the underlying theory purports to have uncovered. To be sure, they would shift the whole balance of the political economy, perhaps irreversibly, if they were put into practice. But the theory from which they are derived offers their advocates no reason for believing that they can be put into practice. Albeit only tacitly, the governing assumption underlying the whole programme is that it will be carried out if a future socialist government wishes to carry it out. If the underlying theory is true, however – if the new centres of meso-economic power are strong enough to blunt the weapons of Keynesian demand management and frustrate the policies of the Keynesian state – the giant firms which wield that power are hardly likely to sit quietly while their wings are clipped. In one way or another, they will resist; and the government will have to decide how to respond to their resistance.

There is nothing in the theory to show that it will respond more firmly than previous socialist governments have done in similar circumstances. Still less is there anything to show that the prevailing balance of social power will allow it to respond more firmly should it wish to do so. The theory, in other words, implies more than its exponents have been willing to recognise. If it is true, then they are right in thinking that social-democratic reformism is no longer feasible. But if the reason why social-democratic reformism is no longer feasible is that new centres of social power have emerged, strong enough to make the weapons traditionally used by social-democratic reformists unworkable, it is not enough to put forward more radical policies. It is also necessary to link such policies to a radical political strategy through which these new centres can be mastered, and their inevitable opposition overcome. And about the possible content of such a strategy the theory is silent.

Neo-liberalism deserves more extended treatment. Neo-liberal theories are not all of a piece, of course. Neo-liberalism should be seen as a cluster of related attitudes and beliefs, not as a single, monolithic creed. That said, the same underlying theme runs through almost all neo-liberal interpretations of the political and economic history of the last twenty years: the theme of what it became fashionable in the 1970s to call 'overload'.[12] The governments of the 1960s and 1970s failed, neo-liberals argue, because too much was demanded of them, and because they tried too hard to satisfy the demands: in the language of the metaphor, the fuses of the political economy blew because the circuits were carrying too much current. Driven by the expectations and ambitions which Keynesian social democracy had generated, government reached further than it could grasp. The result was a paradox. Big government turned out to be ineffective government. The more it tried to do, the more it failed. The more it failed, the more it lost authority. The more authority it lost, the more it failed.

All this applied with special force in the economic sphere. Stagflation, currency depreciation, balance-of-payments crises, even faltering growth and declining competitiveness — in neo-liberal eyes, all the characteristic economic ills of the seventies were symptoms of the same syndrome of encroaching government and ebbing governability. The industrial interventions of hands-on Keynesian social democracy prevented market forces from working properly, and in doing so made the economy less productive than it would otherwise have been. So far from strengthening the supply-side, government was systematically 'picking losers'[13] — necessarily, since, in the long run, only the market can pick winners. That was only the beginning of the story. With the pre-Keynesian doctrine of the balanced budget discredited, and deficit finance made respectable, the 'mooring rope' of the nineteenth-century fiscal constitution had been cut.[14] The result was a rake's progress of swelling public expenditure, paid for either by inflationary increases in the money supply, or by taxes which cut into take-home pay, provoking inflationary wage demands and eroding public confidence in government.[15] Above all, the fundamental Keynesian commitment to full employment, and the corresponding Keynesian faith in demand management, set in motion a vicious spiral of inflationary expectations and currency debasement, in the long run adding to unemployment instead of subtracting from it.

The last point is so central to the neo-liberal diagnosis that the argument behind it must be set out with some care. It starts from the premise that the labour market is a market like other markets. There is therefore a market-clearing price for labour, just as there is a market-clearing price for apples. If sellers of labour offer their wares at a price higher than the market-clearing price, they will find no buyers. Since markets must clear, in the long run, at the clearing price, the only possible cause of unemployment in the long run is that real wages have been pushed above the market-clearing level. In practice, however, there will always be rigidities in the labour market to prevent the market-clearing mechanism from working properly. These rigidities produce a rate of unemployment, different at different times and in different societies, which can be called the 'natural' rate. Keynesian pump-priming can force the actual rate below the natural rate for a while, but by increasing the money supply and so causing inflation. Sooner or later, workers will become used to the going-rate of inflation, and demand wage increases which take account of it. If government still insists on forcing unemployment below the natural rate, it will accommodate these demands with yet more increases in the money supply. The result will be yet more inflation and yet higher wage demands, followed, so long as the distemper lasts, by yet more Keynesian pump-priming and yet more inflation. A favourite neo-liberal analogy is with drug addiction: to produce the required result, each 'fix' has to be bigger, and more destructive, than the last. Sooner or later, the drug will have to be withdrawn. When it is, the distortions which inflation brought in its train will almost certainly have made the natural rate of unemployment higher than it was at the beginning. In any event, the withdrawal symptoms are bound to include high unemployment in the short term.[16]

In themselves, these doctrines were not particularly startling. All neo-classical economics, and not only its neo-liberal varieties, is based ultimately on the 'price-auction' view of the economy, according to which resources are, by definition, most efficiently allocated through 'undistorted' competitive markets, operating through the price mechanism.[17] Most economists in the tradition hold that government intervention is justified only to provide public goods, which the market cannot provide, and to correct market failure. As we have seen, Keynes himself opposed government intervention in the supply-side on classical, market-liberal grounds, and it was only when it had become clear that the arm's length Keynesian social democracy of the 1950s had failed to halt Britain's relative economic decline that his intellectual followers turned towards indicative planning and controls over wages and prices. Whether these interventions could or could not be justified within the accepted neo-classical framework was always a moot point; in arguing that they could not, neo-liberal economists were engaging in a professional dispute with fellow professionals, not mounting a philosophical counter-revolution. The neo-liberal attack on Keynesian demand management was, of course, a different matter. That went to the heart of Keynesian social democracy, raising issues of high political and philosophical controversy. But it was hardly a novel attack: Keynes's opponents had said much the same in the 1930s, and once the dust had settled, few denied that the Keynesians had won the argument. Had the neo-liberals confined themselves to these economic criticisms, they might have made a stir in the journals, but it is hard to believe that they would have had much influence on events.

What gave neo-liberalism its counter-revolutionary bite was its political theory, not its economics: its analysis of the dynamics of alleged overload, not its description of the ills of an allegedly overloaded political economy. As we have seen, Keynesianism was a doctrine of market failure. By the same token, it was also a doctrine of government success. Even more obviously, so were the doctrines that inspired the planning and welfare strands in post-war Keynesian social democracy. All presupposed that government − or, at any rate, liberal-democratic government − is at once inherently benign and inherently competent. The real originality and power of present-day neo-liberalism lie in its attempt to turn that central presupposition on its head. In a late-twentieth-century political economy, with competitive party politics, a mass electorate, big government and strong, well-entrenched, organised interest groups, neo-liberals argue, market failure is in practice less likely and less damaging than government failure. In such a political economy, government cannot be trusted to do better than the market, even when the market has failed and when there is a case, in principle, for government intervention to correct its failure. In the economic sphere, at any rate, late-twentieth-century democratic government is not benign at all. It is malign.

It is malign for three reasons. In the first place, the electoral processes from which democratic governments spring are themselves malign. This is what might be called the 'political market-place' argument, the chief British exponent of which has been the economic commentator, Samuel Brittan.[18] It can be traced back to Joseph Schumpeter's famous suggestion that the essence of democracy lies in a 'competitive struggle for the people's vote', analogous to the entrepreneur's competition for customers.[19] In it, the democratic process is seen as a special kind of market: as a market where votes are exchanged for policies. The party machines are like business firms trying to sell their products. Policies are the products; votes are the currency; office is the profit. But the neo-liberals add a pessimistic twist to a notion which Schumpeter himself presented in an optimistic way. Unfortunately, they point out, there is a fundamental difference between the vote market and other markets. In ordinary markets, the consumer operates within a budget constraint. He trades off competing wants against each other, adjusting his preferences to changes of price. The voter cannot do this. He does not pay directly, as an individual, for the policies he 'buys'; he cannot buy slightly more of one policy when the price goes down, and slightly less of another when the price goes up; more important still, his own decisions have only a trivial influence on the size of the payment he has to make in the end. Even if he is a prudent character, who prefers cheap policies to expensive ones, he will have to pay his share of the cost of the expensive ones if the majority decides to buy them. He is like a skinflint, dining in an expensive restaurant with a party of friends, who have agreed to share the bill equally between them. However tight-fisted he may be, it is not rational for him to order the cheapest items on the menu. If he does, he will probably end by subsidising his fellow diners. It makes more sense for him to opt for the caviar and champagne.

By the same token, it is not rational for policy salesmen to cater for skinflint customers: in the vote market, expensive policies sell best. Because of all this, the political process in a modern mass democracy is, in two senses, inflationary. It is inflationary in the narrow sense that political leaders − unwilling to pay the political costs of resisting excessive demands and expectations – have a built-in propensity to accommodate them through increases in public expenditure, paid for through increases in the money supply. It is also inflationary in the more fundamental sense that the competitive auction for votes, which is the essence of democratic politics, makes demands and expectations excessive even if they were moderate to start with.

The political market-place argument applies to what might be called the demand-side of the democratic process. A complementary argument – it might be called the bureaucratic empire-building argument – applies to the supply-side. The Keynesian social-democratic picture of government as a benign market-corrector and social-problem-solver depended on the assumption that the officials who actually do the correcting and solving are disinterested servants of the public, with no private axes to grind. It is as foolish to make that assumption, say the neo-liberals, as it would be to make the same assumption about entrepreneurs in the private sector. 'Bureaucrats', in Gordon Tulloch's phrase, 'are like other men';[20] they may, in practice, serve the public good, just as private entrepreneurs generally serve the public good, but if they do it will be because it is in their interests to do so. But, whereas competitive markets bring the private interest of the entrepreneur into harmony with the general interest, there is no invisible hand in government to do the same to the private interest of the bureaucrat. In practice, the bureaucratic equivalent of profit is size. Where entrepreneurs try to maximise profits, bureaucrats try to maximise their bureaux. Since they generally have a monopoly of expertise in their own spheres, it is extraordinarily difficult for their nominal political chiefs to prevent them. The result is a continuous, built-in pressure for expanding government, emanating from within the government machine itself, independently of the voters, and also of the politicians who are supposed to represent the voters.[21]

In the political market-place and bureaucratic empire-building arguments, the motor of the process is the timeless appetite of the individual, and the villain of the piece, institutional. Individuals act rationally to maximise their interests, but the institutions of the political and bureaucratic marketplaces condemn them to do so in ways which run counter to their own (and everyone else's) interests in the long term. Implicit in much of the neo-liberal critique of Keynesian social democracy, however, is a third, more nebulous, more time-bound, but equally resonant, set of arguments in which the villain is cultural. Once again, the central thesis is that democracy feeds on itself. This time, however, changing values, rather than the constants of individual behaviour, set the processes of self-mastication in motion.

In its early years, the argument runs, the latent dangers of Keynesian social democracy were held in check by traditional values, traditional systems of authority and traditional methods of social control. By the 1960s, however, these restraints and inhibitions were wearing thin. A change in the *Zeitgeist* had produced 'a generalised erosion in public and private manners, increasingly liberalised attitudes towards sexual activities, a declining vitality of the Puritan work ethic, deterioration in product quality, explosion of the welfare rolls, [and] widespread corruption in both the private and the governmental sector'.[22] It had also disseminated democratic, egalitarian and participatory beliefs more widely than ever before. Groups which had hitherto been, for all practical purposes, excluded from the political process – women, racial minorities, the poor – demanded, and won, a place in the sun. As in the political market-place argument, the result was a paradox. The 'democratic surge', as it was called in a much-cited report for the Trilateral Commission in 1975, over-whelmed the informal barriers of convention and culture which had made democratic government possible.[23] As participation widened, more was demanded of government, making the load on it heavier. As egalitarian and individualistic attitudes became more general, they undermined all forms of authority, making it more difficult for government to carry the load. In its struggles to carry it, government expanded public spending. The imbalanced growth of public expenditure exacerbated inflation. Thus, the dynamics of the democratic process pro-duced a surfeit of democracy. By implication, at any rate, democracy is to adults what chocolate is to children: endlessly tempting; harmless in small doses; sickening in excess.

Once again, the implications are not what they seem at first sight. In principle, a crisis of overload could be overcome in one of two ways. Either the circuits could be strengthened, or the current could be reduced. Here, the neo-liberal position has turned out to be more complex, not to say more ambiguous, than was generally expected when it started to gain ground in British politics. The political economy is in crisis, say the various overload theories, because the state has intruded into economic spheres where it has no business to be; the rake's progress of excessive expectations and inflationary policies started on its way because the old, nineteenth-century barriers between the polity and the economy were destroyed. The obvious solution is to push the state back; to rebuild the barriers; in neo-Marxist language to 'de-couple' the state from the economy, so as to return, as far as possible, to the liberal capitalism of the past. Hence, the familiar neo-liberal agenda of privatisation, de-regulation, cuts in public expenditure, lower taxation and reduced state intervention in industry — all, in essence, different ways of reducing the current.

The trouble is that that part of the agenda, though an essential element in the neo-liberal cure, does not go to the heart of the problems which the neo-liberals claim to have diagnosed. It deals only with the consequences of overload, not with its causes: with the government-induced 'distortions' of an overloaded economy, not with the dynamics of the overload process. If the overload theorists are right, these cannot be countered merely by pulling the state out of the economic spheres it should never have entered. Somehow, the whole mechanism of overload must be stopped and the mix of social expectations and demands changed, so that the state is not put under pressure to re-enter these spheres in future. To do that it is necessary to halt, or if possible to reverse, the spiral of inflationary aspirations, inflationary promises and inflationary policies of which the crisis of overload and ungovernability was the culmination. Not only inflation, but inflationary expectations, must be squeezed out of the system. Along with government-induced distortions, the market must be freed of the non-governmental distortions which helped to cause the failures which government intervention was foolishly supposed to correct.

Here, however, there is a gap in the neo-liberal argument, reminiscent of the gap in the neo-socialist argument which we have just discussed. On the neo-liberals' own showing, all this will require profound changes of attitude and behaviour. But neo-liberalism has nothing to say about the processes through which attitudes and behaviour change: as we have seen, in the classical and neo-classical economic systems, the preferences which men bring to the market, and the factors which shape these preferences, are exogenous. It therefore offers – and logically can offer – no reason to believe that changes of this sort will take place. Indeed, the gap in the neo-liberal argument is even more serious than that. The central premise of all the overload theories we have been discussing is that – for whatever reason – popular expectations and demands have become excessive. In that case, why should the genie suddenly go back into the bottle? Overload, as these theories depict it, does not spring from conscious intent, but from unintentional social processes, through which individuals, acting rationally to maximise their interests, produce an irrational result. Why should such processes stop or go into reverse?

In some neo-liberal writings on these matters, there is an implicit assumption that rational argument will lead to a change of heart, and a change of heart to a change of system. But for neo-liberals that is a form of utopianism, reminiscent of the millenarian defeatism of the neo-socialists. It may have made sense for Keynes, with his mandarin belief in the power of disinterested intelligence, to claim, in his most famous phrase, that the world is ruled by ideas.[24] If they are consistent, neo-liberals must believe that it is ruled by interests; and if the rest of their theories are right, interests are given, impervious to political argument or debate. Abandon that assumption, and the notion that democratic politics can never be anything more than a competitive auction for votes falls to the ground. On the other hand, an appeal to self-interest is hardly likely to do the trick, since *ex hypothesi* those to whom the appeal would have to be made are already pursuing what they believe to be their self-interest. Many neo-liberal writers have suggested that the dilemma can be resolved through institutional changes, such as a constitutional amendment to outlaw deficit financing or the establishment of an independent commission, not subject to political control, to manage the money supply.[25] F.A. Hayek, the most distinguished of the neo-liberal thinkers whose writings helped to change the intellectual climate in the 1970s, has proposed an elaborate set of constitutional changes designed to counteract the forces making for fiscal irresponsibility by destroying the influence of political parties and pressure groups and limiting the suffrage. Under his constitution, a legislature, the members of which would be elected for fifteen years by those over the age of forty-five, would lay down general rules governing the conduct of public business; civil servants, old age pensioners and the unemployed would have no votes. Administration would be left to a subordinate assembly, whose decisions would be binding only if they conformed to the rules promulgated by the legislature.[26] But there is an air of desperation in suggestions of this sort. If the forces making for overload are as powerful as the neo-liberal analysis implies, how can fragile constitutional devices stand up to them? If the source of the problem is democracy, how can it be solved democratically?

The answer bristles with paradoxes. In order to reduce the economic current, neo-liberals conclude in effect, it will be necessary to strengthen the *moral* circuits: if the economy is to be de-coupled from the polity, the barriers of custom and attitude which separated them in the past will have to be rebuilt. To do this, the state will have to have the authority and will to push aside the vested interests whose demands have kept the barriers down for so long: though there is a libertarian, even quasi-anarchistic, flavour in some neo-liberal writings, it is remote from the mainstream. Most neo-liberals hold that the state must be strong as well as limited: indeed, that it has to be strong in order to be limited.[27] A more complicated paradox follows as well. On one level, as we have seen, the over-arching neo-liberal value is freedom of choice. In a market order, men are free to choose their own purposes, without interference from their fellows: it is because a market order gives them this freedom that it is morally superior to other orders. But, on a deeper level, the freedom which neo-liberalism offers is hedged about with limitations. For, as Hayek points out, a market order is possible only if moral values appropriate to it prevail; and, in most late-twentieth-century societies, these values are in retreat. The moral values appropriate to a market economy, he writes:

> were inevitably learned by all the members of a population consisting chiefly of independent farmers, artisans and apprentices who shared the daily experiences of their masters. They held an ethos that esteemed the prudent man, the good husbandman and provider who looked after the future of his family and his business by building up capital, guided less by the desire to be able to consume much than by the wish to be regarded as successful by his fellows who pursued similar aims . . .

> At present, however, an ever-increasing part of the population of the Western world grow up as members of large organizations and thus as strangers to those rules of the market which have made the great society possible. To them the market economy is largely incomprehensible; they have never practised the rules on which it rests and its results seem to them irrational and immoral.[28]

Though Hayek does not spell it out in so many words, the implication is plain. If a market order is to survive, men cannot be free to follow any purposes whatever. They can be free only to follow purposes compatible with, and implied by, the rules of the market. But, if Hayek is right, fallen late-twentieth-century men — products of large organisations and strangers to the rules of the market — will not spontaneously use their freedom in that way. If such men choose freely, the odds are that their choices will impede or undermine the working of the market. Thus, the revival of a market order depends upon the revival of the old market values; only after they have revived will the reign of market freedom dawn. But, on neo-liberal assumptions, argument and persuasion alone cannot revive them. Thus, the only hope is to create (or rather to re-create) conditions which will foster the old values, and impel men to behave in the way that the market order requires: conditions which, in a phrase of Sir Keith Joseph's, will once again promote 'the forward march of *embourgeoisement*, which went so far in Victorian times'.[29] On Hayek's showing, this is likely to require an exercise in social engineering at least as ambitious as any attempted by the Keynesian social democrats in the post-war period. In practice, the only feasible engineer is the coercive state.

Two concrete examples may help to pin down the argument. One of the chief sources of economic overload has been the increase in state-provided social welfare which all developed countries have experienced during the last quarter of a century. Though many factors contributed to this, the erosion of traditional attitudes towards the place of women and the role of the family must have been one of the most important of them.[30] For a variety of reasons − wider economic opportunities, easier contraception, the decline of religion, the spread of an ethic of equal rights and self-realisation − women began to rebel against the old attitudes. Partly because of this, the caring services which they once provided without formal payment to the members of their own families now have to be provided by paid employees of the state. It is hard to see how the growth of welfare spending can be halted, and still harder to see how the existing welfare state can be cut back, unless the old attitudes are resurrected. But they are unlikely to resurrect themselves of their own accord. If they were, they would not have been eroded in the first place. To carry out its economic programme, the neo-liberal state has therefore to become a proselytizing state, preaching and, so far as it dares, imposing a return to 'Victorian values', in order to intervene in the sphere of attitudes and beliefs which, on neo-liberal assumptions, should be left to private individuals.

Unemployment provides another example. If the unemployed are seen as the deserving victims of circumstances beyond their control, it will be difficult to contain the cost of unemployment benefit. If they were to be seen as many saw them in the nineteenth century − as the undeserving poor, unemployed either because mental or moral defects have made them unemployable or because they have chosen to price themselves out of work − it would be easier. Here again, however, attitudes are unlikely to change without pressure by the state, or at least by the politicians in control of it. Thus, the promise of less government and more privacy which lies at the heart of the neo-liberal message turns into its opposite.

As the last example suggests, all this applies with special force to the labour market. In strict neo-liberal theory, of course, all distortions in all markets are harmful; since all organised producer groups distort markets, they are all harmful too. The Bar Council, the National Farmers' Union, perhaps even the Confederation of British Industries are all collusive distortion-carriers, as noxious as the Transport and General Workers' Union or the National Union of Mineworkers. But for most real-world neo-liberals, it is in the labour market that distortions present the gravest menace to freedom of exchange. For unlike business groups, professional associations and farmers' organisations, the trade unions which distort the labour market do not even pay lip-service to the doctrine of free exchange. They are the carriers, not merely of distortion, but of an alternative ideology. They reject the propositions that the labour market is a market like any other, that there is a market-clearing price for labour just as there is a market-clearing price for apples and that if there is a glut of labour the price should fall, in favour of the medieval notion of the just price. For that reason alone, their teeth must be drawn if the neo-liberal project is to succeed.

Partly because of all this, moreover, the labour market — at any rate in Britain — has become the chief arena for tests of ministerial nerve and will. The crisis of ungovernability and overload which the neo-liberals want to overcome was, above all, a crisis in the relationship between government and organised labour. The notion that the British state was becoming ungovernable gained currency in the first place because successive governments were defeated in trials of strength with the unions. With the possible exception of the changes in the international economic environment that followed the 1973 oil shock, the chief cause of the breakdown of Keynesian social democracy was its failure — symbolised by the dimmed street lights during the mining dispute of 1973–4 and the unburied corpses in the 'winter of discontent' of 1978–9 – to find a satisfactory answer to the 'union question'. As we have seen, one of the central objectives of the whole neo-liberal project is to change expectations. Given this history, a government which said it wished to reduce excessive expectations, but flinched from tackling the expectations generated in the labour market, would not be believed.

Quite apart from these psychological and ideological considerations, the labour market was the crucible from which the Keynesian revolution and all its consequences flowed. It is important to remember that Keynes did not dispute the classical view that there was, in principle, a market-clearing price for labour, and that the reason why the labour market did not clear was that the unions had forced real wages above that price. Where he differed from the classics was in thinking that the 'juggernaut theory' of wages, as he called it in one of his most famous polemics,[31] could no longer be applied to the real world. The growth of trade-union power, he believed, and still more the change in the moral climate which had accompanied and fostered that growth, had created a new institutional reality, to which economists had to accommodate themselves. For better or worse, wages had become 'sticky' downwards. But there was no point in bemoaning the fact, still less in vainly attempting to undo the social and institutional changes which had caused it. Instead, unemployment had to be remedied in other ways. For neo-liberals, however, that conclusion is at once cowardly and perverse. In their eyes, the Keynesian remedy merely replaces one disease with a much more dangerous one. Not only does it set off the vicious spiral of pump-priming and inflation; at least as damagingly, the wage and price controls to which Keynesian governments are forced to resort in their doomed attempts to halt the spiral aggravate the distortions which prevented the labour market from working properly in the first place. For such policies cannot work without trade-union acquiescence; the trade unions will not acquiesce without compensating concessions; the concessions almost always include measures to strengthen their already destructive ability to prevent the labour market from working efficiently. And the only other remedy is the one that Keynes ruled out – a vigorous attack on the distortions which prevent the labour market from clearing properly and on the institutions which cause them.

Here, however, the gap in the neo-liberal analysis makes itself felt again. For Keynes, an institutional pragmatist *par excellence*, trade-union power was a fact of life, to which economic principle should bow. Neo-liberals reject Keynes's economic remedy, but they do not offer an alternative institutional diagnosis. If they are right, trade-union power is substantial as well as mischievous. But if it is substantial, how is the mischief to be undone? The trade unions are hardly likely to disarm themselves. If they are as strong as the neo-liberal analysis presupposes, how can they be disarmed against their will? One solution is to change the law, and many neo-liberals have advocated this. But the Heath Government changed the law in the 1970s, only to find that the trade unions were still strong enough to make the new law unworkable and, in doing so, to exacerbate the crisis of ungovernability to which neo-liberalism is supposed to be an answer. Laws that reflect social realities may also reinforce them. Laws that run counter to them are apt to undermine the authority of the legislator.

Once again neo-liberalism is forced back on a paradox. If inflation and inflationary expectations are to be squeezed out of the system, and if incomes policies do more harm than good, government has to use other instruments to do the squeezing; strict monetary controls are the only other instruments on offer. For a while, these will be accompanied by increased unemployment, but on neo-liberal assumptions, they will not cause it. For, as Hayek puts it, unemployment 'has been made inevitable by past inflation; it has merely been *postponed* by accelerating inflation'.[32] Inflationary booms must end sooner or later; when they do, high unemployment is inevitable. But it need not last for long. For, once the authorities follow anti-inflationary monetary policies, the level of unemployment becomes the responsibility of the trade unions. If they insist on keeping wages above the market-clearing level, their members will suffer the unemployment which is bound to follow. As wage-earners realise that government is no longer prepared to accommodate excessive wage levels with lax monetary policies, expectations will change; when expectations have changed, the inflationary distemper will have been cured. This may take time, but provided the authorities do not flinch, it will not take a very long time. For unemployment has another consequence as well. Not only does it lower expectations, it also reduces the bargaining power of the trade unions and, with it, their ability to distort the labour market and to force the natural rate of unemployment above what it would otherwise be. Unemployment is, in short, a kind of purgative, ridding the body politic of dangerous matter. Provided the dose is big enough, it will do its work quickly, and the body's own mechanisms will then maintain it in health.

Unfortunately, this raises two further dilemmas, which neo-liberalism is powerless to resolve. There is no doubt that high unemployment weakens the unions. It did so in the 1930s, and it has done so again in the 1980s. From the neo-liberal point of view, however, a temporary abatement of their power is not enough. Their ability to 'distort' the labour market must be destroyed for good and all. Now high unemployment will presumably not last for ever: or not if the neo-liberal cure works. What happens when it ends? What is to stop the forces which brought the unions into existence in the first place, and then gave them the power to distort the labour market, from coming into operation again? Some neo-liberals put their faith in technological change. The information revolution, they say, has so transformed the conditions of production that union power will not revive, even if unemployment falls. But technological determinism of that kind is a notoriously unreliable ally. A capital- and skill-intensive economy is more, not less, inter-dependent than a backward one and more, not less, vulnerable to the market power of groups of specialists. These specialists may be slow to exploit their power through collective action, but it would be rash to assume that they will never do so. On neo-liberal assumptions, the logical solution is another spell of high unemployment. But even on those assumptions, repeated spells of high unemployment are scarcely compatible with a thriving economy.

The second dilemma goes deeper. To put it simply: for how long can a political order based on the assumption of equal citizenship survive high unemployment? For how long will a system which tolerates a high level of unemployment remain, in any useful sense of the term, democratic? No doubt, it is hard to imagine any advanced western society experiencing a violent revolt of the dispossessed, of the sort Marx foresaw a century ago. But the emergence of an alienated and apathetic underclass, effectively denied the right to full participation in the life of the wider society, and scornful of, even if not actively hostile to, its values, would be equally incompatible with the democratic ideal, and put equal strain on the social tolerances which make democracy possible.

This part of the argument, then, concludes with a series of negatives. The Keynesian social democrats ended their period of ascendancy in an impasse, from which their governing philosophy could provide no escape. Neo-socialism and neo-liberalism – the prospective alternatives which have made most of the running since then – cannot provide solutions to the problems which their champions claim to have uncovered, and take refuge in hopes which their own assumptions condemn as utopian. It may be that no better approach can be found. There is no divine law to say that Britain's problems are soluble. What is clear is that the best way to start looking for one is to explore the economic, political and cultural realities which the doctrines I have considered in the last few chapters have all failed, in different ways, to address. That is what I try to do in the next part of the book; and since the economic realities are in some ways more obvious than the others, I start with them.

Part Two

REALITIES

4

States and Markets

'The taylor does not attempt to mend his own shoes, but buys
them of the shoemaker. The shoemaker does not attempt to
make his own clothes, but employs a taylor . . .

What is prudence in the conduct of every private family, can
scarce be folly in that of a great kingdom. If a foreign country
can supply us with a commodity cheaper than we ourselves can
make it, better buy it of them with some part of the produce of
our own industry, employed in a way in which we have some
advantage.'

Adam Smith, 1776.[1]

'[A] system of the private economy of all the individual persons
in a country, or of the individuals of the whole human race, as
that economy would develop and shape itself, under a state of
things in which there were no distinct nations, nationalities, or
national interests . . . not a scientific doctrine, showing how the
productive powers of an entire nation can be called into
existence, increased, maintained and preserved — for the special
benefit of its civilisation, might, continuance and independence.'

Friedrich List, on Adam Smith's economic theories, 1841.[2]

Whatever may be in doubt about the political and cultural
realities which a new governing philosophy would have to
address, the central economic realities are only too plain. No
western industrial society has found it easy to adjust to the
upheavals which have taken place in the world economy since
the collapse of the post-war boom. Britain has found it
exceptionally, perhaps uniquely, difficult. After the 1973 oil
shock, the inflation rate rose more rapidly than in the industrial world as a whole, and was well above the OECD average
from the second half of 1974 to the second half of 1978, and

from the second half of 1980 to the second half of 1982. The unemployment rate rose more slowly than the inflation rate, but by 1977 it was above the OECD average as well.[3] The economy almost stopped growing; the balance of payments went into heavy deficit; and the currency depreciated at an unprecedented rate. Thereafter, North Sea oil shielded the balance of payments and the living standards of those in work from the effects of lagging international competitiveness, while tight fiscal and monetary policies cut the inflation rate to approximately the OECD average. Behind the oil shield, however, unemployment continued to rise. By the end of 1986, 11.3 per cent of the labour force was out of work, more than twice the percentage in 1979, more than that in any other major industrial country and nearly one and a half times the OECD average.[4]

Meanwhile, a complex process of 'de-industrialisation' seemed to be accelerating. Since 1960, Britain's share of the combined manufacturing output of all the OECD countries together has halved.[5] Since 1970 her share of the aggregate output of the five leading national information technology industries has fallen from 9.0 per cent to 5.0 per cent.[6] By the early 1980s, her trade in manufactures was in deficit, for the first time since the industrial revolution.[7] These gross figures, moreover, conceal even more ominous shifts of direction. Even in the boom of the 1950s and 1960s, Britain was falling behind her competitors in productivity and in expenditure on industrial research and development.[8] Since the early 1970s, British industry has been caught in a kind of pincer movement between relatively unsophisticated, but low-wage, competition from the Third World and relatively high-wage, but sophisticated, competition from the United States, Japan and the rest of the EEC. In response to these pressures, British manufacturers developed new products and moved into new markets. But they shifted, in the jargon, 'down market' — away from the advanced products, with a high added-value, in which the pacemakers of the industrial world specialise, and towards simpler products with a lower added-value. Increasingly, they have found themselves, in the words of a recent International Labour Office report, 'at the less sophisticated end of a new international division of labour'.[9] Proficiency in certain sorts of services, even when combined with an efficient agriculture and temporary self sufficiency in energy, is not an adequate compensation in an industrial society, whose standard of living largely depends on its ability to compete in the world's markets for manufactured goods.

If the realities are plain, their causes and implications are clouded in controversy. The neo-liberal and neo-socialist arguments discussed in Part One provide an ideal starting point from which to penetrate the clouds. As we have seen, both camps interpret the crises of the 1970s as the products of overload — of the social processes which, in advanced capitalist democracies, cause popular demands to press relentlessly against the limits of supply, and, in the neo-liberal version at any rate, of a built-in pressure for bigger government, which emanates from within the state apparatus itself. How valid are these notions, and how far do they explain the economic record outlined above?

Clearly, there is something in them. It is true that the Keynesian social-democratic governments of the post-war period reached into new spheres; that, both as cause and as consequence, new demands were made of the state; that traditional values, traditional systems of authority and traditional methods of social control came under strain; and that, partly because of all this, the political leaders of the 1960s and 1970s found it more difficult to make their will prevail than political leaders had found it in the past. It is also true that public expenditure grew rapidly, both absolutely and as a proportion of the gross domestic product; that the growth sometimes seemed to be taking place independently of the wishes of the politicians who had to take responsibility for it; that, in certain periods at any rate, the effect was probably inflationary; and that, as the post-war boom petered out, it became more difficult to finance the expenditure programmes to which governments had committed themselves in happier days, with the result that conflicts over the distribution of resources became more bitter.

But although all this is compatible with the suggestion that popular demands were pressing against the limits of supply, it does not prove that it is true. It is, of course, a widely-believed suggestion but like many widely-believed suggestions about popular attitudes and behaviour, it does not square with recent research on how public opinion has actually evolved. A study by James Alt shows that, in the 1970s, at any rate, the British public was not in the least irrational, or greedy or short-sighted in its approach to economic questions: that, on the contrary, it was more cautious about the prospects of the economy than the politicians, and correspondingly sceptical about the promises which politicians made to it. As Alt puts it:

> [O]nly 10 to 15 per cent of the electorate believe that politicians of either major party 'very much' keep their promises. Indeed, only 30 per cent of Labour voters in October, 1974 believed that the Labour Party 'very much' kept its promises; only 25 per cent of Conservative voters believed that the Conservative Party 'very much' kept its promises. . .
>
> . . .minute proportions of Conservative voters in February 1974 believed that their party had handled prices 'very well', and only one Labour voter in five believed that had their party been in power it would have done 'very well'. The same realism emerges from the survey of opinions after the October election.[10]

Moreover, Alt points out, the whole notion of excessive popular 'demands' is conceptually flawed. It is easy enough to show that large numbers of people want a higher standard of living: that is hardly surprising. But wants are not demands; and demands are not expectations. What we have called the 'political market-place argument' hinges on the assumption that a credulous electorate votes for the party which makes the most lavish promises. But it is hard to see why the electorate would do this if it thought lavish promises would not be carried out. In the 1970s at any rate, that is exactly what the electorate did think. In Alt's words, 'Even if a majority desired an increased standard of living in 1973, and possibly were demanding it, there is no evidence that they expected it: other survey results show that a derisory *five* per cent of the electorate *expected* their income to go up by more than prices in 1974, and a majority expected their incomes to fall behind prices.'[11]

This is not to deny that voting behaviour was influenced by the electorate's changing appraisal of the rival parties' ability to produce higher living standards. The now classic study of voting behaviour in the 1960s by David Butler and Donald Stokes suggested, among other things, that there was a close correlation between the level of unemployment and the government's standing in the opinion polls, and that changes in the level of unemployment were closely correlated with changes in the electorate's sense of well-being.[12] But the patterns of behaviour to which this finding points are much more complicated than those implied by the political market-place argument. In the political market-place argument, voting behaviour is influenced by promises for the future. The Butler-Stokes finding suggests that it was influenced by per-formance in the past. That may imply calculation, but it hardly implies credulity. To be sure, Butler and Stokes show that the electorate (or sections of the electorate) were apt to punish the government of the day when unemployment rose, and to reward it when unemployment fell. Since governments knew this, this finding supports the view that electoral pressures helped to induce the 'go' phases of the stop-go cycle of the period. But unless we make the further assumption that the 'go' phase did more harm than the 'stop' phases – in other words, that the trend level of unemployment ought to have been higher than it was – it does not follow that they damaged the economy. This, of course, is exactly what neo-liberals do assume, but that is not a reason why the rest of us should agree with them. It is at least as plausible to think that the 'stop' phases did more harm than the 'go' phases: that the long-term rate of growth would have been higher than it was if successive governments had not deflated the economy in order to main-tain the parity of sterling.

At first sight, there is more in the bureaucratic empire-building argument. No one who sat in the House of Commons in the 1960s and 1970s could deny that strong pressures for extra public expenditure came from what Aaron Wildavsky and Hugh Heclo have called the Whitehall 'village',[13] or that the politicians who presided over the spending departments which made up the village often became, in practice, little more than spokesmen for the interests from which these pressures emanated. But it would be wrong to jump to the conclusion that the pressures were therefore irresistible. In the immediate aftermath of the 1973 oil crisis, when governments still hoped that the high rates of economic growth of the previous twenty years would soon return, public expenditure continued to grow at its pre-crisis rate in most western countries. Since the rate of economic growth in fact fell sharply, the share of GDP going to public expenditure rose sharply and, so it seemed at first sight, uncontrollably. That, no doubt, is the chief reason why the overload theories of the period gained currency. But once it became clear that the recession was there to stay, and that economic growth was not going to return to its pre-1973 path after all, the trend line of public-expenditure growth was brought down everywhere.[14]

Britain's experience was particularly striking. Not just the trend line of public-expenditure growth, but the actual amount of public expenditure, was reduced significantly after the 1976 crisis; in 1978–9, the Callaghan government's last year in office, the share of GDP going to public expenditure was 5 per cent less than in 1975–6.[15] Though the total crept up again under the Conservatives, the distribution between different programmes has changed considerably, reflecting the political priorities of the government.[16] To be sure, all this took place after the collapse of Keynesian social democracy, allowing neo-liberals to argue that it does not invalidate their explanations for that collapse. But there are two weaknesses in that argument. In the first place, as we have seen, the bureaucratic empire-building argument held that the pressures for big government were systemic and institutional, operating independently of the politicians who happened at any moment to be in nominal charge. If a change in the governing philosophy could halt them, that is clearly not the case. On at least one occasion, moreover – the post-devaluation cuts of 1968–9 – the same thing happened, though on a smaller scale, under an impeccably Keynesian social-democratic government.[17]

A much more serious objection to all the explanations we have been discussing is that there is, in any event, no evidence that the alleged state of affairs on which they hinge is related to the long-term performance of the economy. Neo-liberals take it for granted, not just that overload has generated inflation in the short term, but that it has made the economy less productive, over the long term, than it would otherwise have been. Neo-socialists make the same assumption about the forces behind the fiscal crisis and the escape of the meso-economy. Yet if the OECD area is considered as a whole, it is impossible to establish a causal connection between any of these, on the one hand, and economic performance on the other.

Most overload theories imply that the best measure of overload is either the proportion of GDP going to public expenditure, or the rate of growth of public expenditure, or some combination of the two. Though the theory of the 'fiscal crisis' is more sophisticated, in that it distinguishes between spending on the 'accumulation' function and spending on the 'legitimisation' function, its practical implications are remarkably similar: whatever may be true of 'accumulation' expenditure, the growth of 'legitimisation' expenditure is held to damage the economy. Unfortunately for the overload theorists, however, Britain – whose economic performance has been, on almost any reckoning, the worst in the developed world – has suffered, by these measures, rather less overload than most other developed countries. She has also devoted a rather smaller share of her GDP to welfare spending – presumably the best indicator of the cost of what neo-Marxists call the 'legitimisation' function.

Sweden, with one of the highest public expenditure/GDP ratios in the western world, has had a much higher rate of economic growth than Britain or, for that matter, than the United States. For most of the last twenty years, the proportion of GDP devoted to public expenditure in the German Federal Republic, one of the most successful economies in the world for most of the post-war period, has been almost identical to the British proportion. In 1979, Britain's ratio of public expenditure to GDP was the second lowest in the European Community; only Greece had a lower one.[18] Much the same is true of the rate of growth in the ratio. In the twenty years from 1960 to

1980 — the twenty years when the overload syndrome is supposed to have been at its most virulent — the proportion of GDP going to public expenditure increased by 12 per cent in Britain, by 14.9 per cent in the German Federal Republic, by 21.4 per cent in Belgium, by 28.8 per cent in the Netherlands and by 31.2 per cent in Denmark. Of the member states of the European Community, only France came below Britain, and then only by the trivial figure of 0.4 per cent. The non-European members of the OECD show the same pattern, or rather non-pattern. Canada apart, all of them devote much smaller proportions of their gross domestic products to public expenditure than do the European members. One of them — Japan — has enjoyed extraordinarily high growth rates for most of the post-war period. Another — the United States — has grown more slowly than any other developed country, except Britain.[19] (See Table III.) What is true of public expenditure in general is equally true of welfare spending in particular. In the 1960s and early 1970s, the share of GDP going to welfare spending rose steeply in all developed capitalist democracies, but wide variations in the level remained. For most of the time, it was markedly lower in slow-growing Britain than in any other member state of the EEC, apart from the Republic of Ireland; fast-growing Germany had the second highest share. Outside Europe, the slow-growing United States ranked below Britain. On the other hand, fast-growing Japan came below the United States.[20]

Much the same applies to the neo-liberal assumption that state intervention in the supply-side of the economy is bound to do more harm than good. As we shall see, the governments of all developed western societies intervene directly in the supply-side, in order to produce outcomes which the market would not have produced had it been left to itself. Of course, methods, instruments and objectives differ, not only between countries, but between different periods — and, for that matter, different spheres of activity — in the same country. Some forms of intervention bulk large in the public-expenditure accounts; others hardly figure in them. Tax concessions may cost the national treasury as much as subsidies do, but they do not count as public spending. Argument and persuasion come cheap, but they may influence behaviour as powerfully as do subsidies or tax concessions. Thus, the amount of public money spent on aid to industry is not an index of the scale or impact of state intervention in the economy. The Japanese state, to take the most obvious example, influences the behaviour of private firms in a whole host of ways, only some of which have consequences for expenditure. Despite generous spending on aid to industry, the British state may well have had less influence than the Japanese on what happened on the ground. Because of all this, cross-national comparison is extraordinarily difficult. Despite the difficulties, however, France, Japan and Sweden all show that, to put it at its lowest, state intervention to promote economic adjustment and growth can sometimes succeed. The evidence, in fact, supports the common-sense conclusion that industrial policies may be either beneficial or harmful to the economy, depending on a range of circumstances which include the values of the society, the character of the state apparatus, the nature of the policies and the political environment in which they are implemented. The neo-liberals may be right in thinking that, in the 1970s at any rate, British industrial policies led to a 'scramble for subsidies'[21] which impeded adjustment and growth. If so, it is important to find out why. But the explanation cannot be derived from an a priori assumption that state intervention is bound to do harm in all circumstances.

Even inflation, in practice the chief bugbear of most neo-liberals, is not necessarily bad for growth, however distressing it may be in other ways. In the period from 1954 to 1978, Japan and France combined high growth and comparatively high inflation. West Germany had high growth and low inflation. The United States had low growth and low inflation. The United Kingdom had low growth and medium to high inflation.[22] Not only was inflation compatible with rapid growth, in some societies it may even have been part of the price of the social and economic changes which made rapid growth possible. France and Japan grew rapidly, John Zysman has argued, only because a powerful and interventionist state was able to establish the conditions in which resources could be shifted from the traditional sectors of the economy (notably, but not exclusively, agriculture) into more advanced sectors. It was able to do this only because it bought off opposition from the traditional sectors; part of the cost of buying it off was expressed in inflation.[23]

If overload does not explain the economic failures with which Keynesian social democracy could not cope, what does? More particularly, what light can international comparisons throw on the question?

Here again the debate between neo-liberals and neo-socialists provides a useful point of departure. In practice, as we have seen, the battle between the two camps is almost always a battle over the *extent* of state intervention in the economy. Most neo-socialists say that Britain's economic ills are due to inadequate state intervention or to the power of private capital to defy or circumvent state intervention. Neo-liberals say that they are due to excessive state intervention. As the last section implied, this whole argument is, on one level, a red herring, diverting attention from the questions which really matter. State intervention is neither markedly more nor markedly less extensive in Britain than in the industrial world as a whole; it is the quality of the intervention which deserves study, not the quantity. On another level, however, the red herring provides important clues to the causes of the British crisis.

At the heart of the neo-liberal diagnosis lies the notion that, in some undefined sense, the market is 'natural' and therefore good. Hence the suggestion that state intervention in the market is a 'distortion' – in some way 'unnatural' and, in principle, bad: at best a necessary evil, and at worst an unnecessary one. But the implicit assumption that the market is more 'natural' than the state has no warrant from history or anthropology, or for that matter from observation. In the real world, as Charles Lindblom has suggested, the exchange relations which are characteristic of markets, and the authority relations which are characteristic of states, co-exist and inter-penetrate each other, and have almost certainly done so from the earliest times.[24] Bureaucracies may appear, from the outside, to depend almost wholly on authority relations. But as anyone who has ever worked in one can testify, the wheels of authority are often oiled by exchanges of favours between the bureaucrats. On the other hand, the private companies which compete with each other in the market are often as hierarchical in their internal structure as are government departments. On a different level, even the Soviet Union relies partly on the price mechanism, while even in nineteenth-century Britain, perhaps the closest approximation to a pure market economy which the world has ever seen, state power constrained freedom of exchange. Adam Smith thought that a 'propensity to truck, barter and exchange one thing for another' was part of human nature,[25] and he may have been right. But there is no reason to believe that it is any more integral or fundamental a part than a propensity to govern, or for that matter than a propensity to want to be governed. If anything the boot is probably on the other foot: governments precede, and could reasonably be thought to be more 'natural', than markets. The truth is that it is as misleading to talk of the state 'distorting' the market as it would be to talk of the market 'distorting' the state. Without the state there would be no market: at the door of the auction room stands the policeman. Indeed, in this perspective, it may even be misleading to talk of the 'mixed economy'. To label an economy 'mixed' implies that some economies are somehow 'unmixed', whereas in reality all economies mix market and authority relations and − on a different level − private and public power. The only questions are, where should the boundary be? And what sort of mixture serves our purposes best?

This is high theory, no doubt, but practical experience points in the same direction. For the state has played a central part in economic development in virtually all industrial societies, with the possible exception of early nineteenth-century Britain. Even in Britain, moreover, the state played an important facilitating role − passing, as Harold Perkin has pointed out, 'the enclosure acts which enabled more food to be grown for a much larger population, the canal, turnpike and railway acts which created the new infrastructure of modern transport, the many private acts and rulings in chancery which, almost literally, cleared the ground for the building of towns, suburbs and factory colonies, the various banking acts which created a network of payment and credit facilities [and] the at first private and later public companies acts which enabled industry and trade to grow beyond the scale of the family firm or partnership.'[26] In the last resort, it also stood ready to stamp out challenges to the new industrial system with armed force. Elsewhere it did much more than this. The classical political economists of the late-eighteenth and early-nineteenth centuries, from whom the neo-liberals of the late-twentieth century draw their inspiration, were generalising, as so often happens, from the case they knew. Unfortunately, it happened to be a unique case. Britain's successors on the path to industrialism did not, almost certainly could not, emulate Britain's methods. If they were to reach the same destination, they had to follow a different route. And in all of them – Prussia and her successor, Imperial Germany; Meiji Japan; Tsarist Russia (which enjoyed remarkably high rates of industrial growth in the period before the First World War); even, in some spheres, the United States – the state used its power to promote and foster the industrialisation process, in a fashion which the teachings of market-liberalism would have ruled out.

Thus, in the middle of the nineteenth century, the Prussian state held shares in five railway companies; owned coalmines which produced, altogether, one-fifth of the country's total production; and operated zinc mines, iron works, salt works and lead mines. In addition, the state overseas trading corporation, the *Seehandlung*, either owned or had a financial interest in paper factories, iron works, worsted weaving sheds, cotton mills, flax-spinning mills, corn mills and engineering works. It also maintained a regular Atlantic service and operated river craft on the Brandenburg waterways.[27] After German unification in 1871, the public sector grew. By 1907, about one-tenth of all the mines, factories and transport facilities in the Reich were publicly owned, while between 20 and 25 per cent of the country's investments were made by public authorities or nationalised undertakings.[28] It was the same story in Japan. Under the slogan *shokusan kogyo* ('develop industry and promote enterprise'), the Meiji regime, established in 1868, promoted a national banking system; built railways, harbours and telegraph networks; established and later sold off publicly-owned plants in the cement, silk-filature, copper and glass industries; and provided start-up loans and subsidies to the private sector.[29] In the United States, often seen as a citadel of market-liberalism, the crucial early stages of industrialisation depended heavily on public power. The federal government did little beyond investing in the Bank of the United States and imposing tariffs against imports from Britain, but state governments were much more active – using the proceeds of state lotteries to finance bridges, roads, paper mills and glass works; granting franchises to protect favoured companies from competition during their early growth; and investing in banks, canals, turnpikes and railways.[30] As Robert Lively writes of the early years of American capitalism:

> [T]he elected official replaced the individual enterpriser as the key figure in the release of capitalist energy; the public treasury, rather than private saving, became the major source of venture capital; and community purpose outweighed personal ambition in the selection of large goals for local economies. 'Mixed' enterprise was the customary organization for important innovations, and government everywhere undertook the role put on it by the people, that of planner, promoter, investor and regulator.[31]

The same applies to the period after the Second World War. In modern times, what Ronald Dore has called 'regulatory' intervention – intervention to protect the public from monopoly, or to prevent fraud or adulteration or other abuses of market power – has become commonplace in all industrial societies. But that is only the beginning of the story. Some societies have also operated a second form of intervention, which Dore calls 'developmental' – a form designed, in his words, 'explicitly to promote the competitiveness of the nation seen as one actor in a cut-throat world economy'.[32]

The prime example of a developmental state is, of course, Japan. As we have seen, state-promoted industrial growth started in the Meiji era, when Japan's ruling élites decided that the only way to stop their country from becoming a western colony was to industrialise on western lines. The relationship between the state and private industry went through a number of phases in the next seventy years. Sometimes the state was the predominant partner and sometimes the great private industrial empires which had grown up in the shadow of the Meiji governments, the so-called *zaibatsu*. No matter who predominated, however, the relationship was always close. By the early 1950s, when Japan emerged from defeat and occupation, she possessed a long tradition of public-private collaboration in the interests of economic development; highly-trained bureaucratic and managerial cadres, many of them graduates of the same élite schools, imbued with the values and assumptions of this common tradition; and a range of institutions with the capacity and will to bend market forces in the pursuit of national goals. What Chalmers Johnson has called the 'economic general staff'[33] – the élite of policy-making bureaucrats and former bureaucrats which straddled (and still straddles) the public and private sectors – set out deliberately to use these assets to transform Japan from a poor and backward country, specialising in labour-intensive products with a low added value and poor growth prospects, into an advanced industrial power. As everyone knows, it succeeded. In 1965, Japan exported 100,000 cars, mostly to other Asian countries. By 1970, her car exports totalled 700,000; and by 1978, the figure was more than 3 million.[34] In the late 1950s, most of her exports still came from unskilled labour-intensive industries, like clothing, light assembly, footwear and toys. By the early 1970s, she had become the chief supplier of ships, steel, motorcycles and cameras to world markets; since then, she has shifted increasingly into knowledge-intensive products, such as computers, fine chemicals and sophisticated machine tools.[35]

The logic and methods of the 'economic general staff' deserve as much attention as the results they produced. In some ways, Japan's is plainly a market economy, with private firms competing fiercely for custom.[36] But it is a market economy which defies many of the precepts of market-liberalism, including the fundamental precept that, except in a few strictly-specified cases, the market knows best. The economic policy makers of the early 1950s, who decided to shift resources into more sophisticated, capital-intensive activities, manipulated market forces to achieve their purposes, and collaborated closely with large private firms, but they did not allow the market to decide what those purposes should be. On the contrary, they believed that private corporations, left to themselves, would be more likely to stick to their existing activities, even if they were in decline, than to branch out into new and more promising activities, of which they had no experience; and that there was therefore no guarantee that the sum total of individual corporate decisions would be in the interests of society as a whole. Like surfers riding a turbulent sea, they harnessed the inevitably short-term logic of the private, profit-seeking entrepreneur, seeking to make the most efficient use of his existing inputs, to a national logic, in which the future weighed more heavily than the present. And although they worked through the market, they did so by rigging it.

Officials of the famous Ministry of International Trade and Industry (MITI) – created in 1949 as the successor to the pre-war Ministry of Commerce and Industry – used a formidable armoury of instruments to prod and twist the economy into the shape they wanted. One of the most important was *de facto* control of the supply of credit. Japanese companies raised most of their capital from the banks, not from an equity market. Since interest rates were deliberately kept low, there was always a queue of would-be borrowers waiting for loans. Because the pressure for bank loans was so heavy, the banks over-lent. They in turn had to borrow from the Bank of Japan, and the Bank of Japan lent to them only on condition that their loan policies conformed to government priorities.[37] But that was only one of a 'panoply' of devices, which also included:

the extensive use, narrow targeting and timely revision of tax incentives; the use of indicative plans to set goals and guidelines for the entire economy; the creation of numerous, formal and continuously operating forums for exchanging views, reviewing policies, obtaining feedback and resolving differences; the assignment of some governmental functions to various private and semi-private associations . . . ; an extensive reliance on public corporations, particularly of the mixed public-private variety, to implement policy in high-risk or otherwise refractory areas; the creation and use by the government of an unconsolidated 'investment budget' separate from and not funded by the general account budget; the orientation of anti-trust policy to developmental and international competitive goals rather than strictly to the maintenance of domestic competition; government-conducted or government-sponsored research and development (the computer industry); and the use of the government's licensing and approval authority to achieve developmental goals.[38]

Japan heads the list of developmental states, but it includes other striking examples as well. One of them is France, in many ways the closest western parallel to Japan. Like Japan, France had a long tradition of state intervention in the economy and a bureaucracy trained to believe that it served a national interest which was more than the sum of private interests. Like Japan's, her policy-making élites emerged from defeat and occupation convinced, in the words of the socialist economist, André Philip, that 'only great industrial states count in the modern world'; and that if she were to remain genuinely independent, she would have to re-structure her economy accordingly.[39] Out of the debates in the Resistance and the political struggles of the early post-war period came the *économie concertée* – a form of planning very similar to the Japanese, in which the state, acting in close collaboration with large, private-sector firms, prodded, bullied, bribed, cajoled and argued a predominantly privately-owned economy into a more advanced and more competitive shape. As in Japan, moreover, the planners tried to channel market forces in directions which the market would not have chosen if it had been left to itself, so as to shift resources into more advanced sectors; as in Japan, they did this by favouring some market actors at the expense of others. Their instruments were reminiscent of the Japanese as well – notably, selective subsidies and tax concessions, and the manipulation of credit allocation through a heavily state-influenced banking system.[40]

A rather different example of the same phenomenon is Sweden, where social-democratic governments, acting in concert with the trade unions, deliberately tried to shift resources from declining to growing industries and to maintain export competitiveness through a combination of solidaristic wage bargaining and an active manpower policy.[41] Even in West Germany, where the official theory of the 'social market' implied that the state should confine itself to holding the ring for market forces and redistributing the fruits of economic growth, governments have in fact intervened energetically in certain markets (notably, the labour market), promoted new technologies, subsidised declining industries and pursued an active regional policy, in all cases for essentially developmental reasons.[42]

In all these cases, and not only in the French one, the metaphor of the *économie concertée* is particularly apt. The developmental state has not suppressed or dictated to the market: it has acted as a sort of conductor, trying to direct and harmonise the efforts of market actors whom it can influence, but not command. In economist's language, it has 'constrained' the market: it has drawn (or re-drawn) the boundaries within which markets operate, and defined the terms on which competition takes place. To be sure, this is not, in itself, remarkable. States have always constrained markets. The notion of a pure market system, totally unconstrained by political authorities, is as fanciful as the notion of a pure state system, in which markets play no part at all in allocating resources. Harold Perkin's list of the economic measures of early-nineteenth-century British governments shows that the state determined the boundaries within which markets functioned even at the high point of market liberalism. But the developmental state has used a wider and more sophisticated range of instruments than previous states have done. It has also been more self-conscious about its objectives. It is in these objectives, and in their implications for its relations with the members of the economic orchestra which it is trying to conduct, that its real originality lies.

This is where Adam Smith and Friedrich List, quoted at the head of this chapter, come into the story. Their respective reputations make an intriguing contrast. Adam Smith was, of course, one of the founding fathers of the orthodox classical and neo-classical tradition which still permeates the economic culture of the English-speaking world; rightly, his is one of the most famous names in the history of ideas. List was one of the prophets of nineteenth-century German economic nationalism, but in English-speaking countries, he is remembered, if at all, as the father of an intellectually disreputable set of errors, the adoption of which can only do harm. Yet if we want to understand the developmental states, where the orthodox Anglo-American tradition is not seen as the source of all economic wisdom, but whose economies have nevertheless been the most successful in the post-war world, List is a much better guide than Smith.

The difference between them centres on Smith's doctrine that if foreigners 'can supply us with a commodity cheaper than we ourselves can make it,' it pays us to 'buy it of them with some part of the produce of our own industry, employed in a way in which we have some advantage.' Not so, said List: Smith had ignored the fundamental political reality of the nation. His doctrine might hold good in a world-state, consisting of millions of private individuals, but it did not hold good in a world of nations. The factors which determined a nation's economic performance were its 'productive powers' – above all, the skill and culture of its people. Some forms of production (notably industry) enhanced productive powers, while others (notably agriculture) did not. Weak and backward nations were weak and backward because they had not developed their productive powers. If they adopted Smith's teaching and concentrated on the kinds of production for which they were best fitted in their present state, their productive powers would remain undeveloped and they would remain weak and backward. Even if they were nominally independent, this would leave them at the mercy of the strong and advanced, who would rule over them 'as England rules over Portugal'. If they were to be genuinely independent, they had to move into the kinds of production which did enhance productive powers, and in which, by definition, their strong and advanced neighbours were at present more competitive than they were. That, List thought, could only be done by protection.[43]

One hundred and forty years later, the vocabulary sounds quaint, but the fundamental insight applies as much to the late-twentieth century as it did to the mid-nineteenth. Poor and backward nations are still unwilling to accept permanent inferiority to the rich and advanced; to become rich and advanced themselves, they still have to overcome the inevitable myopia of the market, and develop productive powers which the market would not develop by itself; the economic tradition against which List protested still offers them little guidance. The orthodox theory of international trade derives from the teachings of the nineteenth-century classical economist, David Ricardo, who gave a more sophisti-cated twist to the Smithian doctrine that it pays to import goods which others can produce more cheaply than one can oneself. With Ricardo, the theory holds that all countries will gain by exporting goods in the production of which they have a comparative advantage, while importing those in which they have a comparative disadvantage. As so often with orthodox economics, however, it is static, not dynamic. It explains what happens with a given set of comparative advantages, but it does not explain how comparative advantages come into existence. More importantly, it does not reckon with the possibility that they can be deliberately created.

In Ricardo's day, that was sensible enough. Comparative advantages mostly reflected natural endowments, which no one could alter. It is less sensible today. God may have decreed that the French would be better at growing grapes than the Irish, but he did not decree that the Japanese would be better at making computers. Nowadays, comparative advantage is primarily a matter of accumulated capital, physical and human; as John Zysman puts it, this is best seen as the 'cumulative effect of firm capacities and government policy choices and not simply as the effect of resource endowments'.[44] Though he focused on absolute, rather than on comparative, advantages, List's argument applies to the latter as much as to the former. Rephrased in modern terminology, the essence of his teaching was that comparative advantages not only can be created, but should be: that in order to improve its chances of prosperity in the long run, a backward country should deliberately set out to exchange its existing set of comparative advantages for a more advanced set. In practice, this is exactly what the developmental states have tried to do. Where the orthodox Anglo-American tradition sees the world market as a vast collection of individual economic agents, competing across national boundaries, they have seen it, in Listian terms, as a collection of national trading units, competing with each other. They have re-drawn the map of competition within the nation in order to strengthen its competitive power in the world. They have been willing to sacrifice the consumer's short-term interest in buying in the cheapest market to the long-term interests of the community of which he is part.

This leads on to a more complicated point. Economic adjustment is always a political process as well as an economic one. It requires disinvestment as well as investment, and it brings costs as well as benefits: death as well as birth. Old activities, old habits, old skills have to disappear to make room for new ones; the new ones cannot appear unless the old ones disappear. In the long run, society as a whole will benefit; in the short run, those who carry on the old activities, who have become used to the old habits, or who have learned the old skills will lose. Not only does economic adjustment redistribute income and wealth, moreover, it also redistributes power and esteem. Somehow, these costs and benefits have to be allocated. In allocating them, society has to settle a series of distributional questions. It also has to resolve − if only by default − the moral issues which those questions raise.[45] The politics of adjustment have to do with the way in which society handles the process of allocation and its consequences, and with the principles which guide it. Losers and potential losers are likely to resist. As Mancur Olson has pointed out, they may resist through the market, by using their market power to slow down the rate of change, or even to prevent it altogether.[46] They may also call upon the state to redress the balance of the market. If their resistance succeeds − if they manage to stop resources from shifting on an adequate scale from declining to growing sectors, to freeze the pattern of activity in its existing shape — adjustment and growth will not take place. Broadly speaking, there are two ways of ensuring that the resisters do not succeed. One is to buy them off: to compensate them for their losses: in effect, to socialise the inevitable pains of adjustment. The other is to coerce them — in one way or another to deprive them of their power to stop adjustment from taking place.

Historically, these processes have taken a bewildering variety of forms, ranging from the free-booting, gun-toting individualism of gold-rush California to the forced industrialisation of Stalin's Russia. In developed western societies, however, three models of adjustment stand out. It may be market-led, as in early nineteenth-century Britain and present-day Hong Kong. It may be state-led, as in Japan and France. It may be negotiated between the state and the 'social partners' — chiefly, the representatives of organised labour and private capital — as in Austria, Sweden and, to some extent, West Germany. As will appear later, the differences between these three forms are of great importance for our theme. For the moment, however, what matters is the difference between the market-led model and the other two. In market-led adjustment, the costs and benefits are allocated by the market; the issues of distributive justice which it raises are concealed. According to the prevailing market-liberal ideology, prices are the unintended outcomes of the preferences of uncoerced consumers. This is as true of the price of labour or the rate of interest as of any other price. Thus, to ask whether the pattern of rewards conforms to some notion of distributive justice is to ask an irrelevant question. Men get what they and their property are worth in the market-place: what freely choosing consumers judge the goods and services they bring to the market to be worth. Justice consists in letting these judgments take effect.[47] In practice, of course, even in a market-led system, the state stands by to guarantee the winners' gains and to crush any attempt on the part of the losers to interfere in the allocation process. But so long as the prevailing ideology is accepted, the political aspects of the process are unrecognised, or at least unacknowledged.

In state-led and negotiated adjustment, the two modes of the developmental state, the political aspects come into the open. It is easy to see that the state is deliberately trying to shift resources from some sectors to others, and those who stand to lose from the shift will probably know that the state is at least part-author of their losses. If they can, losers and potential losers are likely to turn to politics to protect themselves. The adjustment process is politicised, and the distributional issues which it raises are politicised as well. They can no longer be settled by the 'undistorted' market, for the 'undistorted' market is a thing of the past. Instead, they have to be settled through politics. This can happen in a number of ways. By buying off some losers and potential losers, notably in agriculture, the French Gaullists and Japanese Liberal Democrats managed to construct a broad-based, majority coalition for economic adjustment, strong enough to impose its distributional settlement on the minority. In Scandinavia and central Europe, the distributional issues have been settled by a process of negotiation — more or less open to the public view — between the state and the most important groups of organised economic interests. All of these cases, however, have at least one crucial feature in common. In all of them, some losers and some winners strike a bargain, either tacit or open, allocating the gains and losses of adjustment in a way in which the 'undistorted' market would not have done.

Against this background, the neo-liberal and neo-socialist explanations of the crises of the 1970s look like the guns at Singapore, which faced out to sea when the enemy came by land. True or false, they address the wrong problem. The Schumpeterian public-choice arguments were originally put forward to explain what was happening in the United States. If they are valid at all, they are valid for all developed mass democracies with competitive party politics. The same applies to the theories of the fiscal crisis and of the escape of the meso-economy. The fiscal crisis of the 1970s is held to have sprung from the contradictions of a class-divided society. But if these contradictions exist, they must exist in all capitalist societies. The escape of the meso-economy is supposed to be a product of the growing power of multinational companies. By definition, that too is common to the whole of the developed world. But the question we have to answer is not common to the whole developed world. It is specific to Britain. It is not why the world economy ran into trouble in the 1970s. It is why Britain coped with the trouble less successfully than other industrial societies.

Part of the answer, of course, lies in repeated failures of adjustment earlier in the post-war period: in the sluggish growth rates, lagging productivity increases and declining competitiveness of the 1950s and 1960s. Because of these, Britain was more vulnerable to the shocks of the 1970s than were most industrial societies. But that only pushes the question one stage further back: why, in that case, was Britain's economic performance so poor in the 1950s and 1960s? The adjustment failures of the post-war period followed a long series of similar failures, stretching back over three-quarters of a century. Early nineteenth-century Britain was, in some ways, the most successful exemplar of market-led adjustment which the world has ever seen, but her relative decline was already under way by the last quarter of the nineteenth century. With occasional ups and downs, it has continued ever since — under *laissez-faire* market-liberals, protectionist big-business Conservatives, top-down socialist planners and both arm's length and hands-on Keynesian social democrats. Market-led adjustment ceased to work, but neither state-led nor negotiated adjustment took its place. The question we have to answer is, why not? Why has none of the three models of adjustment worked in Britain, not merely in the 1970s, but for nearly a hundred years? Why have successive generations of British political and economic leaders been unable to settle the political issues which lie at the heart of the adjustment process?

What is special about Britain, to put the point another way around, is not that she abandoned market-led adjustment. It is that, after abandoning it, she failed to become a developmental state on the pattern of her more successful competitors on the European mainland and in the Far East. Neither the neo-socialist nor the neo-liberal interpretations of the crisis of the 1970s can explain this dominating feature of her economic experience: indeed, their continuing popularity is a symptom of her inability to adjust. Yet it holds the key to her current economic problems. Almost by definition, the explanation must lie deep in British history.

5

The Politics of Economic Decline

'[N]ever again let anybody in Lancashire hear you talk this childish stuff about foreign competition . . . In the first place, we've got the only climate in the world where cotton piece goods in any quantity can ever be produced. In the second, no foreign Johnnies can ever be bred that can spin and weave like Lancashire lads and lasses. In the third place, there are more spindles in Oldham than in all the rest of the world put together. And last of all, if they had the climate and the men and the spindles — which they never can have — foreigners could never find the brains Lancashire cotton men have for the job.'
A Lancashire cotton manufacturer in 1911.[1]

As we have seen, the origin of Britain's inability to adjust to the economic upheavals of the 1970s and 1980s lies in her failure to become a developmental state. But the story of that failure to adjust is more complex than might be expected. It is, of course, a political story as much as, perhaps more than, an economic one. The political elements in it can be understood, however, only against the background of repeated failures of economic adjustment, to which they are a sort of counterpoint. Hence, I begin with economics, and turn to politics after the economic background has been sketched in.

Though some of the details are in dispute, the broad outlines of the economic story are clear enough. At some point between the depression of the 1870s and the First World War, the astonishing surge of social, technological and economic change which had made Britain the first industrial society in history, and the British the richest people in the world, began to lose momentum. Economic historians disagree about the extent and timing of this deceleration, but they agree that her total output and output per head both grew more slowly in the forty years after 1870 than they had done in the previous half century.[2] (See Table I.) Partly because of this, but much more because a number of newcomers to industrialism attained rates of growth higher than hers had ever been, she lost the economic and industrial supremacy which had seemed. almost beyond challenge in the first half of the century. The German and American economies, in particular, grew significantly faster than Britain's, and saw bigger increases in productivity. Between 1873 and 1913, total output grew by about 1.8 per cent a year in Britain, compared with 2.8 per cent a year in Germany and 4.5 per cent a year in the United States. To some extent, of course, these differences were due to differences in the growth of population. Thanks partly to natural increase, and partly to one of the biggest waves of immigration in history, the population of the United States more than doubled in these years. But that is only part of the reason. Output per head followed the same pattern: an average increase of 0.9 per cent a year in Britain, of 1.4 per cent a year in Germany and of 1.8 per cent a year in the United States.[3] Not only was Britain's actual rate of growth lower than those of her leading competitors; her rate of investment, the key to future growth, was lower too. As a percentage of net domestic product, net domestic capital formation in Britain in the period between 1875 and 1914 was only a little more than half what it was in Germany and the United States; in the decade immediately before the First World War, when fears of German competition were at their height, the British proportion actually fell while the German proportion rose.[4]

At first sight, the differences in rates of growth may appear small, but over a period of forty years, the 'remorseless arbiter' of compound interest[5] can give small differences big consequences. Between 1870 and 1913, industrial production in Britain doubled. In the world as a whole, it quadrupled. In 1870, 32.0 per cent of the world's industrial production had been manufactured in Britain — a substantially bigger share than the American 23.0 per cent or the German 13.0 per cent. By 1913, Britain was only the third industrial power in the world, with 14.0 per cent of world industrial production, against Germany's 15.7 per cent and the United States's 35.8

per cent.[6] Not only had she ceased to be the workshop of the world in respect of absolute totals, she was no longer the world's most efficient or productive workshop man for man. By 1907, the United States had twice as much capital invested per worker as Britain, and used twice as much horse-power per worker; where the value added to the cost of materials by a worker in a range of industries averaged £100 in Britain, the American average for the same industries was £500.[7] In Germany, it is true, productivity was still lower than in Britain. But so were wages; and since the gap between German and British wages was bigger than the productivity gap, German industry had the competitive edge.[8] What alarmed contemporaries most of all was that these weaknesses were increasingly reflected in the pattern of foreign trade. For most of the nineteenth century, her industrial supremacy had gone hand in hand with trading supremacy. Now she was losing the second as well as the first. By a narrow margin, she was still the world's largest exporter of manufactured goods, but the margin was shrinking fast. Between 1880 and 1913, her share of world exports of manufactures fell from slightly more than 40.0 per cent to slightly less than 30.0 per cent while the German share rose from less than 20.0 per cent to more than 26.0 per cent and the American from less than 3.0 per cent to more than 12.0 per cent.[9]

These totals concealed more ominous changes of character and direction. In her industrial heyday in the early- and mid-nineteenth century, Britain had been ahead, not just in manufactures and manufactured exports, but in the most sophisticated manufactured products of the time. Most of the important inventions of the industrial revolution had originated in Britain; in any case, British entrepreneurs soon adopted those which originated elsewhere.[10] But the most sophisticated sectors of the early- and mid-nineteenth century were now comparatively unsophisticated, and at the same time comparatively sluggish. Industry had changed its character; increasingly, industrial sophistication came, not from un-tutored genius or the piecemeal, rule-of-thumb adaptation of craftsmen whose skills had been learned on the job, but from what David Landes has called 'the ever-closer marriage of science and technology'.[11] The most sophisticated sectors of the late-nineteenth and early-twentieth centuries depended far more on applied science than their predecessors had done. It was in exports from these that Britain was most conspicuously outclassed; and she was outclassed there partly because she was still pre-eminent in the old staples of the days of her glory, and therefore had too many resources locked up in them. Out of four major commodity groups — machinery and transport equipment, chemicals, textiles and clothing and other manufactures — she was decisively ahead only in exports of textiles and clothing, where she had more than 40.0 per cent of the world market. In machinery and transport equipment, she was slightly ahead of Germany, but in chemicals her share of the world market was only about half Germany's, while in other manufactures it was about two-thirds of the German share.[12] In 1907, to illustrate the point in another way, 70 per cent of Britain's exports and almost half her industrial output, came from three industries — textiles, coal mining and iron and steel.[13] Only the third saw much technical progress in this period; and it was in the least progressive part of the industry that Britain had the comparative advantage. In the years before the First World War, her exports of pig iron were booming. Meanwhile, she became the world's largest importer of steel.[14]

Britain depended increasingly on comparatively unsophisticated markets, just as she depended on comparatively unsophisticated products. Traditionally, around half of her exports had gone to markets outside Europe and the United States. The late-nineteenth and early-twentieth centuries saw a sharp rise in the proportion. Between 1890 and 1913, the value of British exports to Europe and the United States grew by 26 per cent, and to the rest of the world by 81 per cent. By 1913, around two-thirds of the total were going to semi-industrial and non-industrial countries.[15] More disquietingly still, she was beginning to fall behind her competitors even in some of the unsophisticated markets on which she was becoming more and more dependent. Alfred Maizels has divided the world into industrial countries, semi-industrial countries and the rest. In 1899, Germany was slightly ahead of Britain in exports to industrial countries, and well behind in the other two categories. By 1913, German sales to industrial countries stood at $1285 million against Britain's $572 million. Britain was ahead only in exports to semi-industrial countries (admittedly, by the substantial margin of $810 million to $218 million); and most of these were either British colonies or economic satellites of Britain.[16]

No doubt one reason why Britain was overtaken in exports to the industrial world was that, after their victories in their respective wars of unification in the 1860s and 1870s, the two rising continental empires of Germany and the United States turned more and more decisively towards protection while she still stuck to free trade. This meant that her exporters had to surmount high tariff barriers to penetrate the richest markets of industrial Europe and North America, while German and American exports entered Britain tariff-free. But that is only part of the reason. The test came in third countries in the industrial world, where British exporters competed with Germans and Americans on equal terms, and in these German and American sales grew more quickly than British ones.[17] Comparative efficiency, at least as much as tariff policies, held the key to Britain's trading performance. The increasingly lopsided pattern of her trade reflected the relatively backward structure of her industry. More disquietingly still, each reinforced the other.

Of course, the picture was not all black. On the eve of the First World War, Britain was still, by the standards of the time, a very rich country. In income per head, she was surpassed only by the United States, Canada and Australia. No other European country approached her: for all the Germans' technological sophistication, exporting success and industrial growth, Germany's domestic product per head was still only about 60 per cent of Britain's.[18] London was overwhelmingly the most important financial centre in the world; sterling was easily the world's main trading currency; a third of the world's merchant shipping, and a half of the world's steam fleet, was British; about half the seaborne trade of the world was carried in British ships.[19] By virtue of all this, Britain earned an impressive surplus on invisible trade, amounting to nearly a quarter of her import bill.[20] As well as dominating the world's trade in invisibles, she was far and away the world's largest creditor nation. Her foreign assets amounted to £4 billion, or about 40 per cent of the world's total international investment. Her income from these came to nearly £190 million a year, or around 10 per cent of her national income. Since her surplus on invisible trade was almost as large as her deficit on trade in commodities, most of this enormous investment income was available for re-investment — one reason why she was able to increase the annual total she invested overseas from about £50 million at the turn of the century to about £200 million in 1911–13.[21] There were strong points in the domestic economy too. Britain still led the world in shipbuilding, and in technological sophistication as well as in quantity; after ten years of rapid growth and innovation, her bicycle manufacturers dominated the world market; light industries like pharmaceuticals, soap and confectionary were expanding vigorously; entrepreneurs like Thomas Lipton, J.J. Sainsbury and Jesse Boot were creating a virtual new industry of mass retailing.[22] Looking back from the vantage point of seventy years later, it is easy to see that the path which the British economy was following in 1914 pointed to even sharper relative decline in the future. It was more difficult to see it then.

Partly because of this, the precise nature of the path is a matter of intense controversy. Broadly speaking, there are two schools of thought. 'Pessimists' point to Britain's declining share of world manufacturing exports; to her over-commitment to the old staples which had reached their technological frontiers; to her corresponding over-dependence on markets in the colonies and what would now be called the Third World; to her inferiority in the new, science-based industries where growth was most rapid and productivity gains most marked; to the wide and growing gap between her rate of domestic investment and the rates elsewhere; and to the slowness of British manufacturers to adopt the latest techniques. Many pessimists conclude that the roots of these weaknesses lay in a pervasive failure of entrepreneurship. 'Optimists' argue, often with the aid of sophisticated mathematical techniques, that

British entrepreneurs and investors responded rationally to the market signals they encountered.[23] If British managements failed to adopt the new techniques of their American and German competitors, it was because it would not have paid them to do so. If British investors sent their capital abroad, it was because they earned a higher return by doing so than they would have done by investing it at home. If British entrepreneurs stuck to the traditional staples of the early and mid-nineteenth centuries instead of moving into the new, technologically advanced industries which were to become the pace-setters of economic change in the twentieth, it was because they were still making satisfactory profits in the old ones which, after all, were still expanding. In the optimists' view, the whole notion of entrepreneurial 'failure' rests on a misconception. The entrepreneurs of eighty years ago cannot be blamed for failing to behave in ways which would have given their great-grandchildren a more productive economy than the one we know today. The only relevant question is whether, with the knowledge at their disposal, they used the resources which were available to them as efficiently as they could have done; and the answer is that they did.

In its own terms, the optimistic argument is well-founded. If the test of economic success is whether individual economic agents behave rationally in the market-place, the charge of entrepreneurial failure brought against the business leaders of the late-nineteenth and early-twentieth centuries almost certainly falls. But this is where the real debate starts. The issues here are complex, and they must be defined with some care. The evidence of contemporaries, which filled the Reports and Royal Commissions at the time, and on which literary historians have relied for their impressions of this period since, is, to some extent, misleading. Once other countries began to industrialise, it was mathematically inevitable that some indices would show Britain declining relatively to the newcomers. If they were to develop manufacturing industries at all, Britain's share of total manufacturing output was bound to fall; if they were to develop export industries, Britain's share of total world industrial exports was bound to fall as well. This naturally alarmed contemporaries, accustomed to Britain's manufacturing and exporting supremacy in the early nineteenth century; to the extent that their alarm merely reflected the mathematical consequences of industrial development elsewhere we should discount it.

Yet only part of Britain's relative decline was inevitable in that sense. Though her percentage shares of output and trade were bound to fall, the fall was not bound to be as steep as it was. Still less were German and American rates of growth per head bound to be higher than hers: the once-conventional notion that late-comers to industrialisation are bound to overtake those who start early does not square with the experience of developing countries in our own day. Nor was it inevitable that American levels of productivity should have been so much higher than Britain's by the end of the period, or that the gap between German and British levels should have been so much narrower than it had been forty years before. Last, but by no means least, it was not inevitable that Britain should have been so heavily over-committed to the old staples, and so slow to develop the new, science-based industries in which her competitors were most decisively ahead. The question that matters is not whether the investors and entrepreneurs of this period should or should not be blamed for behaving as they did. Praise and blame are not to the point in any case: economic growth is not a reward for virtue. It is why the sum total of rational individual decisions produced an economy which was gradually declining relatively to competing economies. On that question, the test of market rationality can throw little light.

The pattern of strength and weakness I have just sketched out was self-reinforcing. One reason why Britain was over-committed to the old staples was that they still sold well in the semi- and non-industrial markets on which she was becoming increasingly dependent. One of the reasons why they did so was that so much British capital was invested in semi- and non-industrial countries. One reason why British capital flowed to these countries was that the London capital market was the most developed in the world. Another was that there was less scope for profitable investment at home — partly because the traditional staple industries were slow to invest in new techniques and new machinery, and because the new science-based industries were slow to develop. No individual or group of individuals had planned this pattern; and no individual or group of individuals can be blamed for it. But it was not fortuitous either. On one level, it was the product of a mass of separate decisions, most of them rational from the point of view of the individual decision-maker. On another, it was the product of a century and a half of economic history, which had created the structure of comparative advantages in which these decision-makers were trapped. To say that their decisions were rational is to miss the point. The point is that Britain could have escaped continued relative decline only by springing the trap — in other words, by applying some other test to the whole pattern than that of the market rationality of the individual decisions which had created it. To say that this was, for some reason, impossible is to beg one of the central questions of twentieth-century British history. Some contemporaries wanted to do just that. What we need to know is why they failed.

This is where politics come into the story.[24] As so often, they do so in an untidy, not to say confusing, way. Three great issues confronted the political class of the late-nineteenth and early-twentieth centuries, each calling into question a crucial element in the political and economic order which had emerged from the upheavals of the Industrial Revolution. The rise of Irish nationalism challenged the conventions of Westminster parliamentarianism, and threatened the territorial constitution of the British state. The rise of organised labour challenged the moral and social assumptions of market liberalism, and threatened the existing distribution of property and power. The rise of Germany and the United States, and the relative decline of British manufacturing and trade, challenged the prevailing market-liberal economic assumptions and threatened Britain's position as the world's dominant economic and political power. These issues were intertwined, but in an extraordinarily complex fashion; the bitter, sometimes even savage, political conflicts which they provoked cut across each other in a way which confused contemporaries and still confuses historians.

To complicate matters still further, contemporaries did not see them as we see them now. On the second and third issues, in particular, much of the contemporary discussion was conducted in the fashionable social-Darwinist language of the time, and permeated with biological metaphors which ring strangely in a modern ear. Thus, the notion of 'fitness' weaves in and out of the debate in a way which now seems both unpleasant and bizarre. For many of the protagonists, international trade was a kind of testing ground for national virility. The fact that Britain was losing markets to Germany showed that she was becoming 'unfit', not only economically, but morally and physically. Britain's economic problems, Lord Rosebery implied in a characteristic expression of this mood, were the products of a 'drink-sodden population' reared in 'rookeries and slums'. What was needed was a 'condition of national fitness equal to the demands of our Empire — administrative, parliamentary, commercial, educational, physical, moral, naval and military fitness'.[25] Willy-nilly, the British were contestants in a struggle for survival, in which the victory would go to the deserving — the healthy, the industrious, the self-denying, the disciplined. If they lost, it would show that they possessed fewer of these qualities than their rivals.

Closely connected with this obsession with 'fitness' was an obsession, greatly accentuated by the humiliations of the Boer War, with the political and military implications of economic decline. Because of this, the economic debate focused almost wholly on competition from Germany. The Germans were feared, not only because they were seen to be capturing Britain's export markets, but because they were thought to pose an actual political and potential military threat; the conclusion that Britain should put her economic house in order sprang as much from the latter fear as from the former. By the same token, what now seems to be the central question — how to master or modify market forces, so as to keep abreast of the technological and industrial changes which were transforming the world economy: how to use the power of the state to modify the existing mix of comparative advantages registered by the world market — figure only indirectly. For the most part, the focus was defensive. The question at issue was how to keep Britain's existing markets for her existing products, not how to break into new markets, or develop new products or processes.

That said, the most striking feature of the turn-of-the-century debates on Britain's economic decline is how nearly they foreshadowed the debates of our own day. Anxiety about Britain's relative decline was widespread; though Germany was seen as the main threat, the United States was frequently seen as a benchmark. In the realm of action no less than in the realm of ideas, these anxieties provoked a growing revulsion against the classical, Cobdenite market-liberalism of the middle of the century. In however confused and muddled a way, large sections of the political class could see that the spread of modern industry to Germany and the United States had destroyed the informal, free-trade empire[26] in which the orthodoxies of the past had taken shape, and that those orthodoxies could not inspire solutions to the adjustment problems which this transformation had posed. The same applies to the parallel debates on the 'social question'. Some thought that the answer lay in simple insistence on the rights of property, but these were a minority. Most looked for ways to blunt the edge of working-class demands, and most saw that this, too, would mean breaking with Cobdenism. Naturally enough, there were fierce disagreements about what to do instead, but few disputed that, whatever it was, it would entail a much bigger role for the state. The question at issue was not whether market-liberalism should give way to state intervention, but how.

There were two sets of answers, each cutting across the party divides of the period and, to some extent, across each other. The first was 'Social Imperialism' — the answer given by Joe Chamberlain and the so-called tariff reformers in the Unionist Party. Though the details varied from time to time, the central message was straightforward. As Chamberlain put it, 'the days are for great empires, not for little states'.[27] The lesson of German and American success in the Darwinian struggle for economic primacy, and of Britain's relative failure, was that Britain on her own was too small to struggle effectively. But if the loose-knit, heterogeneous, incoherent congeries of colonies, trading posts, naval bases and protectorates which gave allegiance to the British Crown could somehow be welded into an economic unity, together with Britain herself and the Indian sub-continent, the balance of competitive power would shift decisively in Britain's favour. Ironically, Germany provided the model. Prussia, the core of the German empire, had launched herself on the path to economic and political greatness through the *Zollverein* – a customs union of German states, based on the principle of free trade with each other, combined with a common tariff against the external world. Empire free trade would do the same for Britain. It would also serve another purpose. The revenue from protective tariffs on non-empire products would provide the finance to satisfy working-class demands for social reform, without trenching on existing property rights. The threat of a class war, in which the only recently enfranchised and increasingly demanding working class could gain only at the expense of the property owner, would be averted at the expense of the foreigner. At one and the same time, a coalition of interests cutting across class lines would enhance the competitive power of the nation and transcend the internal divisions which enfeebled it.

The second answer was Social Liberalism – the answer of the intellectuals and politicians who provided the justification and rationale for the domestic policy of the 1906 Liberal Government.[28] In some ways, it ran parallel with the Social Imperial answer. It too broke away from the Cobdenite liberalism of the nineteenth century; it too was heavily impregnated with the ideology of National Efficiency; its exponents too often used the biological metaphors which sprang ultimately from social Darwinism. But the differences between Social Liberalism and Social Imperialism were more important than the similarities. As much as their classical predecessors, the social liberals stood for free trade; and on essentially the same grounds. By the same token, they opposed the whole idea of an imperial *Zollverein* and the vision of a tightly-knit imperial union which went with it. To the extent that they were imperialists – and some of them were – their empire was to be a loose coalition of self-governing nations, held together by sentiment and loyalty, not by interest. Where the social imperialists opposed Irish home rule as a betrayal of the imperial ideal, they supported it as a logical corollary of the sort of empire they believed in.

Like the social imperialists, only much more vigorously, they sought to incorporate the labour movement into the political order through a programme of social reform. Unlike the social imperialists, however, they believed that their social reforms should be paid for by redistributive taxation, at the expense of the property-owner, not by tariffs, and at the expense of the consumer. These differences of policy reflected more fundamental differences of emphasis and ideology. Though most social liberals insisted that they wished to encourage enterprise and maintain the volume of production, that was an afterthought. What really mattered was the distribution of wealth, not its creation.[29] And where the social imperialists challenged classical nineteenth-century liberalism head-on, putting the interests of nation or race above the freedom of the individual, the social liberals redefined it, arguing that the ideal of individual freedom could be realised fully only if the state redressed the balance of the market in favour of the weak.

The story of British politics in the early twentieth century is the story of how the Social Liberal answer defeated the Social Imperial one. The campaign for tariff reform was a dismal failure. Chamberlain launched his campaign in May 1903, with 'a challenge to free trade as direct and provocative as the theses which Luther nailed to the church door at Wittenberg'.[30] But he failed to carry his Cabinet colleagues with him, and left the government a few months later. For his pains, he split the Conservative party, and made possible the crushing Liberal victory of 1906. The implications of the defeat go deeper than appears at first sight. It would be wrong to idealise the tariff reformers. There was a strongly 'defensive', traditionalist element in their campaign. On one level, it can be seen as an attempt to perpetuate on an imperial scale the old pattern of the early nineteenth century, which the rise of Germany and the United States had destroyed – a pattern in which Britain was the keystone of a world trading system, supplying mass-produced manufactures to the rest of the world, while the rest of the world was content with the role of junior partner, supplying food and raw materials to Britain. In effect, Britain would concede third, non-empire markets to the Germans and Americans. But she would eliminate the threat of German and American competition in empire markets by building a tariff barrier around them. The old staples would be able to carry on as before; and the lop-sided industrial structure which sprang from Britain's over-commitment to the old staples would presumably continue.

On the other hand, the tariff reformers recognised much more clearly than did their opponents that the problems of economic retardation which lay behind Britain's relative decline could not be overcome by market forces alone; that the newcomers to industrialism which were overtaking or catching Britain up were doing so, at least in part, because in all of them state power had been used to channel them in directions which they would not have taken of their own accord; and that if the problem of production were to be solved, Britain would have to do the same. On a deeper and more important level, they also recognised intuitively that state intervention to solve the problem of production would depend on a cross-class coalition, embracing employers and employed. From the point of view of production, the opposition to tariff reform, on the other hand, was almost wholly conservative. On the central economic issue of the time, the Liberals' campaign in the 1906 election was a campaign for the status quo and their crushing victory a sign that it was much easier to construct a coalition to defend the status quo than a coalition to change it. Thus, the outcome was a paradox. In some ways, the 1906 Liberal government marks the first really decisive break with market-liberalism in British history. But it did so in the sphere of distribution, not in the sphere of production. Social Liberalism legitimised state action to ameliorate poverty and foster equality of opportunity; state intervention in the process of production remained illegitimate. Not for the last time in British history, the politics of consumption triumphed over the politics of production. The consequences are with us still.

Why, then, did Social Imperialism fail? Part of the answer is that the coalition which would have had to come into being to carry it to success would have had to embrace so many conflicting interests that Joe Chamberlain's political skills were insufficient to build it. Working-class support was indispensable: indeed, part of the point of the exercise was to wean the working class away from what Chamberlain misleadingly described as 'socialism' and towards an embryonic form of developmental capitalism.[31] But the employers were indispensable too: if not the export-orientated employers in coal and textiles, or the bankers and insurance brokers in the City, then at least those manufacturers who stood to gain by keeping out foreign imports and by securing a preference for their products in empire markets. So, moreover, were the landowners who saw protection as a way to halt the ruin of British agriculture, and so — for different reasons — were the colonial governments, without whom the underlying vision of a tight-knit imperial union could not be realised. Aggregating all these interests into a coherent coalition for economic change turned out to be like squaring a circle.

The story is soon told. Partly under pressure from Chamberlain, the Conservative government embarked rather gingerly on a programme of social reform. But it was nothing like ambitious enough to detach the working class from the Liberal Party, which most working-class voters by now supported. Instead, the Social Liberals outbid the Social Imperialists; when the Conservatives left office after 1906, the protectionist wing of the party was ranged alongside the free traders in blanket opposition to the Social Liberals' assault on the rights of property. The same thing happened, more flagrantly, in the battle over the famous Taff Vale Judgement of 1901, which removed the protection from claims for damages which the trade unions thought their funds had been given by the Trade Union Act of 1871. For the trade-union leadership, legislation to overthrow the Taff Vale Judgement was a much higher priority than social reform as such. Following the judgment, a flood of trade-union affiliations poured in to the newly-formed Labour Representation Committee. Thanks, in part, to the bargaining power which its growing membership gave them, the leaders of that Committee were able to persuade the Liberal chief whip to make a secret pact with them, which resulted in the return of thirty Labour MPs in the 1906 election. The result was precisely what Chamberlain had wanted to avert: so far from being incorporated alongside the employers in a Social Imperial coalition to change the conditions of production, organised labour was, by 1906, more firmly enrolled in an emerging Social Liberal coalition to change the conditions of consumption than even the most fervent Social Liberal could have expected at the turn of the century.

But this sequence of events did not take place by accident. The court was called upon to rule in the Taff Vale case in the first place only because the employers had, for some years, been conducting a campaign to whittle away the legal defences of the unions in order to restore the control over the work-place which the growth of the Labour Movement had threatened – in other words, to solve the adjustment problem posed by German and American competition, in classic market-liberal fashion, by attacking the rigidities and distortions which were thought to be coagulating the labour market. Thus, on this fundamental issue – central to both the parties concerned – the interests of two of the putative elements in the Chamberlain coalition were in direct conflict. All this, of course, reflected the change in the party system which had taken place after the Liberal split over Irish home rule in 1885. Since then, the Conservatives had increasingly become the party, not just of the landed interest, but of all property, whether landed or industrial – with the inevitable result that organised labour was increasingly apt to see the Liberal Party as its natural ally.

The conflict of interest between organised labour and the employers was only one of the conflicts which would have had to be transcended for a successful Social-Imperialist coalition to emerge. Another was the conflict over taxes on food: the most emotive issue in the whole debate. For both the agricultural interest inside Britain and the governments of the self-governing colonies, tariffs, at least on Britain's non-empire food imports, were an indispensable part of the whole package. But taxes on food ran counter to the interests of working-class consumers. A different, but equally important, set of conflicts divided the employers against themselves. By a strange paradox, a long upswing of world economic activity, ultimately generated by the new, science-based technologies in which Britain lagged behind her more sophisticated competitors, had produced a kind of Indian summer for the old, unsophisticated staples, in which she was still ahead. Exports of these were booming in the decade before the First World War;[32] and, since the employers in those industries depended heavily on exports, they were bound to free trade by interest as well as by inherited conviction. Much the same was true of the invisible exporters in banking, insurance and shipping. There was, in short, a powerful constellation of interests with a stake in the traditional free-trade system, and these were bound to resist a movement for change.

Yet interest does not tell the whole story. Two other, less obvious, factors played a part in it as well. One was the growing weight of party. As we have seen, the intellectual appeal of Social Imperialism cut across party lines. In some of his moods, at least, Lord Rosebery — Gladstone's successor as leader of the Liberal Party — flirted with it almost as enthusiastically as Chamberlain did. So, in some of theirs, did the Fabian pioneers, Shaw and the Webbs.[33] But once Chamberlain had raised the spectre of Protection, and split the Conservative Party in doing so, all sections of the hitherto divided and demoralised Liberal Party had an overwhelming party interest in joining forces against him. The second factor was inherited ideology; the myth constructed in the high noon of Victorian prosperity to explain what was then the recent past. The proposal to levy taxes on food revived ancient memories of the 'Hungry Forties' and challenged the prevailing free-trade ethos at its most powerful point. Had the economy been unmistakably in crisis, it might have been possible to overcome it. As things were, the most remarkable thing about Chamberlain's attempt to construct a coalition for economic change is not that he failed, but that he had the temerity to try.

Chamberlain's was the first, the most clear-cut, and in some ways the most revealing failure of this sort in twentieth-century British history, but it was by no means the last. Similar attempts were made between the wars, with a similar lack of success. Like Chamberlain's their failures sprang from a complex mixture of interest, ideology and institutional inertia. Like Chamberlain's, they can be understood only against the background of the economic experiences to which they were a response.

Once again, the economic record points in two opposing directions. The depression of the inter-war years was real; the cruelty and suffering it brought with it were real too; the waste of resources it caused has lost none of its power to shock. Yet, in two critically important respects, Britain's inter-war record was significantly better than the pre-war record we have just discussed. In the first place, her performance in output and productivity growth was more impressive, in comparison with those of her competitors, than it had been before 1914. Between 1901 and 1913, the annual rate of growth of industrial production in Britain had been less than half the rates in Germany and the United States. Between 1913 and 1929, the British figure was 2.0 per cent a year; the German, 1.2 per cent; and the American, 2.9 per cent. Between 1929 and 1937, Britain outdid both Germany and the United States. In those years, industrial production in Britain grew by 3.4 per cent a year, against 3.0 per cent a year in Germany and only 0.4 per cent a year in the United States.[34] Secondly, the more sophisticated activities in which she had lagged so markedly before 1914, now developed quite strongly, balancing the decline of the depressed trades and the hardships of the depressed areas. A few examples must suffice.

Before the war, Britain's electrical manufacturers had judged their industry a 'poor third', after those of the United States and Germany. By 1924, British exports of electrical machinery were greater in value than Germany's and only a little behind those of the United States; though German and American exports grew more quickly than Britain's in the late 1920s, Britain's held up better in the early 1930s. Motor manufacturing told a similar story. The British share of the total car exports of the six major producing countries rose from 7.0 per cent in 1929 to 13.0 per cent in 1931 and 18.5 per cent in 1936. Britain's chemical industry continued to lag behind Germany's, but thanks partly to government intervention

during the war, and partly to the creation of Imperial Chemical Industries in 1926, the gap was much narrower in 1939
than it had been in 1914.[35]

As with the period before 1914, this mixed record has
provoked a good deal of controversy among economic historians. There is a debate between 'optimists' and 'pessimists',
reminiscent of the debate over the late-nineteenth and early-
twentieth centuries. 'Pessimists' about the retardation of the
earlier period, moreover, are often 'optimists' about this one.
In essence, the 'optimists' believe that the over-commitment of
the earlier period to 'old' industries with backward technologies ended after the war. The inter-war period saw a healthy,
if painful, shake-out of labour and other resources from the
decaying staples of the past to 'new' industries and activities.
Because of this, unemployment was high; but despite high
unemployment, heavily concentrated in the areas where the
'old' staples were located, the real story of the inter-war period,
and particularly of the 1930s, is of the birth of the 'new', not the
death of the 'old'. Moreover, the latter was a necessary
condition of the former. Had the old industries not been
allowed to wither, had resources not been shaken out of them,
the growth of new industries and new activities would have
been much slower than it was.[36]

The 'pessimists' reply that, in reality, Britain's economic
performance – though more impressive than before 1914 –
was not much more impressive. Though 'new' industries
developed, their development was far from spectacular. To
take only a few examples, the chemical industry's share of total
world production by value was lower in 1938 than in 1913.
Though Britain led the world in the development of rayon in
the 1920s, bad management at Courtaulds, the dominant
producer, caused her international position to deteriorate in
the 1930s. In 1939, Britain's consumption of electricity per unit
of industrial production was only two-thirds the German level.
Despite its growth, the car industry was much slower to take
advantage of modern methods of mass production than were
its American and German counterparts.[37] One reason was that
British manufacturers kept profits high by investing little and
paying low wages; as a result labour productivity was only

one-third of the American level in 1935.[38] Moreover, there were signs of weakness elsewhere, vitiating the successes on which the optimists concentrate. The trade balance deteriorated, suggesting that British exports were losing competitiveness. Productivity continued to lag behind the American level, and in a wide range of industries behind the German level also.[39] More obviously, the so-called 'intractable million' remained out of work until the end of the period, when rearmament took up the slack. This suggests that the switch of resources from new to old did not go very far: that although resources were shaken out of declining activities, they were not absorbed in rising ones, as they would have been in a healthy economy.

What are we to make of all this? From the point of view of adjustment to economic change, the inter-war period unquestionably saw an improvement. Relatively to others (and the whole argument is about relativities), Britain's economic performance was better than it had been before 1914. It was also better absolutely, in that a switch to new activities did take place; and that, as a result, the pattern of British economic life in 1939 was less anachronistic in 1939 terms than the pattern of 1914 in 1914 terms. But there were at least two serious weaknesses in Britain's inter-war record, even apart from the high level of unemployment.

The first has to do with the long-term effects of imperial preference on which the national government embarked in 1932. As we saw in the last section, the turn-of-the-century campaign for tariff reform, of which the switch to imperial preference was a sort of posthumous culmination, had always been Janus-faced: 'conservative' in intention, if in some ways 'progressive' in method. *A fortiori*, the same applies to imperial preference when it was finally consummated. As with arguments over 'entrepreneurial failure' in the period before 1914, we must be careful to avoid hindsight. It would be absurd to blame the policy-makers of the 1930s for failing to foresee that in the 1950s and 1960s the European market would be growing faster than any others, and that advanced industrial countries would depend far more on trade among themselves than on trade with the rest of the world. The fact remains that rational decisions in the context of the 1930s had harmful consequences later. Imperial preference locked Britain into an archaic, nineteenth-century trading pattern; in doing so it also reinforced archaic, nineteenth-century attitudes to Britain's place in the world and to her relationship with the European mainland.

The second weakness concerns the management of the domestic economy, and particularly the relationship between industry and the state. In the 1930s, government played a much more active role in economic life than ever before in peacetime. To be sure, it stuck to budgetary orthodoxy, and refused to accept any responsibility for the demand-side of the economy. On the other hand, it intervened quite heavily in the supply-side, mostly in order to improve the efficiency and competitiveness of the depressed staples through mergers and rationalisation. At first sight, the logic was impeccable. Protection would give over-manned and under-capitalised British producers a breathing space in which to put their houses in order: government intervention would make sure that they did so. Unfortunately, however, the logic was not carried through. The government's interventions were reactive, not initiatory, and employed only carrots and not sticks. In effect, government-sponsored cartels were left to negotiate pricing policies, production quotas, investment levels and marketing schemes with their own members, behind tariff barriers which were available unconditionally, whether greater efficiency resulted or not. In all the great staples concerned, coal, cotton, steel and shipbuilding, the effect was the same. As Neil K. Buxton puts it:

> Tradition, conservatism and uncertainty over the alleged greater efficiency of large-scale enterprise, combined to ensure that the traditional *modus operandi* of these industries remained virtually intact.[40]

State intervention, to put the point another way around, was defensive and industrially conservative, not aggressive and industrially radical. Despite some modernising rhetoric, the interventionists were trying to build a haven where threatened producers could shelter from the world depression, not to make

British industry better fitted to compete in world markets. The effects on the economy, as Keith Middlemas describes them, were:

> diminished innovation and hyper-cautious attitudes to capital investment . . .
>
> Price-fixing at one end, restrictive practices at the other, may have been no more widespread than in the 1920s or indeed the 1890s, but they certainly received greater stimulus from the political environment . . . For all the talk of 'managing the economy', the gap between politicians' advocacy of expansion and the cartelisation that actually went on grew rapidly: the price of avoidance of conflict turned out to be political compromise, industrial featherbedding and low overall growth.[41]

At this point, the economic and political stories intersect again. As before, the political story revolves around a struggle between rival embryonic coalitions, with conflicting approaches to the problems of retardation and relative decline. As before, one of its central themes was a continuing tension between the needs of the domestic economy and the nexus of attitudes and interests which had grown up around Britain's position as a world financial and trading power. Even more than before, it throws a vivid light on the social and institutional factors which have made it impossible for any of the three models of adjustment described in the last chapter — market-led, state-led or negotiated — to work satisfactorily in modern Britain.

Four episodes or sets of episodes convey the gist. The first is the well-known story of Britain's return to the gold standard in 1925. There is no reason to dispute the conventional verdict that, by over-valuing sterling and making British exports more expensive in terms of foreign currency, this inflicted significant damage on the home economy. The critical questions from our perspective are why the decision was taken, and what significance to attach to it. Though Churchill, the Chancellor of the Exchequer at the time, had doubts about its wisdom, and though Keynes attacked it in a famous polemic,[42] it followed no great crisis of national orientation and provoked no great national debate. Like Churchill himself, most of the country's political leaders slipped into it, almost without realising what they were doing.

As in the Conan Doyle story, however, comparative silence was in some ways more significant than noise would have been. What it showed was that the political class took the return to gold for granted: that despite all the upheavals of the war and its aftermath, the assumptions underlying British adherence to the gold standard still kept their old force. Yet there was a paradox in their longevity. The chief of these assumptions was that Britain was bound to remain the hub of the world financial system which she had brought into being in the nineteenth century: that no one else had the economic weight and international ties to supersede her in that role; and that − since it was essential, both for Britain and the world, that someone should play it − it was Britain's destiny to do so. In returning to the gold standard, the British government was saying, in effect, that her destiny had not changed: that she was the same sort of country, and the world the same sort of place, that they had been in the nineteenth century. In saying that, however, it was also saying something more complicated and less obvious. The gold standard was the lynch-pin of the self-regulating market order of the past. It locked national economies into the world-wide financial and trading system, and made it impossible for national governments to follow unorthodox budgetary or monetary policies which diverged from the international pattern. Return to it only made sense on the assumption that Britain would continue to adhere to that order − in other words, that adjustment to economic change would still be market-led.

The trouble was that that assumption carried implications from which the ministers and officials who based their policies on it were almost bound to shrink. The self-regulating market order of the nineteenth century no longer existed. In the conditions of the 1920s, market-led adjustment required much more than benign neglect. To make it possible, Government would have had to launch a determined attack on the trusts, cartels, trade unions and social welfare services whose proliferation had choked the market mechanism. And for that, no serious politician, certainly no serious Conservative politician, had the stomach. The Conservative Party of the 1920s was singularly ill-fitted for the role of trust-buster. It was the party of the trust-promoters who were belatedly dragging British industry along the path already taken by its German and American competitors out of the age of small-scale, liberal capitalism and into the age of organisation and amalgamation. Apart from a brief and uncharacteristic moment during and after the General Strike, moreover, its leaders were understandably more anxious to coax the rising Labour Movement into the political order, even at some economic cost, than to free the labour market of union-induced rigidities.[43] To have asked it to pursue a policy of market-led adjustment would have been to ask it to be a different kind of party, operating in a different political environment.

This leads on to the second episode — the defeat of the programmes for home development put forward by Lloyd George during and after the 1929 election, and by Sir Oswald Mosley in 1930 and 1931. The details need not concern us. The crucial point is that, where the previous episode revolved around a policy implying market-led adjustment, this one had to do, above all, with attempts to grope for a form of state-led adjustment. Lloyd George and Mosley both called for loan-financed public works to bring down unemployment, as one element in a strategy of industrial modernisation; Mosley also advocated sweeping changes in the machinery of government, to strengthen the Prime Minister and improve policy co-ordination.[44] Most accounts of the period focus on the conflict between the budgetary orthodoxy of Philip Snowden, the Labour Chancellor of the Exchequer, and the proto-Keynesianism of the Lloyd George and Mosley unemployment policies. That is, of course, a reasonable focus. The contents of Lloyd George's 1929 election programme and of the famous Mosley memorandum of 1930 were all heavily influenced by Keynes; and it was on the Keynesian elements in them that the Treasury concentrated its fire. From our point of view, however, the chief significance of the episode lies elsewhere. It is that Lloyd George and Mosley were both trying to tread where Joe Chamberlain had trod and that they both failed as he had failed. Both wanted to construct a coalition for economic change which would cut across the divisions of class. Their programmes both entailed what was, for the time, substantial state investment in the infrastructure and intervention in the supply-side. Whether their authors acknowledged the fact or not (on the whole Mosley did, while Lloyd George was more reticent) both programmes logically presupposed supporting measures to insulate the home economy from the deflationary pressures of the outside world. Both were defeated by an unholy alliance between the Whitehall machine and a Labour government.

The battle between Whitehall and the proto-Keynesians around Lloyd George and Mosley was not only, or even mainly, a battle about the propriety of deficit finance. Despite Snowden's fiscal rectitude, political constraints did not allow him to make his budgetary policies as orthodox as they have usually been assumed to be, or as he would doubtless have preferred. Their net effect, at any rate when the remorselessly rising borrowings of the National Insurance Fund are taken into account, was probably neutral at first and expansionary rather than deflationary at the end of the government's life.[45] Albeit less obviously, two other issues — both of greater long-term significance — were equally central to the argument. In the first place, it was also an argument over where and how to look for recovery. The Treasury insisted that soundly-based recovery could come only from where it had always come in the past: from exports, and particularly from exports by the traditional staple industries. The obstacle was the inefficiency, low productivity and resultant lack of competitiveness of the export industries. The solution was a painful, but necessary, programme of 'rationalisation' — the shedding of surplus labour and the closure of small, under-capitalised firms — through which they would put their houses in order. By raising prices and expanding demand in the soft home market, the Liberal and Mosleyite programmes would impede the process of rationalisation, and slow down the adjustment which was necessary for Britain to become competitive in world markets again. The proto-Keynesians replied that, in practice, recovery would no longer come from this source: that it would have to come from home demand instead: and, by implication at any rate, that the balance of payments difficulties which would result from raising the level of home demand while the rest of the world was engulfed in depression would have to be met by protection or devaluation or both. Secondly, and in some ways more significantly, the argument was about the role and structure of the state. Lloyd George and Mosley were asking British ministers and civil servants to assume responsibilities and behave in ways which were alien to their peacetime experience and, on a deeper level, to the whole ethos of British government. Not only did they want the Treasury to abandon its traditional objections to public borrowing for projects which did not offer an immediate monetary return; they also wanted the Ministry of Transport to build roads in a timescale which its slow-moving processes of planning, purchase and consultation ruled out. Their defeat had at least as much to do with the inability of the Ministry of Transport's officials to behave like entrepreneurs as with the Treasury's refusal to behave like an investment bank.[46]

The third episode — the shift in the party system which destroyed the Liberals as serious contenders for power, and turned the Labour Party into the main anti-Conservative party in the state — helps to explain the second. (It was, after all, a Labour government which turned down the Lloyd George and Mosley programmes; and it was the solidity of the Labour vote which frustrated their attempts to build cross-class electoral coalitions.) This shift has been discussed *ad nauseam* of course, but not from the perspective of this book. From our point of view, its significance lies, above all, in what it tells us about the *economic* terms on which organised labour was at last incorporated into the political order. As we have seen, one of the main reasons why the struggle between Social Imperialism and Social Liberalism went the way it did was that the Labour Movement spurned the somewhat hesitant Social Imperial embrace in favour of the much more enthusiastic — but from the point of view of production much more conservative — advances of the Social Liberals. In this, the 1920s and 1930s were a repetition of the 1900s. Where Lloyd George and Mosley followed Chamberlain in groping for a form of state-led adjustment to change the conditions of production, the Labour Party, like the pre-war Liberals, sought only to change the conditions of consumption and stuck to the productive status quo. This was obviously, even painfully obviously, true of its ideology. 'Socialism' focused on distribution and on ownership, not on production. Even more than with pre-war Social Liberalism, the assumption underlying it was that the problem of production had been solved. What applied to the party's ideology, moreover, applied equally to the interests enrolled under the banner of that ideology. Despite a top dressing of intellectuals, Labour was, above all, the party of the relatively-deprived, 'old', heavily-unionised working class, spawned by the 'old' staples and inhabiting the 'old' regions, whose chief aim was to erect a socially-just shelter against the winds of industrial change. In theory, it stood for sweeping extensions in the economic role of the state. In practice, it could no more embrace a policy of state-led adjustment than the Conservatives could attack the distortions and rigidities which stood in the way of market-led adjustment. It was a coalition of those who stood to lose from adjustment in any form.

The fourth set of episodes – the abandonment of the gold standard in 1931 and the devaluation of sterling which followed; the crushing victory of the national government in the subsequent general election; and the switch to imperial preference in 1932 – should be looked at against this background. We must now try and see what the economic implications of imperial preference and the national government's industrial policies together with the decision to go off gold implied for the politics of economic decline, both then and later. The implications are more complex than is sometimes realised. Just as the Lloyd George-Mosley programmes of home development pointed towards an embryonic form of state-led development, so the national government's industrial interventions pointed logically towards negotiated development. As its name suggested, moreover, the government was itself a cross-class coalition of sorts: a successful version of the cross-class coalitions which Chamberlain, Lloyd George and Mosley had all tried and failed to build. In rhetoric, and to some extent in reality, it too stood for class collaboration in the interests of economic change. Whatever else it may have signified, the 1931 election result was a thoroughgoing defeat for the class politics of the Labour Party; and, however strange it may seem in retrospect, the 'doctor's mandate' which Ramsay MacDonald and his colleagues obtained in the election was a mandate for new departures. More importantly, the government's combination of devaluation and imperial preference was in fact a new departure, of a remarkably radical kind. The two together added up to the most decisive peacetime break with market liberalism in British history. By the same token, they also marked a decisive break with the traditional, nineteenth-century view of Britain's place in the world. In effect, the British government announced that Britain was no longer the centre of either a world-wide trading or a world-wide financial system: that she was retreating into a British-Empire-wide system instead, and that she intended to replace market-led adjustment with some other form of it.

Had this announcement gone hand in hand with a vigorous programme of industrial modernisation, it might also have represented a decisive break with the relative decline of the British economy, which was in large part a product of Britain's nineteenth-century role in the world. But, as we have seen, no such programme ensued. The opportunity to lay the foundations of a developmental state was lost. Having protected her external flank and insulated herself from the deflationary pressures of the outside world, Britain sank back into defensive protectionism. Having established close bargaining relationships with the organised producer groups, the state allowed them to call the tune, and made only fitful and half-hearted attempts to ensure that they used the breathing space it had given them to modernise and adapt. What might have evolved into a system of negotiated adjustment in fact became a kind of negotiated inertia.

Against this background, the sharper and more painful relative decline of the 1950s, 1960s and 1970s falls into place. There are two ways of coping with the distributional issues which the process of economic adjustment is bound to raise. One is to push losers and prospective losers out of the way. The other is to buy them off. Once Britain had become a political democracy – and, still more, once the Labour Movement had been incorporated into the political order and the Labour Party had become a partner in the two-party system – the first way was no longer practical. As the majority of the electorate belonged to the working class, cross-class coalition-building could not succeed without their co-operation; and since the working-class movement was too strong to be coerced, negotiated adjustment, in one form or another, was the only method left with much chance of working. But although political and economic leaders made numerous attempts to act on that logic, none of them succeeded.

Like Chamberlain, Mosley and Lloyd George, Edward Heath and Harold Wilson tried to construct cross-class coalitions for economic change. As before, their attempts came to nothing. In its short-lived heroic phase, the post-war Labour government seemed to be groping uneasily for a form of state-led adjustment. As in the inter-war period, the gropings got nowhere, partly because the politicians lacked the will and understanding to make a success of them, but even more because the inherited culture and assumptions of Whitehall – like the inherited culture and assumptions of the Labour Movement – were antipathetic to the whole idea. In the hands-on phase of Keynesian social democracy, successive governments established close bargaining relationships with the producer groups, just as they had done in the 1930s. As before, the outcome was closer to negotiated inertia than to negotiated adjustment. The post-war history of Britain's political economy has to be seen, in short, as the last act of a much longer tragedy of institutional rigidities and missed opportunities. If we are to understand the denouement, we must try to come to grips with the logic and meaning of the opening acts as well.

6

A State of Perfect Freedom

'All men are naturally in . . . a state of perfect freedom to order
their actions and dispose of their possessions as they think fit,
within the bounds of the law of nature, without asking the leave
or depending upon the will of any other man.'

John Locke, 1690.[1]

'Our prevalent notion is . . . that it is a most happy and
important thing for a man merely to be able to do as he likes. On
what he is to do when he is thus free to do as he likes, we do not
lay so much stress . . . We have not the notion, so familiar on the
Continent and to antiquity, of *the State* — the nation in its
collective and corporate character, entrusted with stringent
powers for the general advantage in the name of an interest
wider than that of individuals.'

Matthew Arnold, 1869.[2]

'In a period of freedom for all, we are part of the all.'

Frank Cousins, 1956.[3]

I have tried to show that the origins of Britain's failure to
become a developmental state began with the Social Liberals'
victory over the Social Imperialists before the First World
War. Plainly, the story is extraordinarily complex, and no brief
summary can do justice to it. We have to pick our way through
a forest of detail, much of it still unexplored; paths which seem
promising at first sight often peter out in thickets of scholarly
disputation. All the same, two central themes stand out.
British economic agents have repeatedly failed to adapt to the
waves of technological and institutional innovation sweeping
through the world economy; Britain's political authorities
have repeatedly failed to promote more adaptive economic
behaviour. But if these two themes are clear, they are also

puzzling. In the late-eighteenth and early-nineteenth centuries, British economic agents and political authorities set in motion the revolutionary chain of innovation and adaptation which created the first industrial society in history. Why should their near descendants have found it so difficult to adapt to later versions of the same achievement?

Understandably, perhaps, many have assumed that the most promising way to approach this question is to focus on the changes which have taken place since the early-nineteenth century. After all, the Britain which failed to exploit the new technologies of the 1890s and 1900s, and which lost market shares to Germany and the United States, was, in a whole host of ways, a different society from the Britain of the 1780s or even of the 1850s, while the Britain whose living standards fell behind those of most comparable countries in the 1950s and 1960s was more different still. Prima facie, there are good grounds for assuming that the key to the story must lie in these differences — that if the erstwhile workshop of the world has fallen on hard times it must be because its inhabitants are not the men their grandfathers were — and that if we can identify their causes and consequences, we shall be able to explain what happened. That assumption is specially congenial to those who have been brought up in the orthodox Anglo-American economic tradition, and whose paradigm of a properly working economy is still — whether consciously or unconsciously — the atomistic, market economy which the eighteenth- and nineteenth-century British founders of the tradition saw around them. Britain was the workshop of the world, the implicit argument goes, in the days when she obeyed the rules of market liberalism. Since she no longer obeys them, that must be why her economy has declined since. Thus, many have found the origins of Britain's economic decline in a 'counter-revolution of values',[4] which led the manufacturing bourgeoisie of the late-nineteenth century to abandon the hard-driving, risk-taking entrepreneurialism of the heroic age of British industry in favour of an anti-industrial ethos disseminated by the old universities and public schools. Others have found them in the early emergence of trade unions and cartels, strong enough to 'distort' the working of the

market.[5] Others again have found them in the conversion of
the governing class to a flabby and soft-hearted liberalism,
dominated by a concern for social welfare.[6]

I think the explanation is more complex than this. It is true
that changes have taken place since the early-nineteenth
century. It is true that some of them have played a part in
Britain's relative economic decline. But the changes are more
complicated than they seem; and, in any case, they are less
significant than the continuities. The notion that the roots of
Britain's economic decline lie in her failure to stick to the
early-nineteenth-century, market-liberal model of a successful
economy rests on the assumption that adjustment can only be
market-led. In reality, as we have seen, there are at least three
models of successful adjustment, not one. Market-led adjustment, on the pattern of Industrial-Revolution Britain, repre-
sents one way of coping with economic change. But state-led
adjustment, on the Japanese pattern, and negotiated or
corporatist-consensual adjustment, on the pattern of central
Europe and Scandinavia, represent others. It is true that
Britain abandoned the market-led model. But it does not
follow that that is why her economy declined: when her decline
began, she was closer to it than were her more successful
rivals. Her real predicament is that, having abandoned it,
she has been unwilling or unable to adopt either of the other
two models. And, by a strange paradox of cultural conservatism, the reason is that the 'ethos' of market liberalism –
the web of assumptions, values, understandings and
experiences which gave the market-led model its emotional
power – survived long after the doctrine was abandoned.

At the heart of that ethos lies a set of attitudes to the role of
public power, and to the relationship between public power
and private freedom, which is unique in Europe. The developmental states, which first followed and then overtook Britain
on the path to industrialism, deliberately repudiated the
orthodox classical and neo-classical theories of international
trade and the political assumptions underlying them. As we
saw in the previous chapter, their approach to international
trade differed in at least four ways from the orthodox classical

approach. For them, the world economy was made up of nations, not of individuals. These nations sought wealth as a means to power; they wished to maximise their power in the long term, even if it meant sacrificing individual satisfactions in the short term. They were not content with a pattern of comparative advantages which condemned them to permanent inferiority to the world's economic pacemakers. It was the task of the state to change the pattern.

As we saw, however, Britain did not follow suit. The notion of a welfare state was slowly accepted. The notion of a developmental state, using its power to give its citizens a more sophisticated set of comparative advantages so that it could compete more effectively with other states, met dogged and uncomprehending resistance. At most, the state's job was to distribute wealth. It was not supposed to create it. As in the United States, where Robert Reich has diagnosed a split between a 'business culture' focused on profitable production, and a 'civic culture' focused on equitable consumption,[7] the public sector came to be seen as the domain of the non-economic – of the fair, the concerned and the tender-hearted in the eyes of its supporters, and of the sloppy, the profligate and the uncompetitive in the eyes of its opponents. The notion that it might be the ally of, or even a spur to, competitiveness remained alien to both. Even when governments began to intervene in the supply-side, first in the 1930s and more systematically in the hands-on phase of Keynesian social democracy, essentially welfare considerations – the protection of existing jobs and existing industries – characteristically predominated over developmental ones.

The implications go wide. In a path-breaking essay, Alexander Gerschenkron once observed that the more 'backward' the society undergoing industrialisation, and the wider the gap between its level of technological sophistication and the level of the most advanced economies of the time, the more industrialisation depends on public authorities.[8] Thus, the German state intervened in the economy more than the British, and the Russian and Japanese more than the German. Gerschenkron's insight underlines a paradox which echoes through the last century of British economic history like a tolling bell. The minimalist state of late-eighteenth and early-nineteenth-century England was appropriate for an industrial pioneer, in which economic development could take place slowly and gradually, through a series of small, piecemeal steps within the capacity of a decentralised private sector. Once Britain's old followers had begun to overtake her, however, roles were reversed. She was no longer a pioneer, and began to fall into relative backwardness herself. But the values and assumptions of her pioneering days still survived, inhibiting her from overcoming her backwardness in the way that her imitators of the previous generation had overcome theirs.

This paradox provides a common thread, linking the failure of the campaigns for Tariff Reform before 1914 and for home development in the 1920s, the defensive character of the national government's internal economic management in the 1930s, the confusions and hesitations of the theorists of economic planning in the same period, the switch from the heroic to the arm's length phase of Keynesian social democracy in the 1940s, the speedy collapse of the National Plan in the 1960s and the muddled, irresolute interventionism of the 1970s. Again and again, would-be interventionists were frustrated by the lack of a tradition of developmental intervention, and by the widespread belief that such intervention was either impossible or undesirable. As Andrew Shonfield wrote at the zenith of the hands-on period:

Old fashioned *laissez-faire* had gone; but the old instinctive suspicion of positive government, which purports to identify the needs of the community before the community itself has recognised them, remained as vigorous as ever. It was reflected both in the behaviour of ministers who refused to plan, and by the administrative devices invented for them by civil servants, who were anxious above all to ensure that the exercise of the new powers of government did not saddle them with the responsibility for making choices. Administrative discretion, which is meat and drink to the French, is anathema to the British official. Of course, he has it in practice; without it a modern state could not function. But because it raises awkward problems about the division of responsibility between politicians and officials, the officials hold deliberately to the pretence that they have no initiative of their own, that they are instruments only, wholly passive, in the hands of some masterminding minister. To give this pantomime verisimilitude, the powers attributed to civil servants must be kept to the minimum.[9]

Yet it can scarcely be argued that Britain would not have profited from developmental intervention. In theory, no doubt, different forms of private organisation — for example, a banking system on the German model, attuned to the needs of industrial development and willing to put long-term growth ahead of short-term profit — might have enabled her to break out of the pattern of decline without government intervention. But if her private sector had been so organised, she would not have been caught in the pattern in the first place. Moreover, some of her economic handicaps — above all, her backward education system and the comparatively poor quality of her human capital — sprang directly from the minimalist view of the state, and could have been put right only by adopting a different view. By the same token, there is no reason to believe that the British were, for some reason, technically incapable of creating as entrepreneurial a state apparatus as existed elsewhere. The British administrative machine managed the wartime economies of 1914–18 and 1939–45 with great skill. In the Second World War, Britain may well have been the most efficiently mobilised of all the belligerents — partly, of course, because American aid made it possible to ignore balance of payments considerations.[10] The civil-service élite which had wearily resisted the Lloyd George-Mosley programme of home development on the grounds that the roads it envisaged could not be built in time to make any difference to the unemployment figures now ran a quasi-totalitarian command economy with flair and drive. The barrier to such behaviour in peacetime was not technical. What was it?

At first sight, the obvious answer is that it was the extraordinary longevity of market liberalism among the British political class. But there are two weaknesses in that. The first is that it is not so much an answer as another way of formulating the question. It is a characteristic illusion of intellectuals to imagine that doctrines convert societies. It would be closer to the truth to say that societies evoke doctrines. Smith, Bentham, Malthus, Ricardo and the Mills were giants of social thought, but if their teachings had not resonated in the society around them, they would have had no influence in their own day and would probably have been forgotten in ours. They are remembered because they put intellectual flesh on to a skeleton of attitude and understanding which was already there. If we want to know why market liberalism made headway in the first place, and why its doctrines continued to carry conviction for so long, we shall have to pay more attention to the skeleton than to the flesh. The second weakness is that, in any event, only some market-liberal doctrines continued to carry conviction. Logically, market liberalism is as hostile to the welfare state as to the developmental state: to the Social Liberal programme of 1906–14 as to the Social Imperialist programme of Joe Chamberlain and the tariff reformers. Yet, as we have seen, British politicians and administrators accepted the idea of a welfare state without much difficulty. If they could come to believe that the state had an obligation to maintain its citizens through sickness and unemployment, why did they not also come to believe that it had an obligation to develop the economy?

Part of the explanation, of course, lies in nineteenth-century Britain's unique place in the world economy, and in the web of interests, values, assumptions and loyalties which grew up around it. The developmental states of that era were trying, quite consciously, to break away from economic subordination to her, just as many of the developmental states of the twentieth century have been anxious to break away from economic subordination to the United States. It is not surprising that she found it hard to emulate them when she eventually lost her pre-eminence and when, as a result, the logic of her own internal development began to conflict with the logic of the world-wide trading and financial system which she had brought into existence. For, in a sense true of no other country before or since, she was the child of that system, as well as its midwife. The British state, the British governing class, the British civil service, the British education system, the British economy and the British capital market were all shaped by its imperatives. It was because Britain was committed to free trade and the gold standard, because individual British citizens exported huge quantities of capital all over the world, because the Royal Navy maintained the *pax Britannica*, because British trading posts and naval bases girdled the globe, that the world-wide system came into being; and it was because Britain had been the pivot of that system for so long that later British politicians and opinion leaders could not emancipate themselves from its assumptions. Of course, she would have been better off if she had put the needs of the domestic economy ahead of the claims of the world-wide system, as most of the developmental states of the nineteenth and twentieth centuries have done. As we have seen, that theme has run through a long succession of lost opportunities, from Joe Chamberlain's defeat at the hands of the free traders in the early 1900s and the rejection of the Lloyd George-Mosley programme under the second Labour government to the abandonment of the National Plan in 1966. But the British governments which acted in this way did not do so out of caprice. They were listening to ancestral voices of enormous power. They could have given precedence to internal development instead only by breaking with the tradition which had made them and their countrymen what they were.

Yet this is only part of the explanation. The developmental states also had histories; and their histories also created obstacles to modernisation and adjustment. Looking back from the vantage point of the late-twentieth century it is easy to see that there were strands in the cultural inheritances of Meiji Japan, or early-nineteenth-century Prussia or Gaullist France which favoured the emergence of developmental states, with the will and power to modernise their economies. But it is easy to see this because we know that developmental states in fact emerged. Before they did so, the obstacles to modernisation — the backwardness and poverty of Japan, the archaic militarism of the Prussian Junkers, the political instability of France — all loomed quite large. If we want to understand Britain's failure to emulate them, it is not enough to know that ancestral voices counselled against doing so. We also need to know why the ancestral voices were listened to.

Andrew Shonfield's contrast between the French official, eagerly embracing administrative discretion, and the British official, desperate to pretend that he does not have any, provides an important clue. For the developmental state is inherently discretionary, in a sense in which the welfare state is not. In a welfare state, the authorities treat precisely specified categories of citizens in precisely specified ways. Once the rules have been laid down, the system is, in Alan Cawson's phrase, 'rule-governed'.[11] The developmental state cannot be rule-governed in that way; flexibility is the whole essence of the developmental économie concertée. In it, the state browbeats, bribes and bargains with private economic agents, favouring some at the expense of others, in varying ways and according to varying criteria — choosing from among a panoply of interventionist devices those that seem most appropriate at any given moment. In Britain, that kind of flexibility seems faintly improper; and when governments have engaged in it, as in the 1930s and the 1960s, their efforts have been half-hearted and lacking in legitimacy. The crucial question, then, is why? Why Britain's political culture has been consistently hostile to the notion, not so much of an interventionist state as of a discretionary one?

The answer lies deep in the experiences which shaped that culture. Thanks to the upheavals of the seventeenth century — thanks, in particular, to the victory of the English landed class over the Stuart kings — one cannot speak of a 'British state' in the way that one speaks of a 'French state' or, in modern times, of a 'German state'.[12] The United Kingdom is not a state in the continental sense. It is a bundle of lands (including such exotica as the Channel Islands and the Isle of Man, which are not even represented at Westminster), acquired at different times by the English crown, and governed in different ways. Its inhabitants are not citizens of a state, with defined rights of citizenship. They are subjects of a monarch, enjoying 'liberties' which their ancestors won from previous monarchs. Executive power is still, in an odd way, private rather than public. It lies with named individuals – ministers of the Crown, legally responsible for the activities of their departments – not with the state. The civil servants who advise the minister and implement his decisions are, in constitutional theory, simply that: individual 'servants', hired technicians in administration, not a corporate body with a corporate responsibility to the public and a corporate obligation to pursue the public interest. The political culture which all this reflects and sustains can tolerate reactive intervention, designed to respond to pressures which have already made themselves felt or to buy off trouble which is patently in the offing. It cannot provide a moral basis for discretionary intervention – for intervention designed, in Shonfield's suggestive phrase, to serve 'the community's needs before the community itself has recognised them'.

To be sure, most of the nation-states of mainland Europe started in the same way. Germany was still a patchwork quilt of kingdoms, principalities and city states more than half-way through the nineteenth century. Even France – in many ways the paradigm case of the European nation-state – became a united monarchy much later than England. But by the early nineteenth-century, the Bourbons, the Jacobins and Napoleon had hammered the lands of the French Crown into the French state, while the Hohenzollerns had hammered the Prussian state out of their bleak, unpromising inheritance and the conquests they added to it. Over most of mainland Europe, modernity came by the same route. Weak and fissiparous medieval kingdoms slowly evolved into absolute, but still patrimonial, monarchies.[13] The old medieval estates were neutered or pushed aside. As in the middle ages, however, there was no real distinction between the monarch as a person and the monarch as a ruler. Under the pressure of war, financial exigency and the ideas of Roman law and the Enlightenment, the patrimonial monarchies of the early modern period then evolved into the benevolent despotisms of the eighteenth century, in which the monarch could boast with Frederick II that he was 'the first servant of the state' – the caretaker or trustee of a public power, above and beyond his own person and, by the same token, above and beyond the persons of his subjects.[14] Sometimes monarchies gave way to republics and sometimes not. But from our point of view, that made little difference. What mattered was that, in monarchies and republics alike, patrimonial power was transformed into state power; and that, in republics no less than in monarchies, the state was assumed to be more than the sum of the citizens who made it up.

From the seventeenth century, Britain followed an aberrant path. The Stuarts, like their contemporaries on the European mainland, tried to create an absolute, patrimonial monarchy, strong enough to impose its will on the medieval corporations and the nobility and gentry. For a brief moment, it looked as if Cromwell's Protectorate might take an alternative, republican route to the same destination.[15] But all of these attempts trenched on the freedom of the landed class to do what it wished with its own, and all of them broke on the instinctive resistance of the landowners of the Country Party to the ambitions of a centralising Court. The Revolution Settlement of 1688 marked their final defeat. Instead of being suppressed, the medieval particularism of the past blended with the 'possessive individualism' of emergent capitalism.[16] The old liberties, the old corporations, the old, precedent-bound common law, the old houses of parliament all survived; and they, not the will of a reforming monarch, became the conduits of modernity. The end product was a political culture suffused with the values and assumptions of whiggery, above all with the central Lockean assumption that individual property rights are antecedent to society. In such a culture, the whole notion of a public power, standing apart from private interests, was bound to be alien. Yet without that notion, it is hard to see how a developmental state, with the capacity to form a view of the direction the economy ought to take, and the will and moral authority to put its view into practice, can come into existence.

The victory of the landed class had a more particular consequence as well. A developmental state would have to have a territorial dimension. It would have to favour certain activities in certain places against other activities in other places – to form an independent opinion about what ought to happen on the ground in unfashionable industrial centres like

Birmingham, or Sheffield or Newcastle-on-Tyne, and to take action to make its opinion prevail. To do this, it would have to know what was going on in such places, and it would have to deal directly with the local economic agents whose behaviour it wanted to influence; for both purposes it would need a high-level presence in the parts of the country concerned. Here too the legacy of the seventeenth-century Country Party still stands in the way. In different ways, the Stuart and Cromwellian attempts at state-building all had a territorial dimension, and it was partly because they had a territorial dimension that the landed class saw them as a threat, and made up its mind to resist them. 1688 marked the victory, not only of possessive individualism on the national level, but of a strange kind of possessive territorialism on the local level. The Crown-in-Parliament determined public policy, but it left implementation to unpaid local squires, sitting as justices of the peace. The result, to use Jim Bulpitt's terminology, is that British central government has traditionally fought shy of the 'low politics' through which services are delivered to the public, in order to concentrate on the 'high politics' of foreign affairs, defence, taxation and, in the Keynesian era, of macro-economic management.[17]

As in the colonies and India, in short, it has relied instinctively on a kind of indirect rule. This has not led to genuine local autonomy, of course. In recent times, at any rate, policy has been laid down at the centre, sometimes very tightly. But it has been implemented by a hodge-podge of half-autonomous boards, commissions and local authorities, whose relationships with central government have been uncertain, fluctuating and often impenetrable to the general public. One obvious consequence is the contrast between the career patterns of high-flyers in the British civil service, who characteristically spend their entire working lives in the capital, and those of their French equivalents, who usually spend part of theirs in the prefect's office in a provincial *département*. Another is the attraction of Keynesian arm's length management for the civil service élite, of which Keynes himself was, of course, one of the most distinguished ornaments in history. Yet another is the inability of the hands-on governments of the 1960s and 1970s to develop an entrepreneurial style of intervention.

The same theme runs through the tangled and perplexing story of the state's relationship with the functionally-based groups of producers which proliferate in all advanced industrial societies. In modern times, at any rate, the possessive individualism of the Glorious Revolution has been mirrored in — and buttressed by — a complex set of attitudes and patterns of behaviour which might be called 'possessive collectivism'. Where the former has stood in the way of any form of developmental state, the latter has been particularly hostile to the negotiated or corporatist-consensual version, towards which governments and producer groups alike seemed to be groping in the 1930s, and again in the 1960s and 1970s.

The best way to approach the role of 'possessive collectivism' in Britain's relative economic decline is through Mancur Olson's important study of the causes and 'retardants' of economic growth.[18] Olson argues that Britain's economic decline is due, above all, to the activities of organised producer groups, which he calls 'common-interest organisations'. According to him, it is not rational for a common-interest organisation to pursue those interests which its members share with the rest of the wider society. If it did, it would bear the whole cost of pursuing them, while receiving only a small part of the benefit. The interests which it pursues must be exclusive to its own members, or at least to the population from which it hopes to recruit members. In a very profound sense, then, common-interest organisations are doomed to be anti-social. They exist to provide their members with goods which others cannot share: to distort the working of the market in their members' favour. Unions seek higher wages, cartels higher prices and professional associations lower recruitment levels than the market would provide if left to itself. It follows that a society with a lot of common-interest organisations will be less efficient, and have a lower rate of growth than will a society with a small number.

Some societies, however, have more common-interest organisations than others. For such organisations are slow to establish themselves. The reason is that, from the point of view of the group whose interests it pursues, the organisation provides what economists call 'public goods'. Thus, all members of the group benefit from its activities, whether they belong to it or not. This 'free rider' problem makes it difficult for common-interest organisations to emerge, and they need long periods of peace and stability to do so. Because of this, societies which have enjoyed long periods of peace and stability will have more common-interest organisations, and therefore lower rates of growth, than societies which have not. Britain has a lower growth-rate than mainland Europe because she has had two hundred years to accumulate common-interest organisations, whereas in the rest of the continent their accumulation has been impeded by wars, revolutions and dictatorships. Yet some stable societies have had a happier destiny. If the members of a common-interest organisation are numerous enough to form a large proportion of the total population (Olson's word for this is 'encompassing'), the incentives and disincentives that affect it will be very different. An encompassing organisation will lose significantly from policies that make the wider society less productive than it would otherwise be, and gain significantly from policies that make it more productive. Hence, it *can* rationally pursue the interests which its members share with the wider society. In societies where the common-interest organisations are encompassing, therefore, growth may still be rapid. It is because this is true of Sweden, that she has had a much higher rate of growth than Britain, despite having enjoyed an even longer period of peace and stability.

Olson's argument has obvious weaknesses. He takes for granted a culture permeated with the values of Benthamite, utility-maximising individualism, ignoring the possibility that other cultures may have different values, embodied in different institutions and manifested in different patterns of behaviour. That said, his analysis of the logic of group behaviour in a culture in which the values of Benthamite individualism do predominate is hard to fault. It seems clear that, in such a culture, organised groups will indeed have a propensity to pursue the narrow interests of their own clientèles in a way which runs counter to the interests of the total society, for the reasons he gives. Middlemas's history of the evolution of 'corporate bias' in modern Britain complements Olson's theory rather well. Olson shows that common-interest organisations are in principle likely to retard economic growth; Middlemas suggests that the relationship between the British state and the most powerful of Britain's common-interest organisations in practice retarded it. And although Middlemas's study does not go back to the turn of the century, there is some evidence that the same was true then.[19]

However, the part which common-interest organisations have played in Britain's relative economic decline is more complicated than Olson suggests. If he is right, the crucial variable − at any rate in a mature, peaceful, highly-developed society − is what he calls 'encompassingness'. If such societies are bound to have a large number of common-interest organisations − and it is central to his argument that they are − it is utopian to imagine that they can somehow be wished out of existence. The only relevant questions are whether they are 'encompassing' or 'non-encompassing'. It is a waste of time to ask whether Britain ought to have a large number of common-interest organisations: she is bound to, whether we like it or not. The question that matters is: why have her common-interest organisations been non-encompassing, and what, if anything, can be done to make them encompassing instead?

For Olson himself, encompassingness is a function of size. The bigger the common-interest organisation, the more closely its interests will coincide with those of the wider society, and the more likely it is to behave in a way which conforms with the interests of the wider society. But cross-national comparison suggests that there is more to it than this. It is true that the Swedish trade-union movement organises a much larger proportion of the working population than does its British equivalent (nearly 80 per cent, compared with a British proportion of less than 45 per cent). But it did not do so earlier in the century, when Britain's relative decline was already under way; and in western Europe as a whole, the British level of union membership is fairly near to the middle of the range. It is ahead of the German and Dutch levels, but behind those of

Austria and Denmark; in turn, the Austrian and Danish levels are behind Sweden's.[20] Yet, as Wolfgang Streeck has shown, British trade unions behave in a much less encompassing way, not only than Swedish unions, but than West German unions as well,[21] while a number of studies suggest that, in behaviour, the Austrian unions are at least as encompassing as the Swedish ones, and perhaps more so.[22] Plainly, then, encompassingness in behaviour — and in this context it is behaviour which matters — is not a function of size alone, but of size in combination with other factors.

The most obvious of these other factors is the structure of the common-interest organisation concerned. The British trade-union movement has a fairly encompassing membership, but an exceedingly non-encompassing structure. The Trade Union Congress is, and always has been, a loose-knit confederation of autonomous, often fragmented and ill-disciplined bodies, jealous of their own independence, suspicious of each other, answerable only to their own members and willing to co-operate with each other only on their own terms. The most decisive difference between it and the Swedish confederation of manual workers' unions (the LO) is not that the LO organises a higher proportion of the eligible population, but that the LO is much more centralised; that it has much more authority over the much smaller number of unions which belong to it; and that its member-unions are also more centralised and more hierarchical than their British counterparts. By the same token, the Swedish private-sector employers' association, the SAF, is far more centralised than the British Confederation of British Industries and has far more authority over its member firms. Much the same applies in Austria and West Germany. The German car industry provides a telling case in point. In 1975, the metal workers union and the Volkswagen management agreed to cut the work force by 20,000 in order to restore profitability. Among the key factors in a decision which solved a serious over-capacity problem without industrial disruption or government subsidy, Streeck notes, were:

the comprehensiveness and monopolistic position of the IGM as an industrial union representing all categories of workers in the German engineering industry; the hierarchical control capacity of the union leadership over the works council, and the respective capacity of the central works council over the local works council, and of the latter over the union stewards at the workplace; the legal limitations on the works councils' range of actions; and the institutionalisation in law of the union as a responsible participant in the company's decision-making process through co-determination.[23]

Why, then, are the common-interest organisations in these countries more encompassing in structure than British ones? Streeck's list of the factors which led the German metal workers union to behave in an encompassing fashion over the Volkswagen de-manning provides a valuable clue. Though some of them sprang only from the union's own internal arrangements, most also reflected a wider philosophy of industrial government, embodied in state policies and public law. There is growing evidence that this applies elsewhere as well: that encompassingness is almost always the product of a kind of symbiosis between the government of industry and the conduct of the state. Albeit in varying degrees, Austria, Sweden and West Germany are all examples of what Gerhard Lehmbruch has called 'liberal corporatism' and of what other political scientists sometimes call 'neo-corporatism'.[24] The phenomenon has attracted a vast literature, and only a few broad generalisations can be attempted here. Liberal- or neo-corporatist arrangements, Philippe Schmitter points out, mostly grew, unplanned, out of 'second-best compromises', reflecting particular local circumstances,[25] and they differ from country to country. Yet certain similarities stand out. In a neo-corporatist system, the state shares power with monopolistic and centralised 'peak' associations of producer groups, to which it gives a privileged say in the development of public policy. In return, the associations become 'governing institutions'[26] – helping to implement policy as well as to shape it, and transmitting influence and pressure from the state to their members as well as from their members to the state.

At first sight, much of this seems to be true of Britain as well.

As we have seen, a system of bargaining and mutual accommodation between the state, organised labour and the organised employers started to grow up in Britain between the wars. But there are at least three crucial differences between the loose, informal British system — Keith Middlemas's 'corporate bias' — and the varying neo-corporatisms of Austria, Sweden and West Germany. The neo-corporatist state promotes strong, authoritative producer-group government. In many cases it also uses public law to define the powers and responsibilities of the groups themselves. By contrast, the British approach to industrial relations has usually been one of benign neglect, tempered by a common-law tradition of hostility to the whole notion of collective action. When Conservative governments have intervened in industrial relations, their motives have been neo-liberal, not neo-corporatist. They have been anxious to weaken the unions' ability to 'distort' the labour market, not to pull the loose-knit associations of labour and capital together. Labour's legislation has been designed to restore old trade-union immunities, not to define new responsibilities. No government has contemplated organising the system even-handedly, on neo-corporatist lines.

The second difference goes wider. Pre-eminently in Austria but to a significant extent in Sweden and to some extent in West Germany neo-corporatism has been acknowledged and explicit. Despite some breakdowns in the last two cases, it has also been fairly stable. The institutions through which it has operated have had sufficient time (and been sufficiently successful) to acquire moral authority as well as coercive power, where they have it. In Austria, self-governing Chambers of Commerce, Labour, Agriculture and other groups have a public-law status, and a legal right to be consulted during the legislative process. Since 1957, a quadripartite Joint Commission on wages and prices has met under the presidency of the Federal Chancellor; though its decisions do not have statutory force, the peak associations represented on it are sufficiently centralised and disciplined to ensure that their members comply with them.[27] In Sweden, a Labour Market Board, representing business, organised labour and the government, and playing a somewhat similar role in the economy, has lasted since the 1930s.[28] West Germany's 'Concerted Action' lasted for ten years, until its breakdown in the 1970s. Statutory works councils and co-determination, the institutions of industrial partnership, still promote encompassingness, in the way that Streeck describes. As in Austria, functional chambers with a public-law status – though with fewer powers than their Austrian equivalents – give institutional form to a principle of producer representation which antedates the industrial era.

The British system, by contrast, has generally been covert and inexplicit, concealed behind the traditional façade of Westminster parliamentarianism. As such, it has also been secretive, occasionally even furtive, and easily repudiated. It has operated through tacit, fluid conventions and understandings, not through clearly-defined or generally-known procedures. Partly because of this, it has also been fluctuating and unstable. This was obviously true of the 1930s, when the national government started to intervene hesitantly and defensively in the supply-side of the economy in response to business pressure. Despite the establishment of the National Development Council, the associated 'little Neddies', the Prices and Incomes Board, the Manpower Services Commission and other corporatist institutions, it was only slightly less true of the hands-on phase of Keynesian social democracy from the early 1960s to the middle 1970s. Apart from the 'little Neddies' and the Manpower Services Commission, most of these institutions, as we have seen, were either powerless talking shops, like the NEDC, or very short-lived, like the Prices and Incomes Board. Partly because of all this, each of the partners in the bargaining triangle could shuffle off the blame for failure – or for unpopular policies needed for success – on to the other two. When it suited it, each did so. The whole system was both shifting and opaque: a perfect recipe for protectionist collusion against the public interest. It was also a perfect recipe for ensuring that non-encompassing groups had no incentive to become encompassing.

This leads on to the third, most complex and, at the same time, most important difference. Most of the literature on neo-corporatism focuses on structures. But, as the late George Woodcock used to point out, structure is a function of purpose;

and purposes are shaped by values. It is reasonable to assume that neo-corporatist structures took root in central Europe and Scandinavia partly because their industrial cultures had been influenced by solidaristic social-democratic and social-Christian political philosophies, and therefore offered fertile soil to the solidaristic neo-corporatist values of power sharing and class collaboration. Be that as it may, Britain's industrial culture is plainly antipathetic to them. Power sharing demands a readiness to accept the responsibilities of power; class collaboration demands a sense of class solidarity; neither is possible unless those concerned are prepared to subordinate short-term self interest to a wider long-term interest. All of this is as foreign to the values of British trade unions and employers' associations as to their structures. For, like most British institutions, they grew up at a time when the ethos of market liberalism was at its height. Inevitably, they shared the individualistic, market-liberal values of the society of which their members were part. Despite appearances to the contrary, they have not been able to shake off that legacy since.

This obviously applies to the employers' associations.[29] Less obviously, it applies just as much to the trade unions. As Alan Fox has pointed out, the possessive individualism which triumphed in the Glorious Revolution was double-edged. It sanctified the craftsman's property in the mysteries of his craft as well as the office-holder's property in his office or, for that matter, the landlord's in his estate; and the attitudes and values which inspired collective action to defend the craftsman's right to his craft mysteries were first cousins to the attitudes and values which inspired the common lawyer's hostility to collective action and the employer's insistence on his right to pay what wages and maintain what working conditions he wished.[30] In the nineteenth century, these attitudes and values percolated down from the skilled trades to the non-craft groups which slowly began to mimic the organisations of the skilled. They too fought collectively for what their members saw, in essence, as individual property rights; and they were at least as eager to fight for them against other workers as against the employers. The result was that nineteenth-century British trade unions became, in Robert

Currie's phrase, 'joint stock companies for the sale of labour'.[31] Like ordinary joint-stock companies, they existed to screw the highest possible price for the commodity they had to sell out of the market in which they sold it. Like ordinary joint-stock companies, they operated on the principle of *caveat emptor*, acknowledging no moral obligation to the consumer, to other producers or to the wider society.

In style, language, proclaimed ideology and official rhetoric, they have changed a good deal since. Officially, most of their leaders are socialists, committed to the quite different values of equality, fraternity and social justice. Most of them, moreover, are affiliated to an officially socialist political party, which proclaims its wish to transform the competitive capitalist society in which it seeks power into a harmonious, morally superior socialist society. But whereas, in central Europe and Scandinavia, trade unionism was the child of a social-democratic political movement, committed to an encompassing notion of class solidarity, Britain's socialist party is the child of a fragmented and individualistic trade-union movement. And for the unions, socialism is for tomorrow: or, at most, for the banners at a gala or the slogans in a peroration. In the grubby, weekday world in which leaders and followers actually live and work, the 'operational code' of even the most militant trade-union official – an Arthur Scargill, say, or in earlier days a Frank Cousins – differs hardly at all from those of the respectable, watch-chained Lib-Lab leaders of a century ago, who praised Mr Gladstone and condemned state intervention. In all this, leaders reflect followers, while both reflect the society around them. The sectionalism which has always characterised the British Labour Movement is the product of a culture permeated with Benthamite individualism.

Two morals stand out, one concerning structures and institutions and the other, values and beliefs. Neo-corporatism is not a panacea. Like all human contrivances, it is subject to folly, misjudgment and bad luck; and, like all western industrial societies, the neo-corporatist systems of Scandinavia and central Europe have been badly buffeted by the world-wide upheavals of the 1970s and 1980s. Yet, over the long term, their economies have been among the most successful in the developed world. Part of the reason is that neo-corporatism has generated a virtuous circle in which encompassingness has facilitated open and explicit power sharing, while open and explicit power sharing has fostered encompassingness. Because the peak associations have been encompassing enough to take a broad view of their members' interests, and well-disciplined enough to ensure that their members would honour the bargains made in their name, they have been able to share the responsibilities of power. Because they have shared power openly and explicitly, they have been under pressure to take account of the general interest and to carry out the bargains they have made. Because the power-sharing institutions have been stable and successful, the whole system has built up a reservoir of goodwill, on which its managers can draw in bad times. Britain, by contrast, has been caught in a vicious circle. Her political economy has been too corporatist for the market to work efficiently, yet not corporatist enough for efficiency to be achieved through the 'transparent' bargaining of encompassing, and therefore socially responsible, producer groups. Her producer groups have been too strong for the state to brush them aside, yet too narrow and fragmented to sustain the open forms of power sharing which might have impelled them to become more encompassing.

The second moral is more paradoxical. If Olson is right, non-encompassing common-interest organisations prevent a market liberal order from working properly. But the values of market liberalism prevent common-interest organisations from becoming encompassing.

Much the same applies to the attitudes and values of the businessmen, managers and investors whose decisions are the most important influence on the development of a privately-owned economy. As we have seen, many have traced the roots of Britain's relative decline to a 'counter-revolution of values' in the late-nineteenth century. A good example of the genre is Martin Wiener's account of the decline of the 'industrial spirit'.[32] During the industrial revolution, he thinks, the manufacturing middle class was self-confidently entrepreneurial and unashamedly enthusiastic about the industrial society it was bringing into being. After 1850, however, it began to be absorbed into the landed gentry, and to assimilate the latter's hostility to the money-grubbing vulgarities of commerce and industry. Increasingly, the Church, the public schools and the universities disseminated an ethos of gentlemanly economic conservatism, which slowly undermined the industrial spirit of earlier days. By the end of the century, this anti-industrial ethos predominated among the political class and the professional intelligentsia, and was even beginning to infect many of the owners of industry themselves. All this has produced an élite which is at best ambivalent about, and at worst positively hostile to, the process of wealth creation. That, in turn, has helped to produce a society in which less wealth has been created than in other societies with other values.

Wiener should not be taken neat. He equates industrialism with capitalism, and support for modern industry with support for market liberalism. Many of the social critics whose writings he cites as evidence of an anti-industrial ethos were not hostile to industrial society as such, but only to the version of an industrial society which prevailed at the time they wrote and to the market-liberal ideology which justified it. But although his account of it is flawed, his notion of a 'counter-revolution of values' is extremely fruitful. In a richer account of the same period, Harold Perkin has suggested that the early-nineteenth century was dominated by a struggle for hegemony between three social ideals — the 'entrepreneurial ideal' of the manufacturers, the 'aristocratic ideal' of the landowners and the 'working-class ideal' of the emerging industrial proletariat.[33] The entrepreneurial ideal was the ideal of the owner manager, whose capital was derived from his own 'self-denying abstinence from consumption', and employed by him in the enterprise he owned and managed. It justified, not property as such, but active property, used by its owner to create wealth, as opposed to the passive property of the landlord. By the middle of the century, the entrepreneurial ideal had triumphed over the other two. But within the entrepreneurial camp, the interests of the manufacturing middle class differed from those of the also rising professions. Gradually, the differences became more acute. Increasingly, the professionals abandoned

the entrepreneurial ideal in favour of a counter-ideal of efficiency, expertise, service and social reform; increasingly, the
reforms spawned by this professional ideal conflicted with the
property rights of the manufacturing capitalists.

Meanwhile, the active owner manager of the industrial
revolution was in any case giving way to the functionless
rentier, created by the invention of the limited liability
company in the 1850s and 1860s. The rentier's interest did not
lie in the defence of active property against passive, but in the
defence of all forms of property against attacks from all
quarters. The result of all these changes was a defensive
alliance between the landowners and the business class against
all threats to property, whether active or passive – an alliance
symbolised by the defection of the Liberal Unionists to the
Conservatives after the Liberal Party split over Irish home rule
in 1886, and embodied in the Conservative and Unionist party
which that defection brought into being. Thus, 'the old virile
ascetic and radical ideal of active capital was submerged in the
still older, supine, hedonistic and conservative ideal of passive
property. In a word, the entrepreneurial ideal had triumphed
only to throw in its lot with the seemingly defeated aristocratic.'[34]

There *was* a counter-revolution, in short; and, as we shall
see, it *did* damage British industry. But it was not a counter-
revolution of the enemies of industrialism against its supporters, still less of the enemies of market liberalism against market
liberals. It was a counter-revolution of dividend receivers
against owner managers: of consumers of property against
users of it. By the same token, it damaged British industry in a
much more complex way than Wiener suggests. Perhaps
because twentieth-century Britain still bears its scars, because
its consequences suffuse the social air we breathe, it requires a
leap of the historical imagination to appreciate its full significance. For its psychological and moral implications go
much further than appears at first sight. In the first place, the
victory of the late-nineteenth-century ideal of passive property
over the earlier ideal of active capital helps to explain the
profit-taking myopia which has had so much to do with the
failures of adjustment. Part of the explanation for Britain's

relative industrial decline in the late-nineteenth century, David Landes notes, lies in a contrast between the narrow, pecuniary rationality of the late-nineteenth-century British entrepreneur and the broader, technological rationality of his foreign competitors:

> Even when the British entrepreneur was rational . . . his calculations were distorted by the shortness of his time horizon, and his estimates were on the conservative side.
>
> The significance of this pecuniary approach is best appreciated when it is contrasted with the technological rationality of the Germans. This was a different kind of arithmetic, which maximised, not returns, but technical efficiency. For the German engineer, and the manufacturer and banker who stood behind him, the new was desirable, not because it paid, but because it worked better.[35]

In the long run, of course, what worked better usually paid better too. But that calculation was too sophisticated for the British business class, and by a paradox which is central to Landes's argument, it was too sophisticated precisely because British businessmen were more interested in what paid than in what worked. Variations on that theme are common. There is a good deal of evidence that part of the explanation for Britain's industrial decline lies in the unwillingness or inability of the banking system to supply investment capital on a long-term basis, and in industry's dependence on an equity market more interested in short-term profit than in long-term growth.[36] Another frequent, complementary explanation is that British industry pays too little attention to the quality of its products and too much to the balance sheet: that accountants rank too high in the managerial pecking order and engineers too low: that, as Alistair Mant puts it, too much of British industry behaves as though its primary task is 'laundering money, with production as an irksome constraint on that primary task, instead of vice versa.'[37] In different ways, all these critics are really saying the same thing: that British industry has declined because Britain's capitalism is that of the quick killing rather than of productive investment. It is not difficult to spot the connection between these weaknesses and the moral and psychological changes which Perkin has analysed. Almost by definition, 'passive' property is also 'quick-killing' property.

That is only the beginning of the story. In an overwhelming industrial society, with a democratic suffrage, no peasantry and only a small agricultural sector, economic adjustment is unlikely to take place without the consent of a significant part of the industrial working class, as well as of a significant proportion of the industrial employers. That, of course, was the logic of the attempts to construct cross-class coalitions for economic change. But, as we have seen, none of the would-be coalition-builders of the early part of the century could bridge the differences between workers and employers for long enough for a programme of economic change to get off the ground. Chamberlain and the Social Imperialists lost the early-twentieth-century competition for the working-class vote to their Social Liberal rivals. Lloyd George and Mosley made virtually no inroads on either working-class support for the Labour Party or employer support for the Conservatives. In a rather different way, the same was true of the post-war period. By now, the class-based party system whose evolution Chamberlain, Lloyd George and Mosley had all tried, in different ways, to prevent was firmly established. The politicians who operated it were imprisoned in an adversarial framework which made it even more difficult to win continuing cross-class agreement for a programme of economic change than it had been before the war. The Wilson and Heath governments in the mid-1960s and early-1970s both tried to mobilise support across class lines, but neither succeeded for long enough to settle the distributional conflicts which have to be settled if state-led or negotiated adjustment is to take place.

For Marxists, and for the much larger number of non-Marxists who share the Marxist analysis of industrial society, sometimes without realising it, this sequence of failures presents no puzzles. Class conflict is inherent in the capitalist mode of production, because the capitalists expropriate the surplus value which the workers produce. If it does not manifest itself openly that must be because the workers have been bamboozled into false consciousness; if the working class is mature enough to understand its true interests, open conflict is inevitable. Thus, there is no need to ask why no one has won agreement for economic change across class lines. The reason is simply that the British working class was (and is) too mature for its consciousness to be falsified.[38] For those who reject the Marxist view, things are not so simple. To assume that, because British politics took a class road in the end, they were bound to take it all along – that, because Chamberlain and Lloyd George both failed to construct cross-class coalitions, their attempts were doomed before they started – is to beg one of the central questions in modern British history. After all, workers and employers alike would almost certainly have been better off if they had succeeded. In any case, mature working-class movements and class-based party systems exist in more successful industrial societies too, without the damaging consequences of the British version. To put it at its lowest, the suggestion that the fragmented and ill-disciplined British working-class movement is, in some sense, more mature than its encompassing, well-disciplined counterparts in Scandinavia and central Europe is hard to sustain. Yet the class-based, social-democratic parties of Scandinavia and central Europe have been enthusiastic, and in many cases predominant, partners in the processes of negotiated adjustment described above; and, to judge by the 'outputs' of the system, they have promoted the interests of their working-class supporters at least as vigorously as the British Labour Party has done.[39] If we are to understand why the Labour Party has failed to emulate them – or, for that matter, why the Conservative Party has failed to emulate the German and Austrian Christian Democratic parties – we must dig deeper.

Part of the explanation lies in the fragmented, non-encompassing character of Britain's producer groups, and in the structural and ideological factors which have made them fragmented and non-encompassing. But even that cannot be the whole story. After all, one of the chief characteristics of fragmented and non-encompassing producer groups is that they find it hard to deliver their members. Industrial workers did not vote against Chamberlain and Lloyd George – or, for that matter, fail to rally behind the incomes policies of Harold Wilson and Edward Heath – solely because their union leaders so instructed them. Still less have the trade associations determined employers' political allegiances, or their reactions to government policy. The key to the behaviour of rank-and-file workers and employers lies in a realm of attitudes and feelings, to which the analysis of interests and institutions is, at most, an uncertain guide.

A seminal essay by Ronald Dore, comparing Japan's industrial culture with Britain's, provides a useful clue. One of the most important differences between the two, Dore argues, lies in the nature of the company, and above all in the role of the shareholder. In Britain, company directors are still legally responsible only to the shareholders. A single-union agreement which Hitachi recently made with the EETPU at a plant in South Wales throws a vivid light on the contrasting position in Japan:

> The agreement outlines plans for a works council representing all employees including managers. These are all defined by the agreement as 'members'. The second clause of the agreement says: 'The company exists to promote the interests of the members, the customers, the shareholders, and the local community.' In that order . . .
>
> These are not just differences in rhetoric . . . The shareholder *does* take a back seat in the large Japanese corporation. Japanese firms are *not* primarily defined as the shareholders' property. The directors are usually senior employees who have spent their lives in the firm, not outsiders appointed to care for the shareholders' interests. The resisted takeover is unknown in Japan, so is the conglomerate that trades in companies as if they were bits of real estate and not the livelihoods of a living community of people.[40]

Dore's essay deals with the micro-politics of the plant and the company, as did his earlier study comparing two Hitachi factories in Japan with two English Electric factories in the north of England.[41] But his finding that one of the reasons for the superior 'spirit and efficiency' of Japanese factory workers is that they feel part of a 'living community of people', and that part of the explanation lies in the Japanese conception of the nature and responsibilities of industrial property, bears on the politics of the wider society as well. Class and class politics are not peculiar to Britain. They occur in many, perhaps most, industrial societies. But Britain's class politics have a peculiarly sour, suspicious, dog-in-manger, chip-on-shoulder quality, which does not seem to be found elsewhere. That, rather than class politics *per se*, is the chief emotional obstacle to class collaboration and cross-class coalition-building. And although there can be no proof, it is hard to resist the conclusion that its roots are to be found in the conception of property which Dore describes, and in the resentments and hostilities which that conception breeds.

Once again, the connection between Britain's late-twentieth-century industrial culture and the late-nineteenth-century switch from active to passive property is easy to see. The notion of active property – of property justified by the personal abstinence and entrepreneurial flair of the heroic, self-reliant owner manager, who built up his own capital, risked his own substance, hired his own labour, found his own markets and, in the process, created a new and more productive economic system – had a moral appeal extending far beyond the entrepreneurial middle class itself. It had about it an almost Promethean quality, which forced the paternalist, *noblesse oblige* ethic of the aristocracy on to the defensive, and which the group ethic of the working class could not match. The switch to passive property – to the view of property which makes it possible to treat industrial enterprises like Dore's 'bits of real estate' – destroyed the moral basis of the industrial order. Most people are likely to feel instinctively that active property belongs in a different moral category from passive: that active property owners have a stronger moral claim on the rest of us than passive ones. To be sure, the passive property of the late-nineteenth and twentieth centuries has often been justified on grounds which used to justify active property – namely, that it is a reward for risk and enterprise. But that in itself suggests that those offering the justification have recognised that passive property is inherently more difficult to

justify than active; and, in any event, the justification has rung
less and less true. To put the point another way around, the
collapse of the entrepreneurial ideal of the early nineteenth
century, and the marriage between land and capital which was
both cause and consequence of that collapse, opened the door
to the increasingly vigorous and increasingly plausible socialist
critique of functionless property as privilege – a critique which
was heard more and more frequently from the end of the
nineteenth century, and of which R.H. Tawney was perhaps
the most effective exponent. At the same time, they made it
more difficult for property owners to answer in a convincing
way. And, as Perkin argues, both can be traced back to the
notion of absolute and unconditional property rights which
triumphed in the Civil War and the Revolution Settlement.

Last, but by no means least, among the factors which have
made it difficult for Britain to become a developmental state is
the 'Westminster Model' of parliamentary government. Two
points deserve attention here. The first and most obvious is
that the Westminster Model is, above all, a model of the
minimal state which nineteenth-century market liberalism
advocated and pre-supposed. For it is only in a minimal state,
with a small bureaucracy and a limited volume of legislation,
that the model can work as it is supposed to work. Only in such
a state can the doctrine of ministerial responsibility approximate to reality, and Parliament carry out its legislative functions in the way that the nineteenth-century doctrine of
parliamentary government implied that it should. Secondly,
and in some ways even more importantly, the notion of
absolute parliamentary sovereignty which is central to both
the theory and the practice of the Westminster Model is, by
definition, a formidable barrier to open and explicit power-
sharing between the state and organised groups of producers.

Yet, as we saw in Part One, modern British governments
have systematically flouted the doctrines and assumptions of
Westminster parliamentarianism in practice. In the 1960s and
1970s, they also found it necessary to make repeated changes in
the institutions which embodied those doctrines and assumptions. Partly because of this, there are signs that they have lost

their old legitimacy. There is, in short, a paradox about the present state of the constitutional arrangements which the British political class inherited from its late-nineteenth-century ancestors. They still receive a great deal of lip service. They still stand in the way of economic adjustment and change. Yet, at the same time, they are themselves in disarray. That paradox, however, is so central to the themes of this book that it deserves a chapter to itself.

7

Club Government in Disarray

'Parliamentary sovereignty is . . . complete both on its positive and on its negative side. Parliament can legally legislate on any topic whatever which, in the judgement of Parliament, is a fit subject for legislation. There is no power which, under the English constitution, can come into rivalry with the legislative sovereignty of Parliament. No one of the limitations alleged to be imposed by law on the absolute authority of Parliament has any real existence, or receives any countenance, either from the statute book or from the practice of the courts. This doctrine of the legislative supremacy of Parliament is the very keystone of the constitution.'

A.V. Dicey, 1885.[1]

As well as addressing economic realities, a new governing philosophy would have to address the political factors which are intertwined with them — notably the institutions and conventions of the British state. It would have to do so for two reasons. In the first place, these institutions and conventions have helped to determine the whole shape and structure of the political economy, and in particular to inhibit the evolution of a developmental state. Not surprisingly, in view of its parentage, the Westminster Model of parliamentary government suited market-led adjustment rather well. Unfortunately, it is incompatible both with state-led adjustment and with negotiated adjustment. It is incompatible with state-led adjustment because that requires an active, discretionary state apparatus, which cannot easily be squared with the 'Westminster' conceptions of ministerial responsibility and civil-service neutrality and passivity. It is incompatible with negotiated adjustment, because the fundamental Westminster doctrine of absolute parliamentary sovereignty inhibits the open and explicit power-sharing on which negotiated adjustment depends. High on the agenda of any new governing philosophy would be the question of how to revise constitutional arrangements inherited from the late-nineteenth century, and permeated with assumptions derived from the market-liberal ethos of a still earlier period, to fit the needs of a complex mixed economy a hundred years later.

The second reason is in some ways more urgent. One of the central propositions we considered in Part One was that the collapse of the Keynesian social-democratic consensus of the post-war period had more to do with politics than with economics: that the rival neo-liberal and neo-socialist alternatives gained ground less because they offered solutions to the country's economic problems than because they offered an escape from the political questions which Keynesian social democracy could not answer. These questions were provoked by a deepening institutional crisis, at the heart of which lay the primordial political problem of consent. The policies which Keynesian social-democratic governments believed to be necessary to operate a mixed economy, and to honour their commitments to full employment and the welfare state, would not work without consent, but they found it increasingly difficult to mobilise consent with and through the institutions of the Westminster Model. In different ways, neo-liberalism and neo-socialism both offered to end the search for consent: to find a way out of the institutional crisis, while avoiding the upheaval of fundamental institutional change. If my argument is right, however, the neo-liberal and neo-socialist alternatives lead nowhere; and if that is true, their offers are fraudulent. There is, after all, no escape from the interventions and compromises of the mixed economy. Consent is as indispensable as it always was; and the search for consent remains at the centre of the stage. It follows that there is no short cut out of the institutional crisis. It can be resolved only by facing and settling the tensions and conflicts which have given rise to it. And if they are to be faced, they must first be understood.

The best way to come to grips with them is to look at the way in which the constitution evolved between the late-nineteenth century, when the Westminster Model acquired approximately its modern form, and the apogee of Keynesian social democracy in the 1950s and 1960s, and to tease out the implications. The late-Victorian constitution is best understood as the offspring of a marriage between two different, but complementary forms of possessive individualism — the oligarchic whiggery of the seventeenth century and the democratic radicalism of the nineteenth. The whigs bequeathed to it the parliamentary absolutism, in the name of which they had fought off the royal absolutism of the Stuarts. Partly under Benthamite influence, the radicals differed from the Whigs in holding that Parliament should represent the freely-choosing, atomistic individuals of utilitarian theory rather than natural communities or functional groups. Their doctrine of individual representation was, however, as absolutist in its practical implications as were the Whig doctrines which they repudiated. Since Parliament represented the totality of freely-choosing individuals, to limit Parliament's power would be to limit the power of those individuals. Thus, parliamentary absolutism could be equated with democratic self-government;[2] and both parents pointed in practice in the same direction. As the Victorian jurist, A.V. Dicey, argued in the quotation at the head of this chapter, the 'keystone' of the whole structure was the doctrine of absolute and inalienable parliamentary sovereignty, or, as he put it in another passage, of the 'absolute legislative sovereignty or despotism of the King in Parliament'.[3] Because of this, no Parliament could bind its successor: if an act of Parliament, however trivial, conflicted with a previous act, however important, the previous act would be automatically repealed. It followed that there was, and could be, no basic or fundamental law, superior in status to other laws; that it was impossible legally to entrench protections for individual rights or to reserve certain functions to lower tiers of government; indeed, that the power of the majority of the legislature to legislate as it wished could not be restricted in any way.

This did not mean that Britain was, in practice, administered from the centre or that there were no safeguards against the abuse of power. Most public services were delivered by local authorities of one kind or another, not by local outposts of central government; outside London this applied even to the police. The modern welfare state and mixed economy grew from the bottom up – from the 'gas and water socialism' of reforming municipalities – not from the top down. By the same token, governments did not, in practice, pay less respect to individual rights than in countries where they were constitutionally guaranteed. Dicey insisted that what he called 'the rule of law' – which for him was virtually synonymous with security against arbitrary power – was more firmly established in Britain than anywhere else in Europe, and there was justice in his claim. What it did mean was that the division of function and power between central and local government, on the one hand, and the most important safeguards against arbitrary power, on the other, were, in Max Weber's language, 'traditional' rather than 'legal'. They derived from the inherited customs and conventions of a small and homogeneous political class, not from explicit principles, clearly promulgated in an accessible code. They were embodied in usages, understandings, unwritten rules and particular precedents – in the complex mosaic of the common law, in the procedures of the House of Commons, in the emotional legacy of the 'possessive territorialism' of the seventeenth century, in the standards of fair play and good administration by which ministers, officials and members of parliament felt themselves bound – which drew their force from inexplicit assumptions and sometimes ambiguous values.[4] The atmosphere of British government was that of a club, whose members trusted each other to observe the spirit of the club rules; the notion that the principles underlying the rules should be clearly defined and publicly proclaimed was profoundly alien. 'The Habeas Corpus Acts', Dicey wrote confidently, 'declare no principle and define no rights, but they are for practical purposes worth a hundred constitutional articles guaranteeing individual liberty'. Most of his readers would have found the proposition almost self-evident.[5]

Three other features of the structure need mentioning as well. In the first place, the doctrine of absolute parliamentary sovereignty was buttressed by the doctrine of individual and collective ministerial responsibility. With only a few exceptions, the powers and prerogatives which had once belonged to the Crown now belonged, in practice, to its ministers. But ministers were responsible to Parliament for the use they made of these powers and prerogatives. They were responsible individually, in respect of their actions as departmental ministers, and they were also responsible collectively, in respect of the actions of the government of which they were part. Not only were ministers responsible to Parliament; what was equally important was that ministers alone were responsible. Ministers alone were responsible because ministers alone were supposed to decide policy. The officials who advised them before the decisions were taken, and who executed the decisions thereafter, could not be responsible because they were merely the servants of the ministers. Secondly, the doctrines of parliamentary sovereignty and ministerial responsibility went hand in hand with the assumption – it could hardly be called a doctrine – that the House of Commons, by now overwhelmingly the more powerful of the houses of parliament, represented the electorate. Thirdly, the electorate was held to consist, not of communities, as in the middle ages, or of 'interests' as in the eighteenth century, but of the sovereign, atomistic individuals of liberal theory.

The net effect was to create a chain of representation and accountability, binding the decision makers in the Cabinet to the electors in the constituencies. Members of parliament represented their constituents, and were accountable to them for the votes they cast in the division lobbies. They decided what legislation to pass, and they held ministers to account for the executive acts of government. The Cabinet held office only so long as it had their confidence. Thus, the mighty engine of parliamentary despotism ran in accordance with the popular will. As Dicey wrote:

> [T]he difference between the will of the sovereign and the will of the nation was terminated by the foundation of a system of real representative government . . . Speaking roughly, the permanent wishes of the representative portion of Parliament can hardly in the long run differ from the

wishes of the English people, or at any rate of the electors; that which the majority of the House of Commons command, the majority of the English people usually desire.[6]

In essentials, that was still the formal theory of the constitution when the first Macmillan government took office seventy-two years later. But continuity of form concealed profound changes of substance. In the first place, the expansion of the electorate and the growth of the modern mass party had transformed the relationship between ministers and members of parliament, on the one hand, and between members of parliament and their constituents on the other. Members of parliament were now elected by a party vote, to sustain a party leadership and support a party programme. A general election was no longer a series of constituency elections, in which the constituency's voters decided who should represent them in the Commons. It was a kind of plebiscite, in which the national electorate decided which team of party leaders should govern the country. As a result, the power relationships within the House of Commons were quite different from the days when the Westminster Model took shape. Formally, members of parliament still held ministers to account. But members of the governing party in Parliament — by definition in the majority — had been elected to sustain the government in office and to put its legislation on to the statute book. Ministers rarely had much to fear from them. As for the Opposition, it was by definition in a minority; no matter how successful it might be in debate, it could not hope for significant victories in the division lobbies. To be sure the House of Commons was the chief cockpit where the leaders of the two great parties fought for victory at the next election. It was also a kind of standing gene pool of future ministerial talent. Moreover, ministers and backbench MPs dined at the same tables, drank in the same bars, gossiped in the same tea-room and marched through the same division lobbies; in a thousand subtle and untraceable ways, the mood of the House helped to shape the mood of the government of the day. Precisely because they were subtle and untraceable, however, these informal influences could not provide the kind of accountability which the nineteenth-century Parliament had enjoyed. Whatever constitutional textbooks might say, governments were now accountable to the electorate, rather than to Parliament, and checked much more effectively by the prospect of the next general election than by anything that might happen to them in the House of Commons.

Meanwhile, the huge expansion which had taken place in the scope and size of government had transformed the relationship between ministers and civil servants. The doctrine of ministerial responsibility was still in force. Ministers, and ministers alone, were still responsible for the actions of their departments. But partly because the growth of government had made it impossible for ministers to take all the decisions that mattered, and even more because it had made the policy-making process enormously more complicated, the operational significance of the doctrine had changed. Once it had given Parliament a lever with which to control the executive. Now it gave the executive a cloak behind which it could shelter from parliamentary scrutiny.[7] For the doctrine (or at any rate the doctrine's most influential exponents) held that, since ministers alone were responsible, officials could not be; and that since officials were not responsible, the advice they gave to ministers was no business of Parliament's. Sometimes this meant that Parliament could not get behind the minister who was nominally responsible for a decision to the officials who had actually taken it. More importantly, it meant that the complex processes through which policies are made in large, modern bureaucracies — the provision and evaluation of expert advice, the discussion of alternatives, the weighing up of pressures — went on behind closed doors. Once made, the policies were usually announced to Parliament. But in the act of announcing them, the government publicly committed itself to them. It could no longer change them without loss of face; and the formidable weight of the party system usually guaranteed them a safe passage.

At the same time, the growth of organised interest groups, linked symbiotically with the government departments concerned with their spheres of operation, had had similar effects on the process of legislation. Partly because it was politically expedient, and partly because it had come to be thought right, government departments preparing legislation normally consulted the interest groups likely to be affected by it before putting proposals to Parliament.[8] Keith Middlemas's 'corporate bias' – the informal system of bargaining and mutual accommodation between the state, the organised employers and organised labour which was by now one of the central features of Britain's political economy – operated behind closed doors. On a more humdrum level, so did the consultations between civil servants and interest-group representatives which had become an equally central feature of this pre-legislative stage, when the details of the government's future proposals were still open to argument. Parliament still played an indispensable part in the legislative process, but for most of the time it was a ritualistic one. Its function was not so much to make law as to legitimise the laws which emerged from this informal process of consultation and bargaining. By 1979, the authors of an authoritative study of the role of organised groups in the making of public policy could conclude that 'the traditional model of Cabinet and parliamentary government is a travesty of reality', and that Britain had become a 'post-parliamentary democracy'.[9] With only a few qualifications, their findings would have been equally valid in 1959, perhaps even in 1949.

Parliamentary and 'post-parliamentary' democracy, however, differed in more than their methods of operation. The approach of parliamentary democracy had inspired eager hopes, dire warnings and prolonged debate. In the course of the debate, its advocates had hammered out a doctrine – or, rather, a jumble of overlapping doctrines – to justify it. Though these doctrines were never embodied in an official code or statement of principle analogous to the statements of principle contained in most written constitutions, they slowly conquered the imagination of the political class. In however confused and, in some cases, half-hearted a way, it came to be accepted that, in Gladstone's famous phrase, 'every man who is not presumably incapacitated by some consideration of personal unfitness or of political danger is morally entitled to come within the pale of the Constitution';[10] that the propertyless had as good a claim as the propertied to participate, through free elections, in the government of the country. 'Post-parliamentary' democracy, by contrast, grew up unannounced, almost unnoticed, within the shell of its parliamentary predecessor. No new set of doctrines greeted it; and although its practitioners could see that their system did not operate in quite the way that the old parliamentary system had done, they made only half-hearted and apologetic attempts to justify the differences. Samuel Beer has identified two influential attempts to come to terms with the post-parliamentary realities of this period, embodied in two rival conceptions of democracy. What he calls the 'Tory' conception justified 'government of the people, for the people, with, but not by, the people', and held that Parliament's role was to check public policy rather than to initiate it. Opposing this was a 'Socialist' conception, in which the people, acting through the mechanism of parliamentary election, actually determined the broad outlines of the government's purposes.[11] But although these conceptions could accommodate the phenomenon of the modern mass party, the full complexity of post-parliamentary politics eluded them.

In different ways, both justified the combination of strong governments and weak parliaments which was the most obvious feature of the post-parliamentary age. Neither acknowledged that governments and parliaments alike now had to deal with new centres of power, some public and some private, on which they could not impose their will; that, if backbench MPs had lost power to ministers, ministers had lost power, among others, to permanent civil servants, chairmen of nationalised industries, trade-union general secretaries, foreign exchange dealers, leaders of professional associations and heads of big, private-sector corporations; and that, in this puzzling new world, a conception of democracy which focused almost exclusively on the relationship between politicians and voters was bound to be incomplete. Moreover, both ran alongside older conceptions, drawn from the parliamentary past. The old, nineteenth-century model of parliamentary government might have become a travesty of reality, but it was the travesty, not the reality, which dominated imaginations and commanded allegiance. It lived on in the habits and conventions of the House of Commons and, still more perhaps, in the way in which its proceedings figured in the press and reached the public − in the post-prandial excitement of the closing stages of a censure debate; in the knockabout of Prime Minister's Questions; in the endless speculation about Westminster manoeuvres and Westminster reputations; in an odd, roundabout way even in the relative indifference to scrutiny by select committees as compared with debate on the floor of the House.

To judge by their speeches and writings, it also lived on in the emotions and assumptions of those who maintained these habits and conventions; and although there is no sure way of knowing what the mass of ordinary, non-political voters thought about their system of government, it is safe to assume that they too over- rather than under-estimated Parliament's influence as well as the influence of the individual MP.[12] Thus, Walter Bagehot's familiar distinction between the 'efficient' and the 'dignified' parts of the Constitution received a new twist. The House of Commons, in his eyes one of the 'efficient' parts, had become 'dignified' instead. But just as the mid-nineteenth-century monarchy had owed some of its dignity to the fact that the mass of the population mistakenly believed it to be efficient, so the mid-twentieth-century Parliament conferred legitimacy on the post-parliamentary system because most ordinary voters thought they were still living in a parliamentary one.

Yet the system worked; and, by the standards of most other large countries, it worked exceptionally smoothly and tapped an exceptionally large reservoir of popular support. Whereas France and Italy both had large Communist parties, committed, at least on paper, to the total overthrow of the system, and whereas a populist radical right threatened its opponents' civil liberties even in the United States,[13] Britain had no significant anti-system party or movement of opinion. In striking contrast to its Liberal forerunners before the first world war, the post-war Labour government put through a vast legislative programme without making any significant changes in the constitution it had inherited, and without provoking any significant constitutional conflict. After six years of Labour rule, the Conservatives returned to office and made only minor changes in their predecessors' legislation. In the 1950s, the two major parties, each solidly committed to the constitutional status quo, shared between them around 95 per cent of the popular vote. In the early 1960s, Gabriel Almond and Sidney Verba, the authors of a famous American cross-national study of popular attitudes to national political institutions, found that 89 per cent of their British respondents expected equal treatment from the police, while 83 per cent expected equal treatment from government officials – higher figures than in any of the other countries they examined. Though the British were somewhat less prone than the Americans to believe that they could 'do something' about a proposal to introduce an unjust law, they were far ahead of the other nationalities in the survey.[14] Almond and Verba concluded that of the five countries they studied, Britain and the United States approximated most closely to the model of a 'civic culture' – in other words, to the model of a culture capable of sustaining stable democracy – and the clear implication of their argument was that Britain was the closest of all.[15]

Stability, however, went hand in hand with ambiguity. Because the traditional nineteenth-century model of parliamentary government had been silently displaced rather than noisily overthrown, and because, as a result, the new, post-parliamentary system was clothed in parliamentary forms and legitimised in language, old notions of constitutional propriety jostled uneasily with later ones. What were the proper duties of a member of parliament, and where did his primary loyalties lie? Was he first and foremost a representative of the party whose nomination he had received, and without whose ticket he would never have been elected? If so, was he supposed to act on the views of his party leaders in Parliament, or of his party association in his constituency? Or was he supposed to represent his constituents, irrespective of party? Or should he bring his own, unfettered judgment to bear on the issues before him, in the way that Edmund Burke had insisted he be free to do in his famous letter to the electors of Bristol? To take another example, what was the proper scope of the informal system of group representation which had grown up alongside the formal system of individual representation, centred on Westminster? As we have seen, governments and organised interests alike had come to believe that the interests should be consulted before legislation affecting them was put to Parliament. But what did consultation imply? Was it enough for the government to inform the interests of its intentions, or was it under an implicit obligation to try to reach agreement with them? What was to happen if the consultations did not produce agreement? Plainly, government had the legal right to impose its view. Did it also have the moral right? The legitimacy of the whole system hinged on the assumption that Parliament represented the people. But the notion of representation is much more slippery than it looks at first sight. Was it enough for members of parliament to be elected by the people? Or was the division of party opinion in Parliament supposed to reflect the division in the country at large?

None of these questions could be answered authoritatively. To be sure, authoritative answers were not needed. The system functioned smoothly: a broad consensus prevailed, both on matters of policy and on constitutional matters: no one asked awkward questions. But the ambiguities nevertheless loomed in the background, like rocks hidden by a high tide.

Slowly in the 1960s, and with gathering speed in the 1970s, the tide went out. The hands-on phase of Keynesian social democracy coincided with an unprecedented volume of institutional changes, attempted changes and what might be called 'pseudo-changes', and as we have seen, some sprang directly from the switch to consensual intervention in the supply-side of the economy. Examples include the establishment of the NEDC in the early 1960s and the creation of the Department of Economic Affairs and the regional planning councils. But others had no obvious bearing on the management of the economy. Into that category fall successive attempts to strengthen Parliament's capacity to scrutinise the executive, through 'reforms' of the committee structure of the House of Commons; the first Wilson government's unsuccessful attempt to 'reform' the House of Lords; the reorganisations of London government and later of local government elsewhere in the Kingdom; the unsuccessful attempt to 'devolve' power to elected assemblies in Wales and Scotland; and the introduction of the popular referendum into the country's constitutional arrangements.[16] Even more remarkably, in some ways, more innovations followed the collapse of Keynesian social democracy towards the end of the 1970s. Despite its initial suspicion of institutional 'tinkering', the Thatcher government abolished the regional planning councils; tightened central controls on local authority spending; and pushed through what amounted to yet another local-government reorganisation, abolishing the Greater London and metropolitan counties created in the reorganisations of the previous two decades.[17]

Some may see all this as evidence of a happy (and characteristically British) capacity to adapt incrementally to changing circumstances. Unfortunately, that interpretation fits neither the content of the changes nor the way in which they were made. Some of them were little more than window dressing. Others went deep. Some were made at short notice, in response to the pressures of the moment. Others had been mulled over for years by Royal Commissions or select committees. Even those in the second category, however, did not reflect a coherent view of the system as a whole. The committees of enquiry which preceded them were given restrictive terms of reference, and steered clear of the most sensitive areas. The Fulton Commission on the civil service was not allowed to enquire into the relationship between ministers and civil servants. The Redcliffe-Maud Commission looked at the structure of local government without looking at its finance; the Layfield Committee at its finance, but not at its structure. The Kilbrandon Commission on the constitution looked at devolution for Wales and Scotland without considering the implications for local government. Successive procedure committees of the House of Commons tried to find ways to strengthen Parliament's capacity to scrutinise the executive, without upsetting the doctrine of ministerial responsibility or undermining the power of the party whips. Thus, the huge and complex problem of how to adapt a late-nineteenth-century political order to the needs of an advanced industrial society in the late-twentieth century was parcelled up into discrete bundles, each considered in isolation from the other.

Unlike their great Victorian predecessors, moreover, those who examined the bundles did not share a common conception of politics and political man, or a common view of what the constitution ought to be. Lacking a common moral and philosophical core, the institutional changes of the period pulled in different directions. Some ran with the grain of the existing 'post-parliamentary' system and some against; some concentrated power in the name of efficiency, while some dispersed it (or purported to disperse it) in the name of democracy. The logic and objectives of the local-government reorganisations of the 1960s and 1970s were essentially techno-cratic, derived from a muddled notion of the economies of scale.[18] Though its supporters mostly fought shy of the conclu-sion, the logic of the devolution proposals was implicitly federalist. The referendum is a populist device, which draws its inspiration from a notion of popular sovereignty only dubious-ly compatible with the traditional British conception of representative government. Insofar as parliamentary reform had a more principled objective than keeping restless back-benchers out of mischief, it implied an investigatory House of Commons which could not easily be reconciled with the doctrine of ministerial responsibility and the traditional con-ception of the respective roles of ministers and civil servants.

But these tensions and contradictions were glossed over; and the choices they posed were not made. Partly because of this, many of the changes failed to achieve their stated purposes. It is hard to escape the conclusion that their real purpose was to buy off trouble; and to buy it off in a way which would cause the least possible disturbance to the system as it stood. To be sure, the governments of the period also wanted to preserve their own power and the power of their parties. The refer-endum was first introduced to preserve the fragile unity of the Labour Party during the struggle over membership of the European Community. It was used a second time to preserve the Party's only slightly less fragile unity during the struggle over Scottish devolution. The devolution legislation was introduced to beat off the challenge of the SNP and maintain Labour's hold on its Scottish seats. The Conservatives re-drew the local government boundaries in a way that favoured the counties, where they were strong, at the expense of the boroughs, where they were weak. But although the governments of the period tried to preserve their power, they did not always succeed. The devolution referendum destroyed the Labour government which had introduced the devolution legislation. Local government reorganisation did its authors more electoral harm than good. If the governments had been solely concerned to preserve their power, they would often have been better advised to make no changes at all. They made them because they had come to believe that changes of some sort were inevitable: because when they pulled the levers, the engine often failed to move, and because they had come to the conclusion that they could not get it to move if they left it as it was.

If we are to understand this crucial chapter in recent British history, then, we must try to tease out the nature of, and reasons for, the trouble. It has made itself felt on a number of levels. It manifested itself most obviously in the defeats which successive governments suffered at the hands of the trade unions. But these were only the most dramatic symptoms. One of the most remarkable features of British public life in the 1970s and 1980s has been the force and frequency of what might be called 'insider criticisms' of hallowed political institutions and conventions. Lord Hailsham has denounced what he called 'elective dictatorship'. Lord Scarman has called for a written constitution, judicially enforceable. Samuel Finer, former Gladstone Professor of Government at Oxford, has denounced 'adversary politics' and argued for a greater use of the popular referendum. Lord Crowther-Hunt has called for extensive devolution of central-government functions to elected regional assemblies.[19] Political figures as far apart as Stephen Hastings and Arthur Scargill have come out for proportional representation.

In at least two areas, moreover, this change of mood among the political class has been reflected in changes of behaviour.

The iron party discipline which has been one of the most obvious features of 'post-parliamentary democracy' seems to have lost some of its old force. Partly because some of the most critical issues of the decade cut across party lines, and partly because backbench members of parliament were in any case becoming more assertive, the 1970s saw more intra-party dissension and more cross-voting in the division lobbies than any decade since the turn of the century.[20] Traditional notions of the proper relationship between ministers and civil servants are also showing signs of strain. The neo-liberal right and the neo-socialist left share an instinctive suspicion of the career civil service – neo-liberals because they believe that the self-interested empire-building of the bureaucracy has helped to cause the economic failures of the recent past, and neo-socialists because they assume that the apparatus of the 'capitalist state' is bound to be hostile to socialism. Moreover, emotion reinforces ideology. Civil servants are paid to give ministers dispassionate, non-partisan advice. To passionate partisans, possessed of a monist vision of the truth, such advice is apt to seem pusillanimous, if not obstructive. Thus, denunciations of the conservatism, defeatism and complacency of the civil service, and demands that appointments to what are now civil-service posts should be made on a political basis, come from both ends of the ideological spectrum – Sir John Hoskyns, the head of the policy unit at No.10 Downing Street at the beginning of the Thatcher government, echoing Brian Sedgemore, parliamentary private secretary to Tony Benn during the Callaghan government.[21]

Changes of mood and behaviour have not been confined to the political class. Electoral behaviour has changed too – if anything, more sharply and more visibly. Between 1951 and 1983, the share of the popular vote going to the two big parties fell from more than 95 per cent to 70 per cent. When abstentions are taken into account, the downward trend in their popularity is even more striking. Between 1951 and 1979, the proportion of the total electorate which did not vote for either major party rose from a little more than 20 per cent to a little less than 40 per cent. Attitude surveys tell the same story. In the course of the 1970s, the proportion of the electorate 'strongly' identifying with one or other of them fell from 39 per cent to 20 per cent.[22] In comparison with the past, they have lost even more members than voters. It has been estimated that the membership of the Conservative Party fell from 2,800,000 in 1953 to about half that figure in 1975, and that in the same period the individual membership of the Labour Party fell from a little more than 1,000,000 to something between 250,000 and 300,000.[23] On a different, but related, level there is a good deal of evidence that groups and individuals seeking changes in public policy are more prone than they used to be to work through single-issue protest or pressure groups, and less prone to work through the parties. At the same time, organised and unorganised minorities – trade unionists, motorway protesters, ethnic leaders, even local councillors – have been more apt than at any time since the war to defy laws of which they do not approve, or which seem to them to conflict with their interests. Meanwhile, the actions and even the roles of the police, the security services and the judiciary have become politically controversial, in a sense which has never been true before.[24] Though this is impossible to prove, when all this is set against the background of the institutional crisis of the 1970s, it is hard to resist the conclusion that the decline in the level of support for the established parties reflects a more diffuse and inchoate dissatisfaction with the system as a whole, which has led to a decline in the authority of government as such.

Survey evidence points in the same direction. In 1963, Butler and Stokes found that 50 per cent of their sample thought government paid 'not much' attention to the people; by 1969, the proportion had risen to 61 per cent.[25] An attitude survey conducted for the Kilbrandon Commission in 1970 reported a 'diffuse feeling of dissatisfaction' with the existing system of government. Of those questioned, 49 per cent thought the system either needed 'a great deal of improvement' or 'could be improved quite a lot'; only 5 per cent thought it worked 'extremely well'. Fifty-five per cent of those questioned felt 'very powerless' or 'fairly powerless' in the face of government; and it was among those who felt powerless that dissatisfaction with the system was most marked.[26] In the early 1970s, a comparative study of adolescents' political attitudes in London and Boston found that, on a range of questions, the British teenagers were significantly less enthusiastic about their political institutions than the Americans.[27] A study by Alan Marsh later in the decade probed more deeply into the nature and sources of public dissatisfaction with the system, and into the relationship between dissatisfaction and protest. Three of his findings are of particular interest. First, more than one-fifth of his sample (21.5 per cent) was prepared to engage in illegal forms of protest ranging from rent strikes to blocking traffic and occupying buildings — a minority, no doubt, but still a big one. Secondly, only a minority displayed much confidence in governments or politicians. Only 39 per cent thought government could be trusted to do what is right either 'just about always' or 'most of the time', while 57 per cent trusted it to do so 'only some of the time' or 'almost never'. Forty-eight per cent thought the country was 'run by a few big interests concerned only for themselves', against 37 per cent who thought it was run for the benefit of all. Seventy per cent thought politicians told the truth 'only some of the time' or 'almost never', as against 25 per cent who thought they told the truth 'just about always' or 'most of the time'. Thirdly, the most politically competent — those who understood the system best and were most likely to be active in it; in other words, those closest to the traditional liberal ideal of good citizenship — were the most likely to distrust government and politicians, and had the highest potential for protest. Moreover, these attributes were connected. A high potential for protest was a function, not of distrust alone, but of distrust in combination with a high level of competence.[28]

Repeated defeats make for mutinous armies. Plainly, part of the responsibility for the institutional disarray of the last decade and a half lies with the economic failures discussed in earlier chapters. If the Labour and Conservative parties had been as successful as the German Christian and Social Democrats at delivering high growth rates and increased living standards, it is hard to believe that they would have lost support on the scale that they have, that the nationalist parties would have become as significant as they did in the 1970s, that the Liberals would have gained as much ground or that the Social Democratic Party would ever have been created. It is more likely that the British two-party system would have remained as strongly entrenched as the German, perhaps with the Liberals as a small sect on the fringes, like the German Greens. By the same token, it is hard to resist the impression that some of the 'insider' criticisms mentioned above — notably, the attacks on the civil service — are the products of a rather unedifying search for scapegoats. Probably, the same applies to some of the dissatisfaction uncovered by Marsh's study and the Kilbrandon Commission's attitude survey. Since no such studies were conducted in the early post-war period, we cannot know whether the attitudes they reveal are more widespread than they used to be. To the extent that they are, it is reasonable to assume that that too is, in part, a product of relative economic decline: that, as Denis Kavanagh argues, 'specific' disappointment with the consequences of economic failure has spilled over into 'general dissatisfaction with the system'.[29]

It is hard to believe that this can be the whole story. For there is a chicken and egg problem here, which a narrowly economic interpretation of the recent past cannot address. No doubt, economic failure has undermined confidence in the political system. Yet there are good reasons for believing that lack of confidence in the system has helped to cause economic failure. One reason why the established British parties have been less successful at delivering high growth rates and increased living standards than their German opposite numbers have been is that British governments have found it harder than German ones to make their decisions stick. It follows that there are strong prima facie reasons for thinking that the British public has, for some reason or another, been less apt than the German to believe that the decisions which its government takes in its name ought to be carried out. Declining efficiency has probably eroded legitimacy, but ebbing legitimacy has almost certainly helped to undermine efficiency.

Clearly too, part of the responsibility lies with ideological polarisation. Modern British electoral politics have always been based on the principle that the winner takes all. But in the heyday of Keynesian social democracy, when winners and losers shared the same tacit governing philosophy, the winners' gains and losers' losses were, in practice, modest. Ideological polarisation has raised the stakes, making victory sweeter, but defeat less tolerable. The traditional, inexplicit form of 'club government' presupposed that no one would push his formal constitutional rights to the limit: that governments would not use the huge battery of powers available to them in a way that seemed unfair or unreasonable to their opponents. That presupposition depended, in turn, on the assumption that — because the contestants for power were not very far apart ideologically — no one would want to. No such assumption can be made today. To put the point another way around, if the two big parties had remained as close to each other as they were in the heyday of Keynesian social democracy much of the institutional disarray under discussion here would not have happened. The upsurge in third-party voting would not have taken place; the SDP would never have been formed; and it is safe to assume that much less would have been heard about the dangers of 'elective dictatorship', the need for a Bill of Rights or the case for proportional representation. The theoretical arguments for a Bill of Rights and electoral reform were, after all, as powerful thirty years ago as they are now. Britain was an 'elective dictatorship' then, and had an unfair electoral system then. Few minded, because few feared the consequences. The Westminster Model of the early 1950s worked satisfactorily, in short, partly because agreement over the rules of the game was underpinned by a broad, inexplicit consensus about the way in which the winners would behave on substantive questions of policy. One of the main reasons why the rules of the game have been called into question is that this policy consensus has broken down: and that as a result, the losers no longer trust the winners not to abuse the powers which the rules confer upon them.

Yet that explanation is circular too. One of the main reasons why the parties became ideologically polarised in the first place was that the ideologies to which they turned offered them ways out of the institutional crisis of the late-1960s and 1970s. In any case, it is not ideological polarisation which has led backbench MPs to become more assertive, eminent jurists to complain about the deficiencies of the common law, or retired civil servants to campaign for reform of the Official Secrets Act. For that matter, ideological polarisation is not the sole source of current conflicts over the roles of the police, the judiciary, the civil service or the House of Lords; of the referendums on EEC membership or Devolution; or of the growth of single-issue protest and pressure groups. There is no doubt that it has exacerbated the disarray we have been discussing. The causes, however, lie deeper.

Where, then, should we look for explanations? Marsh's study of political protest provides some helpful pointers. As we saw a moment ago, it showed, first, that a high potential for protest was a product of a high level of political competence, combined with a low level of trust in government and politicians; and, secondly, that distrust was surprisingly widely spread. The implications are worth pondering. The language of 'trust' and 'distrust' carries a heavy emotional charge. Children trust their parents; lovers trust each other; good leaders win the trust of their followers; the religious put their trust in God. To trust someone is to have confidence in him, to be able to rely on him, to believe what he says without checking it, to be sure that he will treat one fairly, to know that he will try to perform what he has promised: in a word, to feel safe with him and, because one feels safe, to be able to lower one's guard. To abandon trust for distrust is to switch from safety to danger, to be forced off the solid ground of unarmoured fellowship into a quagmire of loneliness and doubt. Partly because of all this, distrust is corrosive. If I do not trust others, and behave to them accordingly, they will soon stop trusting me. By the same token, to experience a betrayal of trust is to suffer an emotional wound of a peculiarly painful and disorientating kind. And, in the eyes of the loser at any rate, trust lost is apt to look, in retrospect, like trust betrayed.

What has all this to do with the institutional disarray and political dissatisfaction of the last fifteen years? Simply this. If

Marsh is right, the high protest potential of the politically competent is a product, not just of distrust, but of lost trust: of the sense of betrayal, and the accompanying sense of righteous indignation,[30] which goes with the nagging suspicion that one's trust has been abused. For according to Marsh, a high protest potential is not the property of 'extremists or militants or any other fashionable *bête noir* of professional politicians and communicators'.[31] On the contrary, the politically competent potential protester is a blood-brother to the good citizen of liberal-democratic theory. He is likely to turn to protest, not because he does not understand the system or accept its norms, but because he has been disappointed in it: because he comes to feel that it has let him down. Setting off from a different starting point, Vivien Hart comes to a similar conclusion. For her too, the political discontents of the 1970s were rooted in distrust. Distrust, in turn, was rooted in discrepancy — or, to put it more precisely, in 'the unfavourable evaluation of politics by citizens who see a discrepancy between the ideal and the reality'.[32] So far from being estranged from democratic norms, the distrustful saw themselves 'as democrats in a democratic polity, integrated into its norms and "estranged" only from its current condition'.[33] Their distrust was the reverse of pathological. It was a healthy response to the failure of a supposedly democratic system to live up to its pretensions.

Distrust as lost trust: lost trust as trust betrayed: trust betrayed as discrepancy between ideals and realities — it is not difficult to pick out these themes in the dissatisfaction and disarray of the recent past. Nor is it difficult to spot at least some of the discrepancies which have given rise to them. As we have seen, discrepancies between ideals and realities, between norms and actions, indeed, in some respects, between one set of norms and another, are the hallmarks of 'post-parliamentary democracy'. The ideal of representative democracy has become increasingly discrepant with the under-representation of minority opinion resulting from a first-past-the-post electoral system. The norms implied by the doctrine of ministerial responsibility are increasingly at odds with the realities of monster departments and a regulatory state. The principle that laws should be made by the elected representatives of the people, assembled in the sovereign Parliament, is out of joint with the realities of plebiscitary general elections, mass political parties and Keith Middlemas's 'corporate bias'. The most obvious single feature of 'post-parliamentary democracy', in other words, is that it has broken the chain of representation and accountability which was central to the late-nineteenth-century version of parliamentary democracy, leaving in its place only a fog of ambiguities. Not only is there no coherent set of principles to justify the system as a whole; as John Mackintosh argued, there is a jungle of competing, and in some cases mutually incompatible principles, each of which can plausibly be inferred from one part of the system, and each of which can be prayed in aid by those who have an interest in doing so. His description of the results is hard to better:

> [T]he public do not consider mere passage by a majority in the Commons sufficient to confer a special moral authority on laws. They want to know whether their pressure groups have been consulted and have agreed, whether the proposal was in the party manifesto and whether the measure has evident public support. The old, straightforward parliamentary system of democracy has been added to and been confused by other concepts of legitimacy and other methods of obtaining and demonstrating support, the total result of which is to take away the automatic reverence for the process of law and to make people ask, 'Why should I?' 'What is in this for me?' and 'Can I see the point of this regulation?'[34]

The implications go wider than Hart or Mackintosh acknowledged. Here it is helpful to recall our earlier discussion of the absence of a state tradition, as well as the discussion of 'club government' at the beginning of this chapter. Two crucial points emerge. The first is that, because Britain lacks a state tradition of the normal west European kind, because the British are subjects of a monarch rather than citizens of a state, ambiguity, perhaps even discrepancy, is inherent in the traditional British approach to government and law. For, as we have seen, one of the essential characteristics of the British system is precisely that the 'rights' (or 'liberties') of the subject are protected by fluid, informal usages, understandings and procedures, instead of being grounded in explicit principles, derived from a coherent philosophy of politics and political man; and that the rules of the game are customary and conventional, not legal and rational. Indeed, in the eyes of the whig historians and lawyers whose celebrations of it pervaded the textbooks of constitutional history as recently as a generation ago, this — and the flexibility which went with it — were among its greatest virtues.

This leads on to the second point. If the customs are taken for granted and the conventions respected, such arrangements may work perfectly well. Ambiguities, and even the discrepancies they cloak, may fortify the political order, so long as no one wants to probe into them. The old whig historians were not wrong in thinking that Britain's peaceful passage to democracy owed much to the hazy compromises which unprobed ambiguity makes possible. By the same token, however, once the customs cease to be taken for granted — once the conventions come under critical scrutiny: once the populace outside the club walls start asking what principles they embody, and why those principles should be accepted — arrangements of this sort are bound to run into trouble. The ambiguities inherent in them will be exposed, without being cleared up, the discrepancies will come out into the open and it will become more and more apparent that the question of principle they pose cannot be answered with precision or authority. When that happens, those who want changes (whether 'micro' changes in their personal circumstances, or 'macro' changes in public policy) will be less likely to regard negative answers as legitimate. The losers in substantive disputes will be more likely to feel that they have lost unfairly. Respect for the rules of the game will gradually ebb away. This is what now seems to be happening in Britain. Custom, precedent and convention have lost much of their old magic. Restive backbenchers, picketing strikers, troubled judges, constituency-party activists, animal rights defenders, even First Division civil servants have all begun to chafe against previously-accepted conventions, and to probe ambiguities which were previously veiled in decent obscurity. In doing so, they have focused attention, not just on Mackintosh's discrepancy between parliamentary norms and post-parliamentary realities, or even on Hart's discrepancy between democratic promise and undemocratic performance, but on the hidden presuppositions of club government itself — on the assumptions that a political order is best founded on unspoken understandings and unwritten conventions: that it is better to rely on the good sense and good faith of the rulers than on the clarity and philosophical coherence of the rules. And, as a result, these presuppositions have started to come apart at the seams.

The question is, why? Plainly, it is an extraordinarily complex question. We are dealing with a set of interlocking cultural and institutional changes, to which no simple interpretation can possibly do justice. That said, four lines of enquiry seem particularly promising. The first is implicit in Lord Scarman's original argument for a new constitutional settlement. Social and cultural changes, he maintained, had generated new kinds of conflict, both between individuals and between individuals and agencies of government. These conflicts had to be regulated somehow, but the common law was ill-suited to handle them. If there were no new constitutional settlement, the law might be pushed out of these areas of life altogether. There would then be no protection in these areas against the arbitrary power of a government with a majority of the House of Commons at its back.[35]

The conclusion may or may not have followed, but the premise is hard to fault. Like all other advanced industrial societies, Britain is becoming an increasingly diverse, hetero-geneous, pluralistic society. Thus, it is not only Denis Kavanagh's 'traditional bonds of social class, party and common nationality'[36] which have worn thin. The same is true of all traditional bonds, of all bonds derived from inheritance or custom rather than from the free choice of the individuals affected by them. In such a society, there are likely to be more disputes than there used to be. But the very forces which produce the disputes will also make the protagonists less likely to take the credentials of those who are supposed to regulate them on trust. Authority — whether the public authority of governments, courts, or policemen, or the private authority of party whips, trade-union leaders or university senates — will have to justify itself. Almost by definition, justification by precedent will not be likely to carry conviction: if it were, no justification would have been needed in the first place. Meanwhile, the ethic of equal rights, which has always been latent in the Diceyan doctrine of the rule of law, has spread more widely. Claimants are more conscious of what they see as their rights, and more determined to stand on them. Decisions are scrutinised more carefully for evidence of bias. The net effect is that authority has been de-mystified. It can no longer stand on inherited dignity. It has to prove that its decisions are fair — and, since the processes through which it reaches them are not grounded in explicit principles, embodying the ethic of equal rights, it finds this increasingly difficult to do.

This leads on to the second line of enquiry, suggested most powerfully by Ronald Inglehart's study of the rise of what he (rather misleadingly) calls 'post-materialist' values in western Europe,[37] and by Samuel Beer's subtle account of what he calls the 'romantic revolt'.[38] In different ways, Inglehart and Beer both tried to illuminate the shift of sensibility and aspiration which took place in the late 1960s and early 1970s, and which, in Beer's view, accompanied and sustained a 'new populism' at odds with the collectivist politics of the post-war period. Inglehart found that, in all the countries covered in a survey carried out in the early 1970s, those who gave priority to the 'materialist' objectives of fighting inflation and maintaining order outnumbered the 'post-materialists', who gave priority to protecting freedom of speech and 'giving the people more say in important political decisions'. Everywhere, however, the younger age cohorts contained a significantly higher proportion of 'post-materialists' than the older ones — more so in the richer societies of mainland Europe than in Britain, but appreciably even there.[39] (See Tables V and VI.) Beer saw in the political discontents of the late-1960s and 1970s the effects of a new romanticism, which emphasised 'the heart not the head; emotion not reason; spontaneity not calculation; nature not civilisation'. This romantic revolt was necessarily hostile to hierarchy, but that was only one of its targets. It was equally hostile to 'class identification imposed from outside by inheritance or objective function' — indeed, to all attempts to group human beings in impersonal, externally-determined categories which they did not choose for themselves.[40] Not only did it challenge established authority in ·the name of a radical populism, it also challenged the class and group loyalties of the collectivist polity in the name of a new kind of individualism.

There are obvious weaknesses in Inglehart's interpretation of his own data. Support for a bigger say in political decisions or at the work-place (another of his indicators of post-materialistic values) is not necessarily evidence of such values. One might want more say in order to pursue materialistic purposes more effectively. Even support for beautifying the countryside may have materialistic roots: behind the environmental enthusiasms of the suburban amenity group may lurk a less Wordsworthian concern for property values. Even Beer's sensitive evocation of the new romanticism of the 1960s and 1970s provokes some nagging doubts. It is not clear that class loyalty has ever had much operational significance for the British Labour Movement. On the other hand, narrower loyalties to occupational and functional groups, echoing those of the nineteenth or even eighteenth centuries, were very strongly in evidence in the industrial unrest which helped to destroy the Heath and Callaghan governments.

When all the qualifications have been made, however, few would dispute that the last twenty years have seen a complex cultural mutation, the effects of which ramify out into all kinds of apparently unconnected areas of life, from clothes to eating habits, and from the structure of the family to the organisation of work. In different ways, joggers, single parents, wholefood eaters, do-it-yourself enthusiasts, home computer buffs, Laura Ashley patrons and the members of producer co-operatives all testify to its strength. Indeed, the economic transformation of the 1970s and 1980s is, in part, the product of a new, quality-conscious public, anxious to assert individual tastes and willing to pay for them. As Michael Piore and Charles Sabel argue, this shift of taste is partly responsible for the current decline of mass production, the dominant form of advanced industry since the late-nineteenth century, and the switch of emphasis to the small-batch production and 'flexible specialisation' which have been made possible by information technology.[41] It would be odd if no similar change of mood had made itself felt in politics. The revival of nationalism in Scotland and Wales; the fainter stirrings of regionalism which have appeared in the north and far south-west of England; the switch from party to pressure group as the favoured instrument for attempts to influence public policy; the increasing propensity of those with grievances to use direct action against policies or decisions they believe to be wrong; poll data showing less confidence in the system of government; the growth of intra-party dissent in the House of Commons; the placing of new issues, like the protection of the environment and of individual and minority rights, on the political agenda — whether these are materialistic or post-materialistic, individualistic or non-individualistic is, in the end, a question of semantics. What matters is that they have all happened; and that, in different ways, they all reflect a new emphasis on the values of autonomy and authenticity — a yearning for the direct, the immediate and the face-to-face, a rejection of the large-scale and impersonal, a confused groping for self-fulfilment. It is easy to see that these values conflict with the grey, impersonal, bureaucratic forms of post-parliamentary democracy. Less obviously, but in some ways more importantly, they are equally hard to reconcile with the oligarchic presuppositions of the Westminster Model at its parliamentary height.

In different ways, Scarman, Inglehart and Beer all focus on the consequences of social and cultural change. The third line of enquiry focuses on continuities. It has to do with the failure of successive attempts at cross-class coalition building, and with the social and cultural forces which lay behind that failure. It is sometimes suggested that the political and institutional disarray of the recent past is a product of the decline of 'deference'. But, as Denis Kavanagh has argued, it is not at all clear that the 'deferential' attitudes which were thought to characterise Britain's political culture until the early 1960s ever predominated among the working class.[42] Certainly, 'deference' would be an odd word for the mixture of resentment, suspicion and fatalism encapsulated in Richard Hoggart's famous picture of the emotional divide between 'us' and 'them' in the working-class quarter of Leeds where he grew up:

> 'They' are 'the people at the top', 'the higher-ups', the people who give you your dole, call you up, tell you to go to war, fine you, made you split your family in the 'thirties to avoid a reduction in the Means Test allowance, 'get yer in the end', 'aren't really to be trusted', 'talk posh', 'are all twisters really', 'never tell yer owt' (e.g. about a relative in hospital), 'clap yer in clink', 'will do y' down if they can', 'summons yer', 'are all in a click (clique) together', 'treat y' like muck'.[43]

Indeed, there are good reasons for thinking that the working class (or at any rate, large parts of the industrial working class) was never deferential at all: that, in the nineteenth century, for example, working-class attitudes to political authority varied from the suspicious to the hostile;[44] and that what looked to middle-class observers like deference was, in reality, a resigned acceptance of a state of affairs which working-class people correctly believed they could not change. What happened in the 1960s and 1970s, if this interpretation is true, is that grudging acceptance started to fray at the edges; that, in some cases, at any rate, the bonds of resignation snapped. At least one explanation stands out. An unwritten rule of British industrial politics from the 1870s onwards was that the state should not intervene in industrial relations: that the 'possessive collectivism' of the organised working class should be left undisturbed. The incomes and industrial-relations policies of the 1960s and 1970s broke that rule. Whatever the motives behind them, moreover, they threatened to freeze a pattern of income distribution for which there was no consensus. On a deeper level, their purpose was to sustain an economic order which, for many working-class people at any rate, was only dubiously legitimate. A political system which had been grudgingly tolerated while it kept out of the labour market began to verge on the intolerable when it started to trench on the property rights and hem in the aspirations embodied in the custom and practice of free collective bargaining.

The next line of enquiry takes that thought a stage further. It springs from Jim Bulpitt's distinction between 'high' and 'low' politics. Bulpitt argues that British central government has traditionally left 'low politics' to subordinate tiers of government, in order to keep its hands free for the 'high politics' which have dominated the imaginations of the political class. In his phrase, Britain's has been a 'dual polity', based on a self-denying ordinance which has kept the centre out of local affairs. But in the 1960s, he believes, the dual polity began to break down. Failures in the supply-side of the economy hampered the centre's conduct of high politics. It could put them right only by intervening in low politics; and in order to do this, it had to upset the unwritten division of labour by which low politics had been left to local élites. The disarray which has been such a marked feature of Britain's territorial constitution ever since is one of the results.[45] Bulpitt's insight illuminates much more than the relationship between the centre and the localities. There is an obvious parallel between the territorial disarray which he describes and the disarray provoked by Keynesian social-democratic interventions in the labour market. In both cases, governments trying to kick-start a lagging economy into life were forced to trespass on territory which the unwritten rules of British politics had previously reserved to others. Sometimes their incursions were successful and sometimes not. Even when they succeeded they provoked fierce opposition and a perceptible drain of legitimacy.

At this stage, politics and economics come together again. Club government and market liberalism were both children of the possessive individualism which triumphed in the Glorious Revolution; both long antedated the democratic Westminster Model of the late-nineteenth century, as well as the regulatory state of the twentieth. And just as the ethos of market liberalism survived long after the doctrines were abandoned, so the ethos of club government survived the enfranchisement of the working class, the development of mass political parties and the accompanying expansion in the role and size of the state. New élites were admitted into the club; absorbed its assumptions; and learned to conduct themselves in accordance with its unwritten rules. At the same time, the members of the club acquired new functions and accepted new responsibilities. This smooth transition was the pride of the British political class, and the envy of its counterparts in less happy lands. Yet it had heavy costs. Club government remained legitimate only because it operated by a principle of live and let live which gradually debilitated the economy. The instinct for indirect rule which had traditionally shaped central government's approach to the territorial constitution also determined its approach to economic management. Just as it left Bulpitt's 'low politics' to local élites, so, for the most part, it tried to leave the 'low economics' of the supply-side to the oligopolistic, yet non-encompassing private-interest governments described by Keith Middlemas and Mancur Olson. That worked for a time – indeed, for a surprisingly long time – but at the price of *immobilisme* and continuing relative decline. In the hands-on phase of Keynesian social democracy, however, these comfortable accommodations collapsed. Under the whip of economic necessity, governments were forced to break with the tradition of indirect rule – notably, in the labour market, but to some extent in other markets as well – and, in doing so, to infringe some of the unwritten rules of the polity. Meanwhile, the British version of the cultural mutation common to most advanced societies in this period began to undermine respect for other rules as well. We are still living with the consequences of the crisis of governability which followed.

As at the end of Part One, then, the argument has reached a kind of impasse. If Britain's economy has declined because she failed to become a developmental state, the obvious conclusion is that she should take steps to become a developmental state in future. But the governments of the 1960s and 1970s did try, albeit in a confused and irresolute fashion, to adopt at least some of the features of the developmental states on the mainland of Europe; and the political system began to buckle under the strain. The 'overload' theorists of the 1970s were wrong in thinking that government as such cannot manage the kind of interventionism on which British governments embarked in the 1960s. They may nevertheless have been right in thinking that British government cannot do so without changes in assumptions, practices and conventions which have been taken for granted, in some cases for centuries. To the question of what those changes might be we will turn next.

Part Three

IMPLICATIONS

8

The Public Realm

'[H]e who is unable to live in society, or who has no need to because he is sufficient for himself, must be either a beast or a god.'

Aristotle.[1]

'If it were not for a rich endowment of social instincts, man could never have risen above the animal world. All specifically human faculties, the power of speech, cultural tradition, moral responsibility, could have evolved only in a being which, before the very dawn of conceptual thinking, lived in well-organized communities. Our prehuman ancestor was indubitably as true a friend to his friend as a chimpanzee or even a dog, as tender and solicitous to the young of his community and as self-sacrificing in its defence, aeons before he developed conceptual thought and became aware of the consequences of his actions.'

Konrad Lorenz.[2]

'To be attached to the subdivision, to love the little platoon we belong to in society, is the first principle (the germ as it were) of public affections.'

Edmund Burke.[3]

So far I have tried to answer two overlapping questions. Why has the Keynesian social-democratic governing philosophy which most British political and economic leaders accepted for most of the post-war period now collapsed? What are the main economic and political problems which a successor philosophy would have to address? The enquiry has gone wider than it seemed likely to do at the beginning, and the answers have turned out to be more complicated. The politicians and officials who abandoned the Keynesian social-democratic policy commitments of the post-war period imagined that they were driven by economic necessity. But their judgment of what was necessary was shaped by moral and political values which they and the society around them had inherited from previous generations and which could, at least in principle, have been abandoned. To take only one example, Keynesian demand management had become unworkable partly because the trade-off between inflation and unemployment had deteriorated. Yet a long-term incomes policy agreed between the government and the great producer groups, on the lines of the incomes policies followed in some of the 'neo-corporatist' social democracies of Scandinavia and central Europe, might have offset that deterioration. To be sure, such a policy would have required different attitudes to collective bargaining, differently-structured trade unions and employers' associations, with different conceptions of their functions, and, most of all, a different view of the proper relationship between the state and organised labour and capital. But this only reinforces the point. The full employment commitment which had been fundamental to post-war Keynesian social democracy was undermined, not by economic imperatives, but by moral and political preferences, and by the institutions which embodied and transmitted past moral and political preferences.

What is true of the crises of the 1970s is equally true of the century of relative economic decline which paved the way for them. By the early 1970s, the British economy was among the most vulnerable in the developed world. But that vulnerability was not a fact of nature. It was a product of past choices, reflecting the moral and political preferences of those who made them. Unlike its counterparts on the mainland of Europe and in Japan, Britain's political class had never managed — even in its interventionist periods — to create an entrepreneurial or developmental state. It had also failed to construct an enduring cross-class coalition, with the strength and will to answer one of the central questions which lie at the heart of the politics of economic adjustment: the question of how its costs and benefits are to be distributed. Most fatally of all, it did not see that, in an increasingly complex twentieth-century society, the late-nineteenth-century political institutions and conventions which most of its members took for granted could no longer generate sufficient trust to win consent for the kind of policies which a developmental state would have had to follow.

Behind these choices and failures to choose lay the sediment of three centuries of British history – a complex amalgam of understandings, assumptions, practices and values, held all the more tenaciously for being largely unacknowledged. One reason why the political class did not create a developmental state is that Britain has lacked a state tradition of the sort which has shaped the politics of most other European nations. Part of the reason why she has lacked a state tradition is that the doctrines, and still more the ethos, of early-nineteenth-century market liberalism were more deeply embedded in her culture than in other European cultures. Her political class has failed to revise the constitutional doctrines which it inherited from the late-nineteenth century partly because, lacking a state tradition, it has taken it for granted that its own unwritten rules provide surer guarantees against the abuse of power than any formal code could do. The most important of the doctrines in question derived partly from the Benthamite utilitarianism which encapsulated and justified the ethos of market liberalism. That ethos has also helped to inhibit the emergence of encompassing producer groups, responsive to the interests of the wider society as well as to the sectional interests of their own clientèles. It is partly because Britain's producer groups have characteristically been non-encompassing that occasional attempts to move towards the 'negotiated' version of the developmental state have come to nothing. One reason why British politicians have never managed to construct a stable and successful cross-class coalition for economic change is that British class relations have been unusually embittered. Part of the explanation for their bitterness lies in the late-nineteenth-century transition from an 'active' conception of property to a 'passive' one – a transition which owed much to the possessive individualism which had helped to shape the whole culture.

In this perspective, the 'British crisis' is, above all, a crisis of *maladaptation*. Private companies, trade unions, government departments, political leaders, the political class and the general public have all failed to adapt inherited practices, institutions, expectations and assumptions to the changes which have taken place in the environment in which they originally emerged. But that is only part of the story. Running through most of these failures of adaptation are three other themes – less obvious, perhaps, but at least as important. The first is the theme of consent and lack of consent; of trust and distrust between and among governments and governed. The second is the theme of possessive individualism – of sectional interests taking precedence over the common interest; of short-term profit maximisation inhibiting long-term growth; of the non-encompassing institutions and habits generated by the primitive industrialism of a hundred and fifty years ago running against the encompassing needs of the skill-intensive, quality-orientated industrialism of the late-twentieth century; of a political culture saturated with the negations of the Glorious Revolution inhibiting the evolution of an active state. The third is the theme of Peter Clarke's 'mechanical' reform – of the pursuit of change through manipulation or regulation rather than through persuasion. These four themes mingle with each other in an extraordinarily complex, even baffling way. Like a horse dragged unwillingly to the water, a distrustful public has repeatedly balked at policies designed to cajole or force it into adaptation against its will. Since most policy-makers have taken the ethos of possessive individualism for granted, their policies have usually gone wide of the cultural and psychological factors which make adaptation difficult. Since they (and the society around them) have thought in terms of 'mechanical' rather than of 'moral' change, they have had no basis on which to persuade their fellow citizens to abandon attitudes that inhibit adaptation for attitudes that favour it.

Hence, one of the great paradoxes of contemporary Britain. There has been no shortage of policy or institutional change in recent British history. Since the late-1950s, British governments have switched from arm's length to hands-on Keynesian social democracy, abandoned the central Keynesian social-democratic commitments altogether and carried through a multitude of institutional reforms, many of which were later undone. But most of these changes have been examples of what the organisational theorist, Donald Schon, has called 'dynamic conservatism' – of the tendency of a threatened social system 'to fight to remain the same'.[4] As such, they are symptoms of the crisis of maladaptation, rather than answers to it. Is there an alternative, and what would it imply for the political economy?

The enquiry is bound to follow a circuitous route. It would not be difficult to draw up a list of policy and institutional changes, designed to overcome the various obstacles to adjustment. Obvious examples would include a series of constitutional 'reforms' to correct the disarray of the Westminster Model; changes in company law to bring British practice closer to Japan's and mitigate the consequences of Harold Perkin's 'passive property'; and changes in the relationship between government and the organised producer groups to induce the latter to become more encompassing. If the analysis set out here is right, however, that is exactly the wrong way to push the argument forward. Devising a list of changes to overcome particular adjustment problems piecemeal would amount, in practice, to yet another exercise in the kind of dynamic conservatism which has so often failed. Rather, we should try to tease out the underlying logic of the crisis: to look at the intellectual and moral roots of the inhibitions and constraints which have frustrated adaptation in the past. Only then can we sensibly discuss the possible implications. And in order to tease out the logic of the crisis, we shall have to go back over some of the ground covered in previous chapters, to look for connections which were not apparent at first.

My central thesis is that the roots of Britain's adjustment problems are to be found in a coherent, though often unconscious, set of attitudes to politics and political man – to the relationship between man and society, between individual purposes and social purposes, and to the political dimension of these relationships – and in the reductionist model of human nature which lies behind them. These attitudes are not exclusive to Britain. The intellectual tradition from which they come has been part of the mainstream of western social thought (Marxism, for these purposes, counting as part of the mainstream) for the best part of two hundred years. But, for a variety of reasons, they are more deeply embedded in Britain than in most industrial societies. Central to them is the assumption – no doubt reflecting the reductionist materialism of the seventeenth and eighteenth centuries – that just as the world is made up of solid lumps of matter, so a society is made up of separate, sovereign, atomistic individuals. The obligations which these individuals owe to their society derive ultimately from the fact that it can be shown that it is to their advantage to belong to it. They follow their own purposes, which they choose for themselves. These purposes may be altruistic as well as egoistic, but in either case, they are individual, not social; and even altruistic purposes are pursued in the same fashion as egoistic ones. There is no reason to believe that altruism is more natural to man than egoism; probably, it is less. Firms, or colleges, or research institutes may have common purposes, but whole societies do not. The notion that politics is, or should be, a process through which a political community agrees its common purposes is therefore nonsensical. The community, in Jeremy Bentham's cutting phrase, is a 'fictious body'.[5] Politics is about reconciling conflicts between individually chosen purposes. It has no business with the choice of purposes. Indeed, in some versions of this tradition, the notion that politics might have something to do with the choice of purposes is at least incipiently tyrannical. Freedom means my freedom to choose my own good for myself, and to pursue it in my own way, provided only that I leave others free to choose and pursue their good in their own way. To allow others to take part in the process through which I choose my good would be to allow them to trespass on psychic space which belongs to me – space which it is my right to keep inviolate.[6]

This tradition – the tradition of reductionist individualism – has held the field for so long that no one brought up in its shadow can easily emancipate himself from it. Yet we have not always seen ourselves and our relations with each other in this fashion, and there are increasing signs that the tradition which has led us to do so has trapped itself in a contradiction which it lacks the resources to resolve. As Alasdair MacIntyre has pointed out, Aristotle and the ancient world saw man's relationship with society in a profoundly different way. So did medieval Christendom. It was not until the seventeenth and eighteenth centuries, he writes:

> that morality came generally to be understood as offering a solution to the problems posed by human egoism and that the content of morality came to be largely equated with altruism. For it was in that same period that men came to be thought of as in some dangerous measure egoistic by nature; and it is only once we think of mankind as by nature dangerously egoistic that altruism becomes at once socially necessary and yet apparently impossible and, if and when it occurs, inexplicable. On the traditional Aristotelian view such problems do not arise ... There is no way of my pursuing my good which is necessarily antagonistic to you pursuing yours because *the* good is neither mine peculiarly nor yours peculiarly — goods are not private property ...
>
> For many seventeenth- and eighteenth-century thinkers however the notion of a shared good for man is an Aristotelian chimaera; each man by nature seeks to satisfy his own desires. But if so, there are at least strong reasons for supposing that a mutually destructive anarchy will ensue, unless desires are limited by a more intelligent version of egoism.[7]

The sting here is in the tail: there can be no guarantee that sufficient intelligence will be forthcoming. As successive Keynesian social-democratic governments discovered when their appeals for higher industrial investment and lower wage settlements went unheard, even enlightened self-interest is not a substitute for belief in a common good. Enlightenment is often scarce; and if the majority is unenlightened, intelligent egoists will soon discover that it pays to be unenlightened too. Even the cleverest egoists cannot serve as the building blocks of a society. If men are driven by self-interest, they are driven by self-interest; and, despite heroic efforts to prove that it can do more than this, all that self-interest can tell me is that it is to my advantage for other people to behave well. And — MacIntyre's most powerful, because least familiar, point — the position is not very different if the egoists are capable of spasms of altruism. For there is an important sense in which a spasm of altruism is merely a special case of egoism. It is still freely chosen by the atomistic individual; and what the individual can freely choose he can freely un-choose. ('Inclination', said Kant, 'goes its own secret way; indeed, it can do no other, because it has no principle'.)[8] A society built on self-interest would be built on a chasm. One built on egoism tempered by altruism — Thomas Hobbes for six days a week, and Bob Geldof on Sundays — would be built on a fault line which might, at any moment, collapse into an earthquake.

As we saw in Part One, this contradiction affects the everyday world of practical men as much as, perhaps more than, the rarefied world of moral philosophy. One example must suffice. Since Adam Smith, economists have recognised that, even in a market economy, 'public goods' — goods like national defence, law and order and sanitation which, by their very nature, are consumed by the whole society — must be provided by public authorities if they are to be provided at all.[9] But the notion of public goods, in the plural, is incomplete without a notion of the public good in the singular. If there is to be a public sector — what Daniel Bell has called a 'public household' — supplying public goods, it must operate on some principles; and without some notion of the public good, and of politics as a process of defining the public good, we cannot know what those principles should be or how to determine them. As Bell puts it, the public household is:

> the polis writ large. Yet we do not have any theoretical underpinning for this state of affairs — a political economy of the public household that joins the economic and the political dimensions, or a political philosophy of the public household that provides decision rules for the normative resolution of conflicting claims and a philosophical justification of the outcome . . . Yet the point of philosophy is that it states a rational standard, provides for consistency of application so that actions are not arbitrary or capricious, and establishes a normative justification which satisfies men's sense of fairness. Only on that basis are some consensual principles of political life possible; without them, there is only brute power.[10]

Meanwhile, however, scientific advances have begun to undermine the reductionist model of man which underpins the prevailing view of politics. Man, it appears from modern social cognitive psychology, is above all an infinitely complex learning animal. As such, he engages in a vast range of indeterminate behaviour, which no constructable model can wholly explain and the motives for which are far too varied to be reduced to any single, driving force.[11] Advances in ethology, the science of animal behaviour, also suggest that the view of human nature from which the contradictions of atomistic individualism spring is, in any case, unsound. Some animals are solitary. Some live in complex societies, with elaborate status hierarchies and subtle processes of social learning. Despite our unique capacity for evil, we belong to the second category. Of course, we are egoists. And, of course, we are altruists. We are capable of appalling meanness, selfishness and greed. We are also capable of up-lifting generosity, self-sacrifice and tenderness to others. But the first do not make us, in some way, a- or non-social; and it is not because of the second that we live in society. We do so because, in one crucial respect, at any rate, Aristotle was right. Some beasts may be able to live outside a society. So may some gods. People cannot; and, as Mary Midgley has argued, the idea that they could is simply, among other things, bad biology.[12]

We are not egoistic calculating machines which decided to form a society, because, after careful scrutiny of the evidence, we came to the conclusion that it would be in our interests to do so. The state of nature of the social contract theorists 'would be fine for intelligent crocodiles, if there were any. For people it is a baseless fantasy'.[13] We live in society because we are social creatures, genetically programmed for sociability — because, as Konrad Lorenz pointed out in one of the quotations at the head of this chapter, our remote ancestors were social long before *homo sapiens* appeared on the scene. And for the same reason, we do not choose our purposes in solitary ratiocination on some mountain peak, and then descend to fight for them against our fellows, who have chosen theirs in similar solitude. We choose them through a constant, never-ending process of communication with the other members of our society — with families, friends, colleagues, neighbours, people we meet in the pub and the bus queue, newspaper columnists, television programme makers, advertising copy-writers, politicians, clergymen and barrow-boys. They are our purposes, but they are society's too.

Two implications follow. It is hard to dispute that the reductionist view of man and of the relationship between man and society which British politics has inherited from the seventeenth and eighteenth centuries denies important parts of mankind's genetic inheritance. One obvious inference is that we do not — indeed, cannot — live as though society consisted of the atomistic individuals whom that view postulates; despite the brilliance of its inventors, it is important to remember that no known society has even attempted to live in that way for any length of time. The reductionist model of man and society was first formulated by a handful of intellectuals, with little influence on the everyday lives of their still overwhelmingly agrarian societies. Even when it entered the bloodstream of the western world in the nineteenth century, it had to contend with powerful antibodies — the Christian and Jewish religions; the aristocratic ethos of the 'Old Society'; the instinctive communalism of the peasantry and, to some extent, of the urban workers; the vestiges of the Aristotelian ideal which the educated classes absorbed from the *gymnasium*, the *lycée* and the public school; the ethic of skill and service of the craftsman and the professional; the great mobilisations of the wars of unification of the nineteenth century and the world wars of the twentieth; above all, the habits, values and expectations learned over the millenia during which men and women had lived by a different view, and the institutions and roles which helped to transmit them.[14] Even now, traces of these antibodies survive. Without them, it is hard to see how the elaborate structures of modern life could function.

The second implication is less comforting. Though we *are* programmed for sociability, we can be more or less sociable. A society founded on self-interest would be a contradiction in terms, but it is all too easy to imagine a society permeated with the belief that society is founded on self-interest. The Ik of northern Uganda whom Colin Turnbull studied were so demoralised by the loss of their old hunting grounds that they had given way to a pitiless, despairing egoism, which withered the ties of family, friendship and even sexuality. Yet even the Ik still had a society of sorts – albeit a dying one.[15] Though no society could succeed in living by reductionist, atomistic individualism, it is perfectly possible to try to live by it; and it would be equally reductionist to assume that attempts to do so could not affect the behaviour of those who made them. Our genetic inheritance leaves a vast range of possible ways of life open to us, and some are closer to the reductionist model than others. The closer we move towards it, the more plausible – and therefore more persuasive – it is likely to become. Like most models of man, it is implicitly prescriptive as well as descriptive; if we behave in accordance with the description we are that much more likely to agree with the prescription.

In any case, the prescription attracts one side of our natures. Though we are social animals, we are less social than many. We need company but we also need space. Our relationship with society is full of tensions, and probably always has been. We are rooted in it; we die for it; yet we chafe against its claims and, in some of our moods, we resent it and would half like to be free of it. No doubt, cavemen sometimes felt oppressed by the togetherness of the cave, sometimes stumped off to brood under the stars and sometimes tried to get out of their share of cleaning the spears. That may be why the theme of the solitary – Ulysses wandering the empty seas, the lone ranger riding off into the sunset – speaks to us so strongly, and why so much political philosophy revolves around the antiphonies of freedom and order. So if we are told repeatedly that society is made up of atomistic individuals, driven by self-interest, and pursuing individually chosen goods – that the notion of a common good is a sentimental fantasy, and the notion of politics as a process of deciding what should count as the common good, either absurd or potentially tyrannical – we may come to believe it; and if we believe it, we may start to behave, in some small but destructive degree, as though it were true. To the extent that we do so, the reductionist model will be vindicated; and to the extent that it is vindicated, the bonds of community will be frayed and the chances of following a different way of life made more remote. For membership of a community is like trust: indeed, it may be a precondition of trust. From an economist's point of view, it is a public good: it has to be consumed collectively, or not at all. It is, by definition, reciprocal; it imposes obligations as well as justifying claims; and it is likely to evaporate once it is put in doubt.[16] I can only belong to a community if others belong to it as well; if the other members of my community question its reality, my membership of it will also become unreal.

Indeed, as MacIntyre, Bell and Ghita Ionescu all argue in different ways, that may yet turn out to have been the leitmotiv of post-war history throughout the industrial world. For in our time, the old antibodies have plainly started to decay. Thus, for MacIntyre, the collapse of the Aristotelian notion of a shared good for man has left us in a new Dark Age, reminiscent of the time when 'men and women of goodwill turned aside from the task of shoring up the Roman *imperium* and ceased to identify the continuation of civility with the maintenance of that *imperium*'. The only hope of sustaining the intellectual and moral life, he believes, lies in building 'local forms of community' — twentieth-century equivalents of the monasticism of 1400 years ago.[17] For Bell, the hallmark of the late-twentieth century is the 'loss of *civitas*, that spontaneous willingness to obey the law, to respect the rights of others, to forgo the temptations of private enrichment at the expense of the public weal — in short to honour the "city" of which one is a member'.[18] For Ionescu, it is the erosion of fraternity by a hedonistic and life-diminishing, because death-denying, materialism:

Only when a great humility towards himself as a mortal man, as an ephemeral existence, permeates the conscience of the individual can it be moved by the misery and the humility of all other men. And it is only then especially that the added miseries of inequality and above all poverty, the material misery of other men, become unbearable for the conscience of others. To think first of other human beings in economic, social or political terms is to empty them of their substance and in that sense it runs counter to the essence of the true sentiment of fraternity.[19]

Only the very bold or very foolhardy would dismiss these warnings. It is, after all, a commonplace of tragedy that men are apt to rebel against their own natures, and in doing so to destroy themselves.

All this puts the British crisis of maladaptation into a broader, but at the same time bleaker, perspective. As we have seen, the failures of adaptation of which it is the culmination all reflect the stubborn survival, both on the 'micro' level of the individual enterprise or producer group and on the 'macro' level of the whole society, of the doctrines and — much more importantly — of the ethos of market liberalism. These doctrines are, of course, founded upon the reductionist model of man which we have just been discussing. Though they are not solely British in origin, they have been propagated more insistently and for longer in Britain than anywhere else in Europe. And they, the ethos associated with them and — most of all — the conception of man which underlies them have nibbled at any notion of community or common purpose like air pollution nibbling at an ancient building.

To be sure, they have always been in contest. Ever since they first began to capture minds and influence behaviour, they have provoked indignation and hostility; even when they seemed to be carrying all before them on the level of policy and decision, there was a strong undercurrent of dissent on the level of imagination and reflection. The inarticulate 'moral economy' of the eighteenth-century crowd, which held it to be '"unnatural" that any man should profit from the necessities of others', continued to inspire popular protests against the new political economy until well into the nineteenth.[20] In the 1820s and 1830s, Robert Owen and a number of Chartist publicists tried to develop a 'people's science' of economics, hingeing on the notion of a fair return for labour.[21] High Tories campaigned for the aristocratic ideal of a harmonious, organic society, in which each of a complex hierarchy of ranks would receive its due share of the protection and support of the state.[22] In different ways, Carlyle, Cobbett, Dickens and the young Disraeli all tried to fill the 'moral vacuum' which they sensed in the classical political economy of the day;[23] and it is not difficult to trace a line of descent from them to such disparate figures as Ruskin, Tawney and George Orwell. In the late-nineteenth century, a school of Idealist philosophers tried to reassert the values of community in an idiom partly derived from Hegel.[24] The same applies, even more strongly no doubt, to the level of everyday life. *Homo economicus*, the rational, egoistic pleasure-seeker and pain-avoider of the political economists, was a reified abstraction, not a creature of flesh and blood: not even Dickens's genius could make Mr Gradgrind more than a horrifying caricature.

But all this only qualifies the central point. The early-nineteenth-century dissenters spoke to the heart, not to the head. They had feeling and imagination on their side; but they lacked a convincing theory to give the promptings of the heart an intellectual cutting edge. They could mourn the passing of the old world, and dream of a new one; but they could not make sense of the world which was actually taking shape around them – or not, at any rate, in a fashion which could tell the inhabitants of that world how, in practice, to prevent it from taking shape. Still less could they dislodge the ethos which made the doctrines they opposed resonate among practical men of all classes. It would be wrong to suggest that they did not touch their contemporaries at all. The social reforms of the period owed much to them. But for practical purposes, their visions of society were, at most, uneasy codas to the market-liberal vision: soft-hearted Sunday school pieties which might mitigate, but could not replace, the hard-headed 'realism' of the rest of the week. Much the same was true of the Idealist philosophers who flourished later in the century. They had a theory of sorts, which enjoyed a considerable vogue in academic circles and even among the more highbrow politicians and publicists. But it was too much at odds with the culture to have much influence for long.

Thus, Benthamite individualism and market liberalism both shaped and reflected the common sense of the age; and although the emergence of a regulatory state and the transition from liberal to corporate capitalism gradually undermined the latter, they hardly shook the intellectual and cultural hegemony of the former. For Benthamism can justify state intervention as easily as *laissez-faire*: on Benthamite assumptions, an enlightened bureaucracy, armed with the appropriate analytical apparatus, can maximise total utility as well as, perhaps better than, the market. Hence, one of the most revealing ironies of modern British history. As Karl Polanyi showed, the 'great transformation' from agrarian to industrial society followed a parabola rather than a straight line. In the first, market-liberal, phase, the laws and customs which impeded the growth of a market economy were repealed or done away with. But before that phase had run its course, a reaction had set in; and in the second, interventionist, phase, new laws and customs were introduced to protect society from the consequences of the previous one.[25] In Britain, however, the reaction against full-blooded market liberalism took place under the same philosophical aegis as the movement towards it. Contemporaries, anxious to come to grips with the changes through which they were living, naturally made much of the differences between the 'Collectivism' of the end of the nineteenth century and the 'Individualism' of the beginning.[26] What stands out in retrospect is the continuity between the two. State intervention was tentative, hesitant and reactive; and although it was sometimes justified in other terms, the logic behind it was essentially utilitarian. Moreover, the private producer groups which increasingly 'distorted' the free play of the market shared the individualistic ethos which had paved the way for the market economy and helped to inspire its apologists.

Hence the repeated failures to adjust which we have discussed. They are, at bottom, products of a fragmented society: of the contradictions of atomistic individualism. By the same token, they are also products of the common sense which practical men have taken for granted for the best part of two centuries.

Hard questions follow. How can a fragmented society make itself whole? How can a culture permeated by possessive individualism restore the bonds of community? Granted that the common sense of nearly two hundred years is the chief obstacle to successful economic and political adjustment, how can common sense be redefined?

These questions overhang the search for a doctrine which has dominated the recent past. As we saw in Part One, Keynesian social democracy could not address them, much less answer them. For most of the time, the Keynesian social-democratic view of politics was, in practice, a mixture of bastard Schumpeter and bastard Marx. Democratic politics was a competitive struggle for the people's vote (the Schumpeterian element), in which the voters were motivated chiefly by class interest (the Marxist element). In the halcyon days of arm's length management, that view at least provided a reasonably solid basis for policy making, but, as we saw, it broke down when the effects of economic decline began to bite. The governments of the 1960s and 1970s discovered that they could not honour the fundamental Keynesian social-democratic commitments to full employment and the welfare state unless behaviour changed. Since they could not obtain the kinds of changes that were needed either by manipulating the sticks and carrots of the market or by ministerial *fiat*, they had to turn to persuasion and argument. Since the changes they sought were often painful, they had to argue on non-hedonistic grounds: on grounds of patriotism, or fraternal solidarity or the common good. But their philosophy gave them no basis for arguments of this sort, and no language in which to couch them. It is not surprising that they became progressively more helpless as the crisis deepened. As we also saw, the same applies, even more strongly, to neo-liberalism and neo-socialism. For neo-socialists, community and a common purpose are impossible under capitalism; for neo-liberals, they are impossible under any circumstances. So far from restoring the fraying bonds of community, the practical effect of both is to erode them still further.

One possible alternative merits more extended treatment. This is the rather inchoate cluster of assertions and aspirations which has gathered around the slogan of the 'Social Market'.[27] In essence, the advocates of the 'Social Market' are market liberals with tender hearts. At least in outline, they accept the neo-liberal diagnosis of Britain's economic failures; though they sometimes rebel against them in practice, they cannot logically reject the cures implied by that diagnosis. Yet, at the same time, they wish to distribute the proceeds of economic success according to non-market criteria, derived from some notion of equity or fairness. The slogan has obvious attractions. It appears to go with the grain of the culture, and there is some evidence that there is a potential constituency for it.[28] Like Keynesian social democracy, however, it cannot address the questions under discussion here. For it too is trapped in a contradiction. The redistribution it entails presupposes a sense of community, but if the assumptions underlying it are true, no community is possible.

For the central premise on which the whole market-liberal system is built is that the choices which the market registers are made by the separate, sovereign, atomistic individuals of the reductionist model, and that these individuals pursue their own private goods by and for themselves. If that premise goes, the rest of the system goes too. The competitive market is no longer by definition the most efficient mechanism for allocating resources; and state intervention or producer-group pressures which 'distort' the market are no longer by definition harmful. But it is on that premise that the market-liberal diagnosis of Britain's economic predicament rests. If it is false − if the sovereign, freely-choosing consumer and the rational, profit-maximising entrepreneur are myths: if the choices market actors make are, in reality, shaped by a vast range of factors, including ambition for power and status, resentment against being pushed around, the influence of friends and work-mates, the constant drip, drip, drip of the advertising industry, respect for the moral code of one's society and even a simple unwillingness to change old habits: if, in short, the preferences which the market registers are socially as well as individually determined − then there is no reason to believe the diagnosis or to take the cures it implies. The very notion of timeless, spaceless economic laws, holding good in all societies at all periods of history, becomes untenable. So does the notion that the task of the economic policy maker is simply to ensure that these laws are allowed to operate. Instead, we are left with the familiar compromises and complexities of the mixed economy and the familiar difficulty of deciding how, in practice, to run it. Yet, if the market-liberal assumptions are true − if choices are, after all, made by atomistic, sovereign individuals, pursuing their own goods by and for themselves: if it really is the case that society is simply an agglomeration of such individuals − then the notions of a common purpose and a common good become, once again, chimerical.

Because of all this, the notion of the Social Market cannot provide convincing grounds for the redistribution which its advocates want. For a redistributionist must be able to answer the question, why should I make sacrifices for others? The answer, 'Because it is in your interests' is unlikely to carry much conviction for long, while the answer, 'Because you are a kindly altruist, who feels compassion for those less fortunate than yourself', dodges the real problem. However emollient the language in which it is put, the answer has to be, 'Because it is your duty; because you are part of a community, which existed before you were born, which will endure after your death, which helped to make you what you are and to the other members of which you have obligations; because you are a member of the human race, and no man is an island unto himself'. By definition, no system of belief derived, however distantly, from reductionist individualism can yield that answer: if reductionist individualism is true, men *are*, in principle, islands unto themselves, joined together in a continent only on their own terms, if at all. Redistribution can be justified only by some notion of community or fraternity, for only a notion of community or fraternity can make it a duty − as opposed to a compassionate whim − to help one's fellows. Market liberalism is logically opposed to such notions: since the very idea of the Social Market presupposes a market-liberal conception of economic motivation and behaviour, it must be logically incompatible with them as well. It is, in essence, an attempt to squeeze communitarian conclusions out of individualistic premises. Whatever the intentions of those who engage in it, this is bound to be an unrewarding enterprise.

Even John Rawls's subtle and powerful attempt to ground a

notion of 'justice as fairness' in a new version of the Social Contract falls at this hurdle.[29] Rawls's arguments are now so well-known that there is no need to rehearse them here. The central point is that, for him, a just distribution of goods is one which would be chosen by 'rational persons concerned to advance their interests' in what he calls the 'original position' – in other words, by rational persons who did not know how they personally would fare under the arrangements they chose. According to him, such persons would take their decisions on the assumption that they might be among the worst off under the dispensation for which they opted. They would therefore opt for the dispensation which would put the worst off in the best possible position. It follows that a just distribution is one which achieves this: that inequalities can be justified only if they make the position of the least advantaged better than it would otherwise be. The conclusion is attractive, even noble. It implies that no one should seek advantages for himself, unless in doing so he benefits the weakest members of his community – an implication embodying, as Rawls points out, an essentially fraternal ideal.[30] The trouble is that the premises of the system are individualistic. It hangs together only if rational individuals, concerned to further their own interests, would behave as Rawls says they would. But, as so often in the history of social thought, Rawls's definition of rationality turns out to be restrictive. Everything depends, in practice, on the tacit assumption that rationality can be equated with risk aversion: that it would, by definition, be irrational for someone in the original position to gamble on being among the better off. The rational person in the original position is, in short, an example of the psychological reductionism we were discussing earlier. He is first cousin to the rational utility maximiser of the Benthamites, and as remote from the pain, sweat and multiple motivations of real people in real societies. The sort of people who become professors at Harvard probably do tend to be risk-averse, but Harvard Yard is not (alas?) the world. The sort who make fortunes on the stock exchange, who lead armies into battle, who write great poetry, who become prime minister or, for that matter, who run successful grocery shops usually have a fairly strong streak of the gambler in their make-up. A theory which excludes that streak from rationality cannot inspire solutions to the problems we have been discussing in these pages.

Where, then, should we turn instead? One possible answer, of course, is that there is nowhere to turn: that the crisis of maladaptation cannot be resolved, and that the most likely prospect is one of continuing social and political fragmentation, perhaps leading, in the end, to the collapse of the political order. No one who has lived through the last fifteen years of British history could dismiss that answer out of hand. If this book has any single thesis it is that the roots of Britain's predicament lie deep in her history and culture. Most past societies caught in a predicament of that sort have failed to escape, and there is no reason to believe that Britain will find it any easier to do so. Yet this does not mean that escape is, by definition, impossible. The conventional British view that culture is in some sense given, impervious to argument and incapable of being changed, is as dangerous as any other sort of determinism. Man is shaped by culture, but culture is made by man. The weight of the past lies heavy on any settled society, but not so heavy that it cannot be lifted. Inherited values and assumptions can be jettisoned; the institutions which embody and transmit them can be reformed or abolished. What it does mean is that change of the kind which might resolve the crisis – change which goes deeper and lasts longer than the changes brought by the 'dynamic conservatism' of recent years – is unlikely to come easily or quickly if it comes at all; and that the obstacles to it may be too strong to surmount.

It also means that new versions of the *methods* of recent years are unlikely to surmount them: that the reductionist individualism which those methods reflected is unlikely to yield anything more fundamental than more 'dynamic conservatism', if of a slightly different kind. For reductionist individualism can encompass only two ways of living together in society, and therefore only two conceptions of politics and political man and only two modes of social change. One is the command mode, and the other the exchange mode. Change may be commanded from the top down, or it may result from free exchanges of one kind or another. People change either because they are told to, or because it is worth their while (or made worth their while) to. Society is either a kind of hierarchy, held together because those at the bottom obey those at the top, or it is a kind of market, held together by the calculating self-interest of its members. Hobbes, in some ways the greatest of all the thinkers in the reductionist tradition, painted a marvellously coherent, if chilling, picture of a society operating by the command mode. The seventeenth-century English whigs, and their eighteenth-century American intellectual descendants, drove out their respective rulers in the name of the exchange mode. Both modes are, of course, omnipresent; it is hard to conceive of a society in which neither played a central part. Change can come by either of them, and frequently does. Almost by definition, however, neither can generate profound cultural changes — changes of value, belief and assumption — of the kind which will have to take place if Britain is to adjust more successfully in the future than she has in the past.

Once we abandon the reductionist straitjacket, however, we are no longer limited to these two modes. And, in the real world, there is also a third — more elusive, less often studied, but, potentially, much more significant for our theme. Charles Lindblom calls the relationships on which it depends 'preceptoral',[31] but they could equally well be called 'persuasive', 'educational' or even 'moral'. They are the relationships, not of masters to servants or buyers to sellers, but of pupils to teachers and teachers to pupils. Change in the preceptoral mode comes neither from commands nor from exchanges, but from persuasion, discussion, indoctrination, conversion — in short, from learning. People change, not because they have been ordered to or given incentives to, but because they have learned to see the world and themselves in a different way: because, in some measure, they have become different people. If a society operating by the command mode would be rather like a regiment, and in the exchange mode like a bazaar, a society operating by the preceptoral mode would be more like a classroom, a debating chamber, a Quaker meeting or a Jewish Yeshiva. This does not mean that preceptoral relationships are, in themselves, morally superior to the others. They can be abused by tyrants and exploiters, just as the others can. If Gladstone's Midlothian campaign was one spectacular example of preceptoral politics, Mao Tse Tung's Cultural Revolution was another. But that is only to say that all human relationships have a potentiality for evil as well as for good, and that all social ideals can be twisted and debased. What matters for our present purposes is that — although no society could operate by the preceptoral mode alone — it is, as Lindblom points out, as omnipresent in most, perhaps in all, real-world societies as the other two. Because reductionist individualism cannot make sense of it, it has eluded most of the theorists whose teachings the common sense of the last two hundred years reflects. Yet it exists. Men and women do not only command and obey, and exchange one good for another. They also teach and learn, persuade and are persuaded.

What part might preceptoral relations play in the matters we have been discussing? Subject to an important *caveat*, action science provides a useful way of looking at this question. Schon and his collaborator, Chris Argyris, have distinguished between two models of the ways in which organisations may learn how to adapt to change.[32] The first is what they call 'single loop learning' — a form of learning which enables the members of an organisation to 'detect and correct errors' in such a way as to maintain the central features of the organisation's existing network of 'norms, strategies and assumptions'. Sometimes, that form of learning can solve the organisation's problems and maintain its effectiveness. All too often, however, changes in its environment have posed problems with which its existing norms, strategies and assumptions cannot cope. When that happens, sticking to them is a recipe for failure, and single loop learning is no longer enough. What is needed then is 'double loop learning' — an enormously more demanding form, in which conflicts of value and purpose are resolved instead of being suppressed, and in which solutions emerge out of frank discussion instead of being imposed by the victors in a struggle for power. In double loop learning, the members of the organisation deliberately and explicitly confront the internal contradictions within its existing norms, and try to resolve them. The object is not just to make the organisation's performance more effective, but to revise the norms which define effective performance.

There are obvious dangers in applying these ideas to the questions which we have discussed in earlier chapters of this book. Argyris and Schon derived them from studies of micro-organisations with defined objectives — firms, colleges, research institutes and the like — and there are fundamental differences between such organisations and the governments of states. The technocratic assumption that government and politics can be equated with management, and whole societies with business firms, is as misleading as it is widely held: 'Great Britain Ltd' is not so much a nightmare as a nonsense. As Leo Pliatzky has put it, government 'is about the management of dilemmas, not about the management of resources'.[33] In it, there is no simple, unambiguous test of success or failure comparable to a company balance sheet: no 'bottom line'. Yet the problems of a firm which has to adapt to a changing market have something in common with the problems of a country which has to adapt to a changing economic order; and approaches derived from studying the first may throw much-needed light on the second. The notion of double loop learning is particularly illuminating. At its core lies the common-sense proposition that really fundamental organisational changes are best made through a process of mutual education, in which the members of the organisation concerned discover and resolve conflicts between incompatible values and assumptions, and in doing so redefine their common purposes. That proposition does not, in itself, offer a solution to the crisis of maladaptation. It does, however, provide an approach to a solution.

We cannot redefine our common purposes if we cannot have common purposes. We cannot educate each other if we have no spaces in which to speak to each other. We cannot learn from each other if we will not accept the responsibility for our mistakes. Transferred to the political sphere, the notion of change through mutual education implies a notion of politics as mutual education: of the political domain as a public realm, where the members of a political community listen to, argue with and persuade each other as equal citizens, so as to find solutions to their common problems. Central to it is man the learning being, subject to a vast range of motives, continually influencing and influenced by his fellows, and with immense potentialities for good and evil. From that follows an Aristotelian, as opposed to a Schumpeterian, view of politics. The political arena becomes a forum where whole human beings, with their loves and hates, hopes and fears, traditions and histories, engage with each other as living persons, instead of a battleground or auction room, where the disembodied abstractions of the reductionist model pursue individual or class interests. At least in principle, the citizen must be a reflective and open-minded being, capable of rising above his particular interests in order to make a disinterested judgment of the general interest, and willing to revise his judgments in the light of the arguments advanced by his fellow citizens. Above all, politics as mutual education implies some notion of a common good transcending private goods: of membership of a political community as partnership in a common enterprise, which endures beyond the lifespans of the individuals who make it up: of politics itself as, in Brian Crowley's words, 'a civilised and civilising' process[34] through which free men and women assume the burdens of social choice and decision, instead of handing them over to a charismatic leader or an impersonal social process.

In implying all this, politics as mutual education also implies a different approach to policy making and political leadership. Most current discussion about these is based implicitly on one of two models of the way in which policy might be made. In the first (it might be called the social engineering model), 'problems' are identified, 'solutions' are proposed, and the 'problems' are duly 'solved' or not 'solved'. In the second (it might be called the procrustean model), policy makers judge their society against the benchmark of a set of principles, discover where it diverges from them and then formulate 'policies' to adjust it accordingly. For both, society is an inert lump to be re-shaped by the policy-maker: a patient lying on an operating table, whose ills the policy maker removes or fails to remove. Political leadership is either an exercise in charisma and will or an attribute of technical expertise. Both models are, of course, wildly misleading. In reality, society is not in the least like a patient lying on the operating table. It is engaged in a perpetual wrestling match with the surgeon. Indeed, as we saw in Part One, it was largely because the governments of the 1960s and 1970s forgot that — because they imagined that complex changes of attitude and behaviour could be imposed from the top down — that they failed to win consent for the changes they tried to promote. Politics as mutual education, on the other hand, implies that society 'solves' its own 'problems', through argument and negotiation. If there is a medical metaphor for it, it is not that of surgery, but of Freudian psychotherapy. The patient cures himself; the therapist can at most act as the catalyst for the process of self discovery through which he does so. The leader is neither a charismatic hero, carrying salvation in his saddle-bags, nor a technocratic manager, pushing through an objec-tively 'correct' solution. He or she is a kind of pastor or moderator or chairman — if possible, wiser and more experi-enced than the rest of us, and as such entitled to respect, but with no special technical knowledge and no pretensions to heroism — whose role is to set off the learning process, to bring us face to face with the contradictions in our values and, if possible, to elicit a latent consensus.

A further implication follows. In the prevailing view of politics, the public are not only passive, they are also irrespons-ible. The politicians answer to them, but they answer to nobody. All they have to do is to express their privately-determined preferences in the secrecy of the polling booth. Responsibility for translating these preferences into action lies conveniently with someone else; and there is always someone else to blame if things go wrong. One powerful element in the neo-liberal critique of Keynesian social democracy is precisely this: that the welfare state becomes a nanny state, in which free citizens are transformed into dependent and therefore irre-sponsible clients. But neo-liberalism has no place for politics as mutual education; and its only solution is to narrow the scope of the state and rely more on the market. If the argument set out here is right, however, that is no solution at all: though the details of the mix may change from time to time, the mixed economy is here to stay. On a deeper level, moreover, the kind of responsibility which comes from free exchanges in the market is very limited. It is true that, as a market actor, I have to take responsibility for the impact of my transactions on myself. But the market has no mechanism for making me face my responsibility for their impact on others. If I give my custom to a firm which pollutes the environment, and thereby help to perpetuate pollution, I can still shuffle off the blame for the consequences of my actions on to someone else. The notion of politics as mutual education entails a different way of looking at social choices. Politics ceases to be a specialist activity, reserved to alien beings known as 'politicians'. All citizens are politicians. Once we see politics in that way, the irresponsible public of the prevailing view disappear along with the charismatic leader and technocratic manager. In their place are members of a political community − inescapably responsible, by the very fact of belonging to it, for what it does or fails to do. There is no distant 'they', government or market, to bear the blame for the mistakes we make in common. There is only us.

Two sets of questions arise, one concerning the practicality of this approach to politics and the other its relevance to the realities we discussed in Part Two. Of course, it has a distinguished lineage. To mention only a few examples, the suggestion that politics ought to be a form of mutual education would not have surprised Rousseau, John Stuart Mill, de Tocqueville or G.D.H. Cole. But that very fact gives it a rather antiquated ring. What can it have to do with the world of the manufactured television news item, the headline-grabbing press release, the public relations consultant, the computerised mail-shot, the mass-circulation gutter press? How does it square with the well-known fact that only a small proportion of the population participates in politics more actively than by casting an occasional vote?[35] How, for that matter, does it square with the increasing complexity of the issues with which politicians have to deal − with the need to decide such matters as the rate of increase in the money supply, or the British line on reform of the common agricultural policy, or the future of the tax and social security systems in an ageing society? Quite apart from its practicality, how could such an approach help to overcome the adjustment problems with which this book is chiefly concerned?

Part of the answer to the first set of questions is that some of the obstacles are less formidable than they seem. It is true that the issues which politicians have to decide nowadays often seem too complex for the ordinary public to grasp. One reason why they seem so is that the fallacy of 'Great Britain Ltd' spreads ever more widely — that politics are increasingly equated with management, and the role of the politician with that of the technocrat. As we saw a moment ago, this is to confuse two quite different activities. Politicians sometimes manage and managers sometimes engage in politics, but politics is not management and management is not politics. Politics has to do with questions of value, not with questions of technique; with appraising, debating and deciding between different ends, not with discovering the most efficient means to achieve ends which have already been agreed. Experience, wisdom and judgment can help in finding the answers to political questions, but there are no Ph.D.s in wisdom or judgment. They can be learned, but they cannot be taught; and they are learned through practice, not through books. As anyone who has taken part in any kind of politics will know, they are quite independent of formal qualifications. Highly qualified academics or business leaders, brought up in the cult of the fact and unschooled in the arts of political argument and evaluation, are often extraordinarily silly when they turn to public affairs: wisdom and judgment can be found in people whose formal education ended at fourteen.

Technical knowledge, on the other hand, cannot provide the answers to political questions, indispensable though it may be for elucidating the nature of the questions. The question of whether Britain should or should not remain in the European Community — the only question so far put to a nation-wide referendum in the United Kingdom — raised a host of technical issues, but it was, at bottom, a question of principle which the general public were perfectly capable of deciding, and did in fact decide. To be sure, it is often difficult to disentangle the political element in a complex issue from the technical detail surrounding it; and, partly because of this, it can also be difficult to prevent self-interested technical lobbies from imposing their political values on lay politicians. But that problem exists in all political systems, even highly authoritarian ones. No approach to politics can eradicate it; and the best way to mitigate it is to force the lobbies to argue their case in public. Equally, the notion of politics as mutual education does not imply that the people are always right or that there is no need for safeguards against the possible tyranny of the majority. Communities sometimes oppress some of their members; and mass publics sometimes do cruel and stupid things. So, however, do technocratic élites. It is true that in an under-educated society, most of whose existing political and industrial arrangements deny the whole notion of man, the learning being, and the conception of human possibilities which that notion implies, large numbers may well be incapable of a politics of mutual education. But that is a reason for changing the arrangements, not for abandoning hope that, if men and women are given the opportunity to learn, some of them will take it.

Another partial answer is that the notion of politics as mutual education does *not* square with some of the realities of present-day politics, and is not intended to. It is intended to challenge them. It springs from the belief that the ills of the political and economic order which we discussed in Part Two are, at bottom, products of the view of man from which many of these realities stem, and that the first step towards curing them is to adopt a different view. One of the central assumptions of this book is that behaviour cannot be divorced from attitudes and values. If we start to think about politics in a different way, and try to realise different values in and through our politics, political realities will change. Moreover, as we saw in the last chapter, there is some evidence that this is beginning to happen. The prevailing view of politics is not a universal view. One of the reasons why the Westminster Model is in disarray is that the limitations of the prevailing view have become more apparent; and that, partly because of this, some of the spectators in the stands have begun to descend on to the field.

This is not to say that the confused, incoherent, sometimes even contradictory yearnings which we have been discussing reflect a settled new view of politics, or even a settled will for change on the part of all those who experience them. To put it at its lowest, however, they do imply deepening dissatisfaction with the existing political order, and growing scepticism about the values and assumptions underlying it. To be sure, the dissatisfaction is not all of a piece. Some of it springs from an impatient, hedonistic egocentricity — the dead-sea fruit of the reductionist model — alien to the values of community and common purpose, and closer to neo-liberalism than to any approach to politics based upon those values. Notoriously, today's yuppie is often yesterday's hippie in a pin-stripe suit. But, like similar episodes in other periods of history, the complex cultural, technological and industrial mutation which seems to be taking place in most developed western societies opens up a bewildering variety of possibilities. Though some of them conform fairly closely to the reductionist model, others are at odds with it. Political argument and debate, not inexorable cultural or technological trends, will determine which of them eventually become realities.

As we have seen, Piore and Sabel believe that this mutation is partly responsible for the growth of small-batch production and 'flexible specialisation' in industry. They also argue persuasively that the political analogue to flexible special-isation is what they call 'yeoman democracy' — a late-twentieth-century equivalent to the Jeffersonian ideal of a republic of smallholders, in which property is held in trust for the community, instead of being owned unconditionally by individuals.[36] This does not mean that yeoman democracy is necessarily the wave of the future. The point is simply that current cultural and technological trends are as compatible with it as with the neo-liberalism which dominated the political agenda of Britain and the United States in the early 1980s. The search for authenticity, the demand for participation and decentralisation, the longing for roots, the revolt against uniformity — all these expressions of the mood of the late-twentieth century have communitarian features as well as individualistic ones, and some, at least, of the emotions behind them point in the direction we have been groping towards in this chapter.

Yet it is not enough to leave the argument there. The notions of double-loop learning and of politics as mutual education cannot serve as blueprints for a new society, still less as programmes for a future government. They offer an approach: a standard for judgment: a way of thinking about, and ultimately of appraising, familiar realities which, in present-day Britain at any rate, has become unfamiliar. No one can tell in advance what would happen if more people adopted this approach: the whole essence of it is that, if they did, change would come through negotiation and debate rather than through direction from the top. But although there is no way of telling what substantive changes it would bring, Britain's existing political arrangements are clearly inimical to it. Even if the answers are bound to be tentative and sketchy, it therefore makes sense to ask what, in broad terms, it implies for those arrangements. Given the persistence and weight of the obstacles to adjustment which we discussed earlier, moreover, it also makes sense to ask how it relates to them.

Some of the implications are plain enough. The notion of politics as mutual education obviously implies the widest possible access to the means of education. If we are to educate each other through politics, government must be as open as possible; institutions ranging from public enquiries to parliamentary committees must have as many teeth as possible, so as to raise the quality of public information and debate. But that is only the beginning of the story. 'We do not learn to read or write, to ride or swim, by being merely told how to do it,' wrote John Stuart Mill, 'but by doing it.'[37] We learn the arts of government by practising them; we become responsible by taking responsibility. Part of the point of a politics of mutual education is to enlarge the scope of the disciplines of choice and decision. That must entail the widest possible diffusion of responsibility and therefore of power – not only in the sphere of formal politics, but, as Mill insisted, in 'the business of life':[38] at the work-place, in the school system, indeed wherever discussion and debate can help to determine common purposes.

This leads on to a more complex set of implications. The best starting point for exploring them is Burke's famous insight, quoted at the head of this chapter, that love for the 'little platoon we belong to in society' is the germ of wider 'public affections'. Intuitively, it seems almost self-evident that small groups are more likely than big ones to develop a sense of community and common purpose. Other things being equal, they are easier to identify with; and it is also easier for a small group to manage its affairs in a participatory, non-authoritarian way. For all these reasons, it is reasonable to assume that politics as mutual education will be easier to practise in a small group than in a big one. But Burke meant more than that. Like Durkheim, who thought that the division of labour and the proliferation of specialist functional groups fostered 'organic solidarity' in the wider society, he obviously believed that small groups were the building blocks for big ones: that the emotions which held a whole society together were rooted in and developed by the groups of which it was made up. Most good infantry officers, managing directors and university vice chancellors would probably agree. Bruno Bettelheim's searing description of the way in which the Nazi concentration camps tried to destroy group loyalties among their inmates in order to break their will to resist points towards a similar conclusion.[39]

In this perspective, a flourishing political community will be a mosaic of smaller collectivities, which act as nurseries for the feelings of mutual loyalty and trust which hold the wider community together, and where the skills of self-government may be learned and practised. Some of these will be public, for example parish councils, regional assemblies or the governing bodies of schools or hospitals. Others – trade unions, employers' associations, producer co-operatives – will be private. Plainly, this implies that political decisions should be taken on the lowest possible level of government. It also implies something less obvious. As we saw in Part Two, there is a built-in tension between group interests and community interests. Small, non-encompassing groups are inherently likely to see the interests of their members in a narrow, inward-looking way; if the argument set out in Chapter 7 is right, it is partly because that tension has been particularly acute in Britain that she has found it particularly difficult to adjust to economic change. There is no reason why participatory, non-authoritarian methods of group government should, of themselves, lead a non-encompassing group to behave in an encompassing way. A participatory, non-authoritarian group of bank robbers may rob with more sense of mutual loyalty than an authoritarian one, but that does not mean that it will be any more considerate to bank clerks. No set of procedures can eliminate this tension altogether, but some procedures may mitigate its effects. As Robert Goodin argues, 'Certain kinds of argument, powerful though they may be in private deliberations, simply cannot be put in a public forum': when men have to justify their demands in public, before their peers who also have demands to make, a form of self-censorship leads them to 'launder' their preferences, making them less egoistic than they would have been otherwise.[40] As we saw in Chapter 7, Scandinavian and central European experience suggests that the same is true of organised groups. If they have to argue their case in the open, and share public responsibility for the ultimate decisions, they are likely to behave in a more encompassing way than if they do not. As well as the devolution of decision making, then, politics as mutual education implies power sharing — not just between the state at the national level and sub-national tiers of government, but between the state and private groups within society.

Of course, this is not an all-embracing formula, and it would be self-deception to pretend otherwise. Small is not always beautiful and big is sometimes best. Many questions can still be settled satisfactorily only on the national level. Others are too vast even for national governments. While some functions and powers could perfectly well move down, from the national to sub-national level, others ought to move up, to a level above the nation-state. As a broad generalisation, however, decentralisation and power sharing are the most obvious implications of the approach put forward above. Yet that is only the beginning of the story. Structures may help to bind communities together, but only if their procedures and the outcomes they produce command allegiance. The values of community and common purpose, and the notion of politics as a process of mutual education to define a common purpose, can have no substance without some consensus about outcomes and procedures. People will not feel that they belong to a community to the other members of which they have duties — that they *are* part of a whole greater than the sum of its parts — if the proceeds of community action are distributed in a way, or by procedures, which offend their sense of what is fair.

Against that background, the relationship between politics as mutual education and the failures of adaptation which we have been discussing in this book is clear enough. For a common theme runs through all these failures. It can be detected most easily in the disarray of the Westminster Model, and in the dwindling legitimacy of its institutions and conventions. This disarray has come about because the Schumpeterian assumption that democratic politics revolve around a competitive struggle for the people's vote — and the corresponding, essentially Benthamite, assumption that the victors in that struggle are entitled to make what use they wish of the power placed in their hands — can no longer provide the basis for a legitimate political order. The institutions and procedures which depend upon these assumptions still exist, and for the most part the decisions which emanate from them are still obeyed. But they are plainly losing authority; and they are losing authority because those who operate them are no longer trusted. Trust is ebbing partly because the conventions and assumptions of club government are no longer respected by the members of the club themselves, but even more because an increasingly sceptical public no longer believe that they provide adequate safeguards against the abuse of power.

The result is a paradox. As we have seen, the conception of power and authority summed up in Dicey's famous notion of the 'absolute legislative sovereignty or despotism of the King in Parliament', and the cluster of attitudes and assumptions which has grown up around that conception, have traditionally lain at the heart of Britain's political culture. Indeed, they have gone well beyond politics: current obsessions with the right of industrial management to manage almost certainly spring from the same emotional sources. For those who hold these attitudes, power is, in some sense, unshareable: something finite, which one has or does not have. To share it is to lose it: to divide it is to diminish it, and in doing so, to diminish its holders. The whole notion of federalism – the notion that state power should be divided between different tiers of government, each supreme in its own sphere – is alien. So is the central European view of democratic government as a process of consensus-building, based on power sharing between different social and political interests: the 'consociational', as opposed to majoritarian, conception of democracy.[41] The same applies to the suggestion that private bodies should share in public decision making, and, for that matter, to the suggestion that workers should share in the government of the firms that employ them. On one level, the traditional conception still holds the field. Governments still conduct themselves in accordance with it; and it still gives them an enormous capacity to make outward changes of form and structure. Yet on a deeper level, it is in retreat. The institutions and practices which it has underpinned for so long are losing legitimacy; and, because of this, the powers it gives are becoming, in certain crucial respects, illusory. They still make 'mechanical' change easy – perhaps all too easy. They make it more difficult to win consent for the deeper changes of attitude and custom without which a backward political economy cannot expect to adjust to the current upheavals in the outside world.

The same theme runs through the complex story of Britain's failure to become a developmental state. Almost by definition, political institutions which have lost legitimacy cannot sustain state-led adjustment on the Japanese or Gaullist pattern. In any case, as we saw in Chapter 7, negotiated adjustment on the central European pattern is more likely to work in a highly industrialised society, with a strong Labour Movement and only a tiny agricultural sector. Negotiated adjustment depends upon consensus building, and that in turn depends upon a form of power sharing. Instead of the secretive, collusive and transitory quasi-corporatism of the 1930s and the post-war Keynesian social democrats, government and the organised producer groups would have to establish British equivalents of the explicit, stable neo-corporatist institutions of the Scandinavian and central European social democracies. One possibility would be to adopt John Mackintosh's proposal to replace the House of Lords with an 'Upper House' representing the unions, the employers and other organised interest groups which already have systematic relationships with Whitehall. Another would be to extend the NEDC and give it a voice in policy making. A third would be to set up a 'house of industry', on the lines recently proposed by Sir Ian Gilmour.[42] A fourth, complementary rather than alternative to the others, would be to create neo-corporatist institutions in the regions, and to devolve developmental functions down to them — implying, in a way, the emergence of a number of developmental states, region by region. It is, after all, worth noting that the countries where the negotiated approach works best are the small nation-states of northern and central Europe, perhaps because they have a stronger sense of community than big ones. Other things being equal, moreover, regional bodies are more likely than national ones to display the flexibility which is even more essential in a time of rapid technological change than at other times. As well as, and more important than, any changes of structure, however, this sort of power sharing would require changes of attitude and belief. Politicians and public would have to accept that, in complex industrial societies, parliamentary election should not be the sole channel of representation: that, in their capacities as producers, 'the people' are likely to be represented better by groups organised on functional lines than by members of parliament elected on a territorial basis; and that it is therefore right, as well as expedient, for governments emerging from territorial elections to share power with functionally based producer groups. And such changes of attitude and belief are, of course, incompatible with the current British conception of parliamentary sovereignty, and with the assumptions underlying it.

The patent inability of recent British governments to follow

an independent economic policy in an increasingly interdependent world points to similar conclusions. In this respect,
at any rate, the classical European nation-state is obsolescent.
Plainly, national governments can overcome the consequences
of their obsolescence only by sharing power with international
or supranational authorities. If the world economy is to escape
from the present deflationary impasse, economic decision
making must somehow transcend national boundaries. The
experience of the 1970s and 1980s suggests, however, that the
mere co-ordination of national policies is not enough: as
Michael Stewart has shown, the temptation to exploit the gains
accruing to the free rider is likely to be too strong.[43] Since
national economic sovereignty stands in the way of recovery,
the world needs an international economic sovereign. The
trouble is that no such sovereign is in sight. The days have
passed when the United States was strong enough to assume
the burdens of sovereignty, at any rate in the western world,
and there are no new candidates for the post. In the case of
European countries, however, the logic of inter-dependence
points towards further devolution upwards to the EEC, which
alone can cope with the macro issues for which the nation state
is too small. For, in default of an international economic
sovereign, the most likely development is a world of mercanti-
list trading blocs; if this happens, 'Europe's' chances of
weathering the transition now taking place in the world
economy will partly depend on its ability to turn itself into one
of these blocs. The logic is, in fact, remarkably similar to the
logic which led the founding fathers of the EEC to reject
intergovernmental co-operation *à l'anglaise* in favour of the
'Community method' and the Jenkins Commission to re-
launch the concept of monetary union in the late-1970s: with
all its faults, the EEC is still the best available prototype of the
sort of transnational power sharing the times demand. From the
perspective set out earlier in this chapter, it is true, this raises
all sorts of problems. The EEC is, in some ways, a monument
to the technocratic fallacy that politics can be equated with
management, and its opaque, only dubiously accountable
decision-making processes are far removed from the ideals of
double-loop learning and politics as mutual education. But

that is an argument for strengthening the European Parliament, and making the other Community Institutions accountable to it. And here again, the absolutist view of power which permeates Britain's political culture stands in the way.

In a rather more complicated fashion, much the same applies to the fundamental distributional question which lies at the heart of the politics of adjustment. As we saw in Part Two, there are two ways of approaching it. One is to try to negotiate a settlement, socialising the pains of adjustment and allocating its costs and benefits in a way in which the undistorted market would not have done. The other is to try to push the losers out of the way. As we also saw, neither approach has worked in Britain since the late-nineteenth century. The losers have been too strong to push aside, but successive attempts to construct a cross-class coalition, based on a distributional consensus of some sort, have come to nothing. The reasons include the suspicions and resentments partly engendered by the late-nineteenth-century switch from 'active' to 'passive' property and the fractured, non-encompassing character of the British Labour Movement — none of which is likely to disappear in a hurry. But although no one could pretend that it would be easy to reach a consensus in any circumstances, it is more likely to come through power sharing and negotiation than in any other way. Certainly, approaches based on reductionist individualism have repeatedly failed. The proclaimed egalitarianism of the revisionist Labour politicians of the 1960s and 1970s turned out to be of little use. Equality of outcome conflicts with an intuitive sense that risk, enterprise, self-sacrifice, skill and deferred gratification deserve some reward. Equality of opportunity, on the other hand, is in practice vacuous. Yet devil-take-the-hindmost reliance on the market cannot generate a consensus either. Losers and potential losers will not accept it, in any case. Much more importantly, it too conflicts with an intuitive sense of what is fair: why *should* the losers have to bear the brunt of changes in the environment, which cannot possibly be their fault? Negotiation and power sharing would work, however, only if government abandoned its exclusive control over such sensitive matters as tax policy, welfare policy and perhaps even macro-economic policy and treated them as items in the bargaining agenda. It hardly needs saying that this would entail at least as profound a break with the traditional British approach to politics as would any of the others.

In all these spheres, the conception of power and authority which has underpinned Britain's political order since the eighteenth century has become an obstacle to successful adjustment. The notion of politics as mutual education is not only alien to that conception; it is also subversive of it. If it were adopted, the traditional conception would have to be abandoned, and the practices and institutions which it has fostered would have to be changed. Of course, this does not guarantee that the communitarian, power-sharing and participatory approaches which politics as mutual education implies would be any more successful. Guaranteed success belongs to Utopia. The only certainty is that the approaches of the last hundred years and more have failed. If the argument set out here is right, they have done so because the view of man and society on which they rest narrows horizons, restricts opportunities for moral growth and inhibits individual and social learning.

The alternative rests on a richer, more complex and in some ways more generous view of human nature and human possibilities, but it is not, for that reason, easier or more comfortable. On the contrary, it is more demanding. It rules out manipulative short cuts to change, imposed 'reforms', technocratic fixes. Its style is humdrum, not heroic: collegial, not charismatic: consensual, not ideological: conversational, not declaratory. It depends on the slow processes of argument and negotiation. It requires patience, open-mindedness and, above all, humility before the astonishing and sometimes exasperating diversity of others. At its core lies the belief that men and women may learn if they are stretched; that they can discover how to govern themselves if they win self government. But the key words in that sentence are 'may' and 'can'. No one who has lived through any of this century would be foolish enough to replace them with 'will'. To substitute the politics of mutual education for the politics of command and exchange would be to gamble — not, it is true, on the altruism or moral excellence of others, but on their sociability and capacity for growth.

No doubt, some will flinch from the risks involved. Yet that has been man's gamble since he descended from the trees.

TABLE I *Growth of Output (GDP at Constant Prices) per Head of Population, 1700–1979 (Annual average compound growth rates)*

	1700–1820	1820–70	1870–1913	1913–50	1950–73	1973–79	1820–1979
Australia		(n.a.)	0.6	0.7	2.5	1.3	(n.a.)
Austria		0.7	1.5	0.2	5.0	3.1	1.5
Belgium		1.9	1.0	0.7	3.6	2.1	1.7
Canada		(n.a.)	2.0	1.3	3.0	2.1	(n.a.)
Denmark		0.9	1.6	1.5	3.3	1.8	1.6
Finland		(n.a.)	1.7	1.7	4.2	2.0	(n.a.)
France	0.3[a]	1.0	1.5	1.0	4.1	2.6	1.6
Germany		1.1	1.6	0.7	5.0	2.6	1.8
Italy		(n.a.)	0.8	0.7	4.8	2.0	(n.a.)
Japan		0.0	1.5	0.5	8.4	3.0	1.8
Netherlands	−0.1	1.5	0.9	1.1	3.5	1.7	1.5
Norway		1.0	1.3	2.1	3.1	3.9	1.8
Sweden		0.6	2.1	2.2	3.1	1.5	1.8
Switzerland		1.7	1.2	1.5	3.1	−0.2	1.6
UK	0.4	1.5	1.0	0.9	2.5	1.3	1.4
USA		1.4	2.0	1.6	2.2	1.9	1.8
Arithmetic average	0.2	1.1	1.4	1.2	3.8	2.0	1.6

[a] 1701/10–1820
Source: Angus Maddison, *Phases of Capitalist Development*

TABLE II *Growth of Output (GDP at Constant Prices), 1700–1979 (Annual average compound growth rates)*

	1700–1820	1820–70	1870–1913	1913–50	1950–73	1973–79	1820–1979
Australia		(n.a.)	3.2	2.1	4.7	2.5	(n.a.)
Austria		(1.4)	2.4	0.2	5.4	3.1	2.0
Belgium		2.7	2.0	1.0	4.1	2.3	2.3
Canada		(n.a.)	3.8	2.9	5.2	3.2	(n.a.)
Denmark		1.9	2.7	2.5	4.0	2.1	2.6
Finland		(n.a.)	3.0	2.4	4.9	2.3	(n.a.)
France	0.6[a]	1.4	1.7	1.0	5.1	3.0	2.0
Germany		2.0	2.8	1.3	6.0	2.4	2.6
Italy		(n.a.)	1.5	1.4	5.5	2.6	(n.a.)
Japan		(0.4)	2.5	1.8	9.7	4.1	2.7
Netherlands	0.1	2.4	2.1	2.4	4.8	2.4	2.7
Norway		(2.2)	2.1	2.9	4.0	4.4	2.7
Sweden		(1.6)	2.8	2.8	3.8	1.8	2.5
Switzerland		(2.5)	2.1	2.0	4.5	−0.4	2.4
UK	1.1	2.4	1.9	1.3	3.0	1.3	2.0
USA		4.4	4.1	2.8	3.7	2.7	3.8
Arithmetic average	0.6	2.1	2.5	1.9	4.9	2.5	2.5

[a] 1701/10–1820
Source: Angus Maddison, *Phases of Capitalist Development*.

TABLE III *Rate of Growth of Total Output in Europe 1950–70*

| | annual average compound growth rate | |
	1950–1960	1960–1970
Austria	5.8	4.7
Belgium	2.9	4.9
Denmark	3.3	4.8
Finland	5.0	5.1
France	4.6	5.8
Germany	7.8	4.8
Greece	5.9	7.5
Ireland	1.7	3.9
Italy	5.8	5.7
Netherlands	4.7	5.1
Norway	3.2	5.0
Portugal	3.9	6.2
Spain	5.2	7.5
Sweden	3.4	4.6
Switzerland	4.4	4.5
UK	2.7	2.8
Average for Western Europe	4.4	5.2
Bulgaria	6.7	6.9[a]
Czechoslovakia	4.9	3.2[a]
East Germany	5.7	2.9[a]
Hungary	4.6	4.6[a]
Poland	4.6	4.9[a]
Rumania	5.8	6.3[a]
USSR	6.6	5.3[b]
Yugoslavia	5.7	4.7[a]
Average for Eastern Europe	5.6	4.9

[a] 1960–1968; [b] 1960–1969
Source: Carlo M. Cipolla (ed.), *The Fontana Economic History of Europe, Twentieth Century 2*

TABLE IV *Public expenditure/GDP ratios on a standardized basis*

The data in this table are measured according to the standard definitions of the outlays of government' which is the sum of lines 23, 28, 29 and 30 less line 26 in Table 9 countries for which information is available.

	1960	*1961*	*1962*	*1963*	*1964*	*1965*	*1966*	*1967*	*1968*	*1969*
A. EEC—EUROPE										
1. Belgium	30.3	29.8	30.5	31.5	30.8	32.3	33.5	34.5	36.3	36.1
2. Denmark	24.8	27.1	28.1	28.6	28.4	29.9	31.7	34.3	36.3	36.3
3. France	34.6	35.7	37.0	37.8	38.0	38.4	38.5	39.0	40.3	39.6
4. Greece	17.4	17.4	18.4	18.7	19.8	20.6	21.5	23.6	23.5	22.5
5. Ireland	28.0	29.7	29.5	30.5	31.8	33.1	33.6	34.8	35.2	36.6
6. Italy	30.1	29.4	30.5	31.1	31.8	34.3	34.3	33.7	34.7	34.2
7. Luxembourg	30.5	30.3	32.2	32.1	32.3	33.3	35.0	37.5	37.3	34.1
8. Netherlands	33.7	35.4	35.6	37.6	37.8	38.7	40.7	42.5	43.5	43.9
9. United Kingdom	32.6	33.4	34.2	35.6	33.9	36.4	35.6	38.5	39.6	41.5
10. West Germany	32.0	33.4	35.2	35.9	35.7	36.3	36.5	38.2	37.6	37.6
B. OTHER EUROPE										
11. Austria	32.1	32.3	33.6	34.7	38.2	37.9	38.3	40.5	40.6	40.3
12. Finland	26.7	26.0	27.4	29.2	30.5	31.3	32.5	33.4	33.4	31.8
13. Iceland	28.2	24.0	23.9	26.0	27.6	28.4	28.4	32.2	33.8	30.2
14. Norway	29.9	29.7	31.5	33.1	33.1	34.2	34.8	36.4	37.9	39.9
15. Portugal	17.0	19.3	18.8	20.3	20.4	20.1	20.3	20.9	20.9	20.9
16. Spain	13.7	13.0	12.8	13.0	18.7	19.6	19.5	21.1	21.3	21.7
17. Sweden	31.1	31.0	32.4	34.6	34.8	36.0	38.1	40.0	42.6	42.8
18. Switzerland										not
19. Turkey	—	—	18.0	19.1	20.5	20.6	20.6	21.0	21.9	23.1
20. Yugoslavia										not
C. NON-EUROPE										
21. Australia	22.1	23.7	23.5	23.3	23.7	25.6	25.6	26.3	25.1	25.1
22. Canada	28.9	30.0	30.0	29.5	28.9	29.1	30.1	32.1	33.0	33.5
23. Japan	20.7	20.6	23.1	23.2	23.2	22.7	23.3	22.7	22.6	21.5
24. New Zealand										not
25. United States	27.8	29.2	29.0	29.0	28.4	28.0	29.2	31.2	31.3	30.8
D. TOTAL OECD	28.5	29.5	29.9	30.2	29.9	30.1	30.8	32.2	32.5	32.1

Source: Table R8 of OECD (1982c).

OECD–UN system of accounts. The definition of public expenditure used is 'total of OECD (1982a) Vol. II. The entry for 'Total OECD' is a weighted average for those

1970	1971	1972	1973	1974	1975	1976	1977	1978	1979	1980	Increase in percentage points 1960–1980
36.5	38.0	38.8	39.1	39.4	44.5	45.1	46.6	47.9	49.5	51.7	+21.4
40.2	43.0	42.6	42.1	45.9	48.2	47.8	48.9	50.6	54.0	56.0	+31.2
38.9	39.3	38.3	38.5	39.7	43.5	44.0	44.2	45.2	45.4	46.2	+11.6
22.4	22.8	22.0	21.1	25.0	26.7	27.4	29.0	29.9	29.7	30.3	+12.9
39.7	40.5	38.8	39.0	43.0	47.5	46.8	45.5	46.4	48.9	–	n/a
34.2	36.6	38.6	37.8	37.9	43.2	42.2	42.5	46.1	45.5	45.6	+15.5
33.1	36.3	37.0	35.7	36.1	48.9	49.7	52.7	51.8	52.1	60.2	+29.7
45.5	47.5	48.1	48.7	50.8	55.9	55.9	56.0	57.5	59.5	62.5	+28.8
39.3	38.4	40.0	41.1	45.2	46.9	46.1	44.1	43.7	43.5	44.6	+12.0
37.6	38.9	39.7	40.5	43.4	47.1	46.4	46.5	46.5	46.4	46.9	+14.9
39.2	39.7	39.8	41.3	41.9	46.1	46.9	46.8	49.7	48.8	48.5	+16.4
31.3	32.8	33.2	31.9	32.9	37.1	38.3	39.5	39.1	38.5	38.2	+11.5
29.6	32.6	33.6	35.5	36.6	38.7	33.9	34.0	–	–	–	n/a
41.0	43.0	44.6	44.6	44.6	46.6	48.5	50.2	52.3	51.4	49.4	+19.5
21.6	21.3	22.7	21.3	24.7	30.3	35.1	–	–	–	–	n/a
22.2	23.6	23.2	23.0	23.1	24.7	26.0	27.5	29.3	30.5	32.4	+18.7
43.7	45.5	46.4	44.9	48.1	49.0	51.9	57.9	59.6	65.1	65.7	+34.6
available											
21.9	22.1	22.5	–	–	–	–	–	–	–	–	n/a
available											
25.5	26.2	26.3	26.8	30.4	32.4	32.9	34.3	33.7	33.2	34.1	+12.0
35.7	36.6	37.2	36.0	37.4	40.8	39.6	40.6	41.0	39.3	40.7	+11.8
19.3	20.8	21.8	22.1	24.5	27.3	27.9	29.0	31.1	31.6	32.7	+12.0
available											
32.2	32.2	31.9	31.2	32.9	35.4	34.4	33.5	33.1	32.8	33.2	+ 5.4
32.6	33.1	33.3	33.1	35.0	38.2	37.7	37.7	38.2	38.6	39.4	+10.9

TABLE V Trends in Public Expenditure in Fourteen Countries, 1955–79 Percent of GDP

Country	1955–57[a] Total spending[b]	Government consumption	Transfers and subsidies	1967–69[a] Total spending[b]	Government consumption	Transfers and subsidies	1977–79[a] Total spending[b]	Government consumption	Transfers and subsidies
Austria	29.0	12.6	11.8	36.4	14.7	14.7	46.4	17.8	19.9
Canada	25.1	13.2	6.2	33.0	17.2	8.2	40.0	20.0	12.2
Denmark	25.5	12.6	7.4	35.5	17.2	11.8	46.7	24.3	17.8
Finland	29.2	12.1	9.1	33.4	16.2	10.8	39.1	18.7	15.7
France	33.5	14.1	15.0	39.4	13.7	19.2	44.4	15.0	25.0
Italy	28.1	11.9	10.9	35.5	13.5	17.1	46.1	15.8	21.3
Japan	18.6	9.7	4.0	19.2	8.4	5.2	29.8	9.7	11.0
Netherlands	31.1	15.1	9.3	42.6	16.0	18.1	57.6	18.5	32.4
Norway	27.0	11.3	11.1	37.9	15.4	16.0	50.8	19.6	23.1
Sweden	30.2	15.6	8.2	41.3	20.2	12.3	59.9	28.4	24.1
Switzerland	n.a.	9.4	6.0	25.0	10.3	8.8	33.9	12.9	14.7
United Kingdom	32.3	16.6	7.9	38.5	17.7	11.3	43.5	20.3	15.7
United States	25.9	16.7	4.5	31.7	19.2	7.1	33.9	18.1	11.2
West Germany	30.2	12.5	12.5	33.1	14.4	13.2	43.8	19.9	18.3
OECD average (unweighted)	28.5	13.0	8.8	34.5	15.3	12.2	44.0	18.3	18.2
Standard deviation (OECD countries)	3.37	22.23	3.07	5.95	3.11	4.44	8.72	4.18	6.12

Sources: Organization for Economic Cooperation and Development, Public Expenditure Trends (Paris: OECD, 1978), table 2, pp. 14–15, and 'Public and Social Expenditure Trends' (OECD, October 1981).
[a] Three-year averages, at current prices.
[b] Includes interest on public debt and investment.

TABLE VI *Value Types by Age Cohort: Combined 1970 and 1971 Data* (Percent of Materialists [Mats.] and Post-Materialists [P.-Mats.])

Age Range of Cohort in 1971	Germany			Belgium			Italy			France			Netherlands			Britain[a]		
	Mats.	P.-Mats.	N	Mats.	P.-Mats.	N	Mats.	P.-Mats.	N	Mats.	P.-Mats.	N	Mats.	P.-Mats.	N	Mats.	P.-Mats.	N
16–25	22%	22%	(544)	20%	26%	(487)	28%	21%	(757)	25%	20%	(754)	26%	20%	(770)	29%	13%	(508)
26–35	36	14	(895)	29	16	(429)	37	13	(650)	38	13	(726)	25	14	(696)	28	10	(680)
36–45	47	9	(768)	19	16	(473)	39	9	(735)	40	12	(697)	38	11	(717)	31	8	(556)
46–55	47	7	(663)	30	11	(378)	46	6	(710)	43	10	(649)	34	12	(547)	35	6	(796)
56–65	58	4	(593)	36	9	(409)	48	6	(571)	50	5	(533)	39	7	(455)	41	6	(662)
66+	55	4	(474)	46	5	(474)	55	3	(400)	52	3	(700)	52	5	(324)	47	4	(748)
Difference between youngest and oldest groups	−33	+19		−26	+21		−27	+18		−27	+17		−19	+15		−18	+9	
Total difference	52 points			47 points			45 points			44 points			34 points			27 points		

[a] Results from a survey carried out in 1971 by the British Social Science Research Council are combined with those from our own British sample in this table.

Source: Ronald Inglehart, *The Silent Revolution.*

TABLE VII Goals of Western Publics, 1973

(Percentage choosing given goal as 1st and 2nd most important out of twelve)

Goal:	Belgium	France	Luxem-bourg	Ger-many	Nether-lands	Den-mark	Britain	Ireland	Italy	Mean Nine European Countries	United States
Fight rising prices (E)[a]	52%	43%	29%	44%	26%	24%	50%	44%	41%	39%	25%
Economic growth (E)	19	18	33	24	14	23	29	29	31	24	16
Fight crime (S)	21	20	9	21	26	21	17	25	37	22	22
Stable economy (E)	12	12	22	39	16	28	25	24	16	22	21
Maintain order (S)	10	21	28	18	18	31	11	16	17	19	20
More say on job (B)	18	13	22	12	24	20	15	20	9	17	16
Less impersonal society (B)	17	28	11	11	26	17	12	8	14	16	12
More say in government (B)	11	9	19	9	14	8	15	15	11	12	16
Protect free speech (A)	17	14	7	11	13	11	11	6	9	11	10
More beautiful cities (A)	15	9	7	4	10	7	6	5	3	7	18[b]
Ideas count (A)	7	11	9	3	10	7	4	3	5	7	8
Strong defense forces (S)	2	3	3	5	4	2	6	6	7	4	16

[a] Letters in parentheses indicate category of the given goal: (E) = Economic, (S) = Safety, (B) = Belonging, (A) = Self-Actualization.
[b] In the United States, the item was: 'Protect nature from being spoiled and polluted'.

Source: Ronald Inglehart, The Silent Revolution.

Notes

INTRODUCTION: DOCTRINE AND REALITY

1 R.H. Tawney, *The Acquisitive Society*, G. Bell & Sons, London, 1921, p.1.
2 For the notion of 'deflationary bias' see Michael Stewart, *Controlling the Economic Future: Policy Dilemmas in a Shrinking World*, Wheatsheaf, Brighton, 1983, pp. 47–81.
3 See, in particular, C. Freeman and L. Soete, *Information Technology and Employment: An Assessment*, Science Policy Research Unit, University of Sussex, 1985.
4 For the broad outlines of this story see Chapter 4.
5 I have borrowed the term 'Keynesian social democracy' from David Heald, *Public Expenditure*, Martin Robertson, Oxford, 1983.
6 F.S.L. Lyons, *Ireland Since the Famine*, Fontana, London, 1973, pp. 54–70.
7 For an illuminating discussion of this point, see Commission of the European Communities, *Eurofutures: the challenges of innovation*, (the FAST report) Butterworths, London, 1984, pp. 84–90.
8 For a characteristic expression of this view, see Michael Meacher, *Socialism with a Human Face: The Political Economy of Britain in the 1980s*, George Allen & Unwin, London, 1982.
9 Charles E. Lindblom, *Politics and Markets: The World's Political-Economic Systems*, Basic Books, New York, 1977, p. 65.
10 Harold Perkin, *The Origins of Modern English Society 1780–1880*, Routledge & Kegan Paul, paperback edition, London, 1972, pp. 17–62.
11 Andrew Gamble, *Britain in Decline: Economic Policy, Political Strategy and the British State*, Papermac, London, 1981, pp. 41–63.
12 For the utilitarian influence on the 'Westminster Model', see Ghita Ionescu, *Politics and the Pursuit of Happiness: An inquiry into the involvement of human beings in the politics of industrial society*, Longmans, London, 1984, pp. 121–5; Anthony Lester, 'Fundamental Rights in the United Kingdom: the Law and the British Constitution', *University of Pennsylvania Law Review*, vol. 125, no. 2, December 1976, pp. 337–63.

I KEYNESIAN SOCIAL DEMOCRACY

1 *Employment Policy*, Cmd 6527, HMSO., London, 1944, p. 3.
2 Harold Macmillan, *The Middle Way: A Study of the Problem of Economic and*

Social Progress in a Free and Democratic Society, Macmillan, London, 1938 (reissued 1966), p. 185.

3 Aneurin Bevan, *In Place of Fear*, republished by EP Publishing, Wakefield, 1976, pp. 144–5.

4 Quoted in Martin Holmes, *The Labour Government, 1974–9: Political Aims and Economic Reality*, Macmillan, London, 1985, p. 92.

5 For 'permeability' and the self see Brian Lee Crowley, 'The Limitations of Liberalism: The Self, the Individual and the Community in Modern British Political Thought with special reference to F. A. Hayek and Sidney and Beatrice Webb', London University Ph.D., 1985, pp. 218–77.

6 For the distinction between 'moral' and 'mechanical' reform, see Peter Clarke, *Liberals and Social Democrats*, Cambridge University Press, 1978, pp. 1–8.

7 John Maynard Keynes, *The General Theory of Employment, Interest and Money*, Macmillan, London, 1954, pp. 378–9.

8 R.J. Skidelsky, 'The Decline of Keynesian Politics', in Colin Crouch (ed.), *State and Economy in Contemporary Capitalism*, Croom Helm, London, 1979, pp. 63–4.

9 Cmd 6527 (op. cit.), para. 53.

10 William Beveridge, *Full Employment in a Free Society*, George Allen & Unwin, London, 1944, p. 199.

11 Leslie Hannah, *The Rise of the Corporate Economy*, Methuen, London, second edition, 1983, chapter 3. See also, Alan Bullock, *The Life and Times of Ernest Bevin, Vol. 1, Trade Union Leader, 1881–1940*, Heinemann, London, 1960, pp. 345–416.

12 The phrase is A.D. Chandler's, *The Visible Hand: The Managerial Revolution in American Business*, Harvard University Press, Cambridge, Mass., 1977.

13 Liberal Party, *Britain's Industrial Future: being the report of the Liberal Industrial Inquiry of 1928*, Ernest Benn, London, second impression 1977.

14 Arthur Marwick, 'Middle Opinion in the Thirties: Planning, Progress and Political "Agreement"', *English Historical Review*, vol. lxxix, 1964, pp. 293–6.

15 Robert Boothby *et al.*, *Industry and the State: A Conservative View*, Macmillan, London, 1927, p. 41.

16 Eustace Percy, first Baron Percy of Newcastle, *Democracy on Trial: a preface to an industrial policy*, John Lane The Bodley Head, London, 1931, chapters III and IV.

17 Harold Macmillan, op. cit., chapters X–XIII.

18 Douglas Jay, *The Socialist Case*, Faber & Faber, London, 1937.

19 Evan Durbin, *The Politics of Democratic Socialism: An Essay on Social Policy*, Routledge & Kegan Paul, London, 1957 impression, especially pp. 75–150 and 283–321. For a different interpretation of the 'New' Fabians of the 1930s, see Elizabeth Durbin, *New Jerusalems: The Labour Party and the Economics of Democratic Socialism*, Routledge & Kegan Paul, London, 1985.

20 G.D.H. Cole, *Guild Socialism Re-stated*, Leonard Parsons, London, 1920; Sidney and Beatrice Webb, *A Constitution for the Socialist Commonwealth of Great Britain*, Longmans Green, London, 1920. For an illuminating discussion of the debate on planning between the wars see Trevor Smith, *The Politics of the Corporate Economy*, Martin Robertson, Oxford, 1979, pp. 3–92.

21 Derek Fraser, *Evolution of the British Welfare State*, Macmillan, London, 1973; José Harris, *William Beveridge: A Biography*, Clarendon Press, Oxford, 1977, chapter 16, pp. 378–418. For a useful discussion of the historical background see Douglas E. Ashford, *The Emergence of the Welfare States*, Basil Blackwell, Oxford, 1986.

22 T.H. Marshall, *Citizenship and Social Class and other essays*, Cambridge University Press, 1950, p. 56. (My italics).

23 A.W. Dilnot, J.A. Kay and C.N. Morris, *The Reform of Social Security*, Clarendon Press, Oxford, 1984, chapter 1.

24 Barbara Wootton, *Freedom Under Planning*, George Allen & Unwin, London, 1945.

25 Friedrich A. Hayek, *The Road to Serfdom*, republished by University of Chicago Press, 1976.

26 Paul Addison, *The Road to 1945: British Politics and the Second World War*, Quartet Books, London, 1977, pp. 129–31 and 160–3; Angus Calder, *The People's War: Britain 1939–45*, Jonathan Cape, London, 1969, pp. 351–7; W.K. Hancock and M.M. Gowing, *The British War Economy*, HMSO., London, 1949, pp. 491–511.

27 Quoted in Paul Addison, op. cit., p. 19.

28 The key text is C.A.R. Crosland, *The Future of Socialism*, Jonathan Cape, London, 1956.

29 Ian Gough, *The Political Economy of the Welfare State*, Macmillan, 1979, pp. 76–8; Alan T. Peacock and Jack Wiseman, *The Growth of Public Expenditure in the United Kingdom*, Oxford University Press, London, 1961, p. 86.

30 Crosland, op. cit., pp. 390–1.

31 Keith Middlemas, *Politics in Industrial Society: The Experience of the British System since 1911*, André Deutsch, London, 1979.

2 THE COLLAPSE OF CONSENSUS

1 Quoted in Leo Pliatzky, *Getting and Spending: Public Expenditure, Employment and Inflation*, Basil Blackwell, Oxford, revised edition, 1984, p. 150.

2 Quoted in Patrick Cosgrave, *Margaret Thatcher: Prime Minister*, Arrow Books, London, 1979, p. 197.

3 Alec Cairncross, *Years of Recovery: British Economic Policy*, Methuen, London, 1985, p. 303.

4 For 'planning' under the post-war Labour Government see Cairncross, op. cit., (especially chapter 11); Jacques Leruez, *Economic Planning and*

Politics in Britain, (trans. Martin Harrison), Martin Robertson, London, 1975, pp. 17–77; Joan Mitchell, *Groundwork to Economic Planning*, Secker & Warburg, London, 1966, pp. 55–120; Kenneth Morgan, *Labour in Power 1945–51*, Clarendon Press, Oxford, 1984, especially chapters 2, 3, 8 and 9; Andrew Shonfield, *Modern Capitalism: The Changing Balance of Public and Private Power*, Oxford University Press, London, 1965, pp. 88–99.

5   Mitchell, op. cit., chapter IV.

6   Cairncross, op. cit., pp. 328–32.

7   Angus Maddison, 'Economic Policy and Performance in Europe', in Carlo M. Cipolla (ed.), *The Fontana Economic History of Europe: The Twentieth Century, Part Two*, Collins/Fontana Books, London, 1976, p. 478.

8   For the 'stop-go cycle' and its effects see Samuel Brittan, *Steering the Economy*, Secker & Warburg, London, 1969; Richard N. Cooper, 'The Balance of Payments', in Richard E. Caves and associates, *Britain's Economic Prospects*, George Allen & Unwin, London, 1968, pp. 147–97; Christopher Dow, *The Management of the British Economy 1945–1960*, Cambridge University Press, 1964, especially chapters III, XV and XVI; Peter Oppenheimer, 'Muddling Through: the economy 1951–64' in V. Bogdanor and R. J. Skidelsky (eds), *The Age of Affluence*, Macmillan, London, 1970, pp. 117–67; and G.D.N. Worswick, 'The British economy 1950–1959' in G.D.N. Worswick and P. Ady (eds), *The British Economy in the Nineteen-Fifties*, Clarendon Press, Oxford, 1962, pp. 1–74. For the view that it did not lower the rate of growth see Alec Cairncross, 'The Post-War Years 1945–77' in Roderick Floud and Donald McCloskey (eds), *The Economic History of Britain since 1700, Vol. 2, 1860 to the 1970s*, Cambridge University Press, 1981, pp. 370–416.

9   Christopher Dow, op. cit., p. 398.

10 For these arguments see F.T. Blackaby, 'Narrative 1960–74' in (ed.) *British Economic Policy 1960–74*, Cambridge University Press, 1978, pp. 11–76; Brittan, op. cit., especially chapter 6; Dow, op. cit., especially chapter 16; and Leruez, op. cit., pp. 81–95. For later arguments for an incomes policy see Hugh Clegg, *How to Run an Incomes Policy and Why We Made Such a Mess of the Last One*, Heinemann, London, 1971, and Aubrey Jones, *The New Inflation: the politics of prices and incomes*, Penguin Books, Harmondsworth, 1973.

11 My account is based on Blackaby op. cit., Brittan op. cit., chapters 7 and 8; R.J. Flanagan, David Soskice and Lloyd Ulman, *Unionism, economic stabilisation and incomes policies: European experience*, The Brookings Institution, Washington D.C., 1983, chapter 7; Leruez, op. cit., pp. 96–285; Keith Middlemas, *Industry, Unions and Government: Twenty-One Years of NEDC*, Macmillan, London, 1983; Pliatzky, op. cit., chapters 3–5; Trevor Smith, op. cit., pp. 138–92; and Michael Stewart, *The Jekyll and Hyde Years: Politics and Economic Policy since 1964*, J.M. Dent, London, 1977.

12 Flanagan, Soskice and Ulman, op. cit., pp. 429–30.

13 Samuel H. Beer, *Britain Against Itself: the political contradictions of collectivism*, Faber & Faber, London, 1982, chapters IV and V.

14 Between 1960 and 1974 the United Kingdom's share in total OECD manufacturing output fell from 9.6 per cent to 5.7 per cent; manufacturing imports as a percentage of sales plus imports minus exports rose from 8 per cent in 1960 to 19 per cent in 1974. C.J. Brown and T.D. Sheriff, 'De-industrialisation: a background paper', in Frank Blackaby (ed.), *De-Industrialisation*, Heinemann Educational, London, 1978, pp. 233–62.

15 For the 'Green Book', and the Government's treatment of it, see Middlemas, *Industry, Unions and Government*, pp. 23–5.

16 Angus Maddison, op. cit., p. 478.

17 Angus Maddison, *Phases of Capitalist Development*, Oxford University Press, New York, 1982, p. 44.

18 Flanagan, Soskice and Ulman, op. cit., chapter 7.

19 In August 1978 a MORI poll showed 41 per cent preferring Labour's policies on industrial relations against 32 per cent who preferred the Conservatives' policies. By February 1979 the proportion preferring Labour was down to 26 per cent and the proportion preferring Conservative up to 39 per cent. David Butler and Denis Kavanagh, *The British General Election of 1979*, Macmillan, 1980, p. 131.

20 Sam Brittan, op. cit., pp. 273–5.

21 For an interesting discussion of this point, see Alan Cawson, *Corporatism and Welfare: Social Policy and State Intervention in Britain*, Heinemann Educational, London, 1982, especially chapters 4–6.

22 For the inability of successive governments to answer the 'union question' see Denis Barnes and Eileen Reid, *Governments and Trade Unions: The British Experience 1964–79*, Heinemann Educational, London, 1980.

23 Between 1965 and 1974, gross fixed capital formation per head of employed labour in manufacturing increased from $460 to $920 in the United Kingdom, from $772 to $2357 in Belgium, from $905 to $2288 in France, from $367 to $1469 in Italy and from $460 to $2141 in Japan. Brown and Sheriff op. cit., p. 247.

24 For a good example of the analogy see J.P. Mackintosh, chapter 5, 'Political Institutions' in *Reshaping Britain*, PEP broadsheet no. 548, December 1974, quoted in David Marquand (ed.), *John P. Mackintosh on Parliament and Social Democracy*, Longman, London, 1982, pp. 112–35.

25 For a characteristic expression of dismay at the unions' failure to deliver see Denis Barnes and Eileen Reid, op. cit., pp. 221–8.

26 Quoted in Leruez, op. cit., p. 283.

3 NEO-LIBERALS AND NEO-SOCIALISTS

1 Sir Keith Joseph, *Stranded on the Middle Ground*, Centre for Policy Studies, London, 1976, p. 25.

2 Tony Benn, *Parliament, People and Power: Agenda for a Free Society*, Interviews with New Left Review, Verso Editions and NLB, London, 1982, p. 33.

3 For a neo-socialist expression of this view see Claus Offe, *Contradictions of the Welfare State*, (ed. John Keane), Hutchinson, London, 1984, especially chapter 8.

4 Friedrich Engels, *Anti-Duhring*, Foreign Languages Publishing House, Moscow, 1954, p. 389.

5 Albert O. Hirschman, *The Passions and the Interests: Political Arguments for Capitalism before Its Triumph*, Princeton University Press, 1977.

6 For examples of these attitudes see W.H. Greenleaf, *The British Political Tradition, Vol. 1 The Rise of Collectivism*, Methuen, London, 1983, pp. 211–21.

7 For characteristic expressions of this view see Milton Friedman, *Capitalism and Freedom*, University of Chicago Press, reissued 1982; F.A. Hayek, *The Constitution of Liberty*, Routledge & Kegan Paul, London, reprinted 1976.

8 For a brilliant exposition of this point so far as Hayek and the Webbs are concerned see Brian Lee Crowley, op. cit.

9 The clearest expression of this thesis by a British writer is in Ian Gough, op. cit., The *locus classicus* is James O'Connor, *The Fiscal Crisis of the State*, St Martin's Press, New York, 1975.

10 See in particular Stuart Holland, *The Socialist Challenge*, Quartet Books, London, 1975.

11 For the outlines of the 'alternative strategy' see Michael Meacher, op. cit., pp. 171–96.

12 For 'overload' see Michel Crozier *et al.*, *The Crisis of Democracy: Report on the governability of democracies to the Trilateral Commission*, New York University Press, 1975; James Douglas, 'The Overloaded Crown', *British Journal of Political Science*, vol. 6, pp. 483–505; Anthony King, 'Overload: Problems of Governing in the 1970s', *Political Studies*, vol. 23, 1975, pp. 162–174; Richard Rose, 'Ungovernability: is there fire behind the smoke?', *Political Studies*, vol. 27, 1979, pp. 351–70; Richard Rose and Guy Peters, *Can Government Go Bankrupt?* Macmillan, London, 1979.

13 John Burton, *Picking Losers..? The political economy of industrial policy*, Hobart Paper 99, Institute of Economic Affairs, London, 1983.

14 J.M. Buchanan, John Burton and R.E. Wagner, *The Consequences of Mr Keynes*, Hobart paper 78, Institute of Economic Affairs, London, 1978, p. 57.

15 This is the central thesis of Rose and Peters, op. cit.

16 For characteristically lucid expositions of these arguments see F. A. Hayek, *1980s Unemployment and the Unions: The Distortion of Relative Prices by Monopoly in the Labour Market*, Hobart paper 87, Institute of Economic Affairs, London, second edition 1984 and *The Constitution of Liberty* (op. cit.), chapters 18 and 21.

17 For the 'price-auction' view see Lester Thurow, *Dangerous Currents: The State of Economics*, Vintage Books, New York, 1984.

18 Samuel Brittan, 'The Economic Contradictions of Democracy', *British Journal of Political Science*, vol. 5, April 1975, pp. 129–59; 'Inflation and Democracy' in Fred Hirsch and John H. Goldthorpe (eds), *The Political Economy of Inflation*, Martin Robertson, London, 1978, pp. 161–85; *The Economic Consequences of Democracy*, Temple Smith, London, 1977, especially chapters 21 to 23 and *The Role and Limits of Government: essays in political economy*, Temple Smith, London, 1983, especially chapter 1. For critiques of the 'political market-place' argument see Nick Bosanquet, *After The New Right*, Heinemann Educational, London, 1983 and Brian Barry, 'Does Democracy Cause Inflation? Political Ideas of Some Economists?' in Leon N. Lindberg and Charles S. Maier (eds), *The Politics of Inflation and Economic Stagnation*, The Brookings Institution, Washington DC, 1985, pp. 280–317.

19 Joseph Schumpeter, *Capitalism, Socialism and Democracy*, George Allen & Unwin, London, 1979 impression, p. 269.

20 Gordon Tullock, 'Bureaucracy and the Growth of Government' in *The Taming of Government*, IEA Readings 21, Institute of Economic Affairs, London, 1979, p. 24.

21 Gordon Tullock, *The Vote Motive*, Hobart paperback 9, Institute of Economic Affairs, London, 1976.

22 James M. Buchanan and Richard E. Wagner, *Democracy in Deficit: The Political Legacy of Lord Keynes*, Academic Press, New York, 1977, pp. 64–5, quoted in Brian Barry, op. cit., p. 284.

23 Crozier *et al.*, op. cit.

24 'the ideas of economists and political philosophers, both when they are right and when they are wrong, are more powerful than is commonly understood. Indeed the world is ruled by little else'. J.M. Keynes, *The General Theory* (op. cit.), p. 383.

25 For the first see Buchanan, Burton and Wagner, op. cit. One of the chief exponents of the second was the economic commentator, Peter Jay (William Keegan, *Mrs Thatcher's Economic Experiment*, Penguin Books, Harmondsworth, 1984, p. 79).

26 F.A. Hayek, *Law, Legislation and Liberty*, vol. 3, *The Political Order of a Free People*, Routledge & Kegan Paul, London, 1979, pp. 111–27.

27 For an illuminating discussion of this point see Andrew Gamble, 'The Free Economy and the Strong State' in Ralph Miliband and John Savile (eds), *The Socialist Register 1979*, Merlin Press, London, 1979, pp. 1–25.

28 Hayek, *The Political Order of a Free People*, pp. 163–5.

29 Sir Keith Joseph, *Reversing the Trend – a critical re-appraisal of Conservative economic and social policies*, Barry Rose, Chichester and London, 1975, p. 57.

30 For the public-expenditure implications of changes in family structures see Andrew Shonfield (ed. Zuzanna Shonfield), *The Use of Public Power*, Oxford University Press, 1982, p. 23; for the correlation between increasing public expenditure and increases in the participation rates for women see Rudolf Klein, 'Public Expenditure in an Inflationary World' in Leon N. Lindberg and Charles S. Maier (eds), *The Politics of*

Inflation and Economic Stagnation, The Brookings Institution, Washington D C., 1985, pp. 202–3.

31   J.M. Keynes, *The Economic Consequences of Mr Churchill*, Hogarth Press, London, 1925, p. 23.

32   Hayek, *1980s Unemployment and the Unions*, p. 21.

4 STATES AND MARKETS

1   Adam Smith, *An Inquiry into the Nature and Causes of the Wealth of Nations*, ed. with an introduction by Edwin Cannan, University of Chicago Press, 1976, pp. 478–9.

2   Friedrich List, *The National System of Political Economy*, translated by Sampson S. Lloyd, Longmans Green, London, 1909, p. 138.

3   OECD, *Economic Outlook*, vol. 41, OECD, Paris, June 1987, pp. 166–7.

4   Ibid.

5   Frank Blackaby, 'Deindustrialisation', paper presented to Manchester Statistical Society, 13 January, 1981.

6   National Economic Development Council, *Information Technology*, NEDC (84) 40, 22 May 1984.

7   House of Lords, Session 1984–85, Report from the Select Committee on Overseas Trade, (the 'Aldington Report') volume 1, *Report*, HMSO, London, 30 July 1985, p. 7.

8   For productivity see Richard E. Caves, 'Productivity Differences among Industries', in Richard E. Caves and Lawrence B. Krause (eds), *Britain's Economic Performance*, The Brookings Institution, Washington DC., 1980, pp. 135–86; for R and D expenditure, C. Freeman, 'Technical Innovation and British Trade Performance', in Frank Blackaby (ed.) *De-industrialisation* (op. cit.), pp. 56–77.

9   Margaret Sharp, Geoffrey Shepherd and David Marsden, 'Structural Adjustment in the United Kingdom Manufacturing Industry', World Employment Programme research working paper, ILO, Geneva, 1983, p. 52.

10   James E. Alt, *The Politics of Economic Decline: economic management and political behaviour in Britain since 1964*, Cambridge University Press, 1979, p. 264.

11   Ibid., p. 265.

12   David Butler and Donald Stokes, *Political Change in Britain*, Macmillan, London, 1969, pp. 401–18.

13   Hugh Heclo and Aaron Wildavsky, *The Private Government of Public Money: Community and Policy inside British Politics*, Macmillan, second edition, London, 1981.

14   James E. Alt and K. Alec Chrystal, *Political Economics*, Wheatsheaf, Brighton, 1983, chapter 10.

15   Pliatzky, op. cit., p. 218.

16   Between 1978–79 and 1985–86 the proportion of public expenditure

going to health and personal social services increased from 13.9 per cent to 15.0 per cent; on law and order from 3.7 per cent to 4.6 per cent; on defence from 11.3 per cent to 13.1 per cent; and on agriculture from 1.5 per cent to 2.1 per cent. In the same period, the proportions going to aid to industry fell from 5.1 per cent to 2.9 per cent; to housing from 7.6 per cent to 4.0 per cent and on education from 14.3 per cent to 12.7 per cent. H. M. Treasury, *The Government's Expenditure Plans 1986–87 to 1988–89*, vol. 1, Cmnd. 9702–I, HMSO, London, January 1986, p. 20.

17 Pliatzky, op. cit., pp. 83–5.

18 David Heald, op. cit., table 2.3, pp. 30–1.

19 Ibid.

20 For 'social expenditures' as a percentage of GDP in the EEC of the 1960s and early 1970s see Peter Flora and Arnold J. Heidenheimer, *The Development of Welfare States in Europe and America*, Transaction Books, New Brunswick, New Jersey, paperback edition, 1982, p. 319; for 'transfers and subsidies' as a percentage of GDP in selected OECD countries in the 1950s, 1960s and 1970s see Rudolf Klein, 'Public Expenditure in an Inflationary World', op. cit., p. 204.

21 For the alleged 'scramble for subsidies', see Beer, op. cit., pp. 63–76.

22 John Zysman, 'Inflation and the Politics of Supply', in Lindberg and Maier, op. cit., pp. 140–71.

23 Ibid.

24 Lindblom, op. cit.

25 Adam Smith, op. cit., p. 17.

26 Harold Perkin, 'The State and Economic Growth: An International Perspective', lecture delivered at Salford University, 15 September 1983.

27 W.O. Henderson, *The Rise of German Industrial power 1834–1914*, Temple Smith, London, 1975, pp. 7–80; for the *Seehandlung*, W.O. Henderson, *The State and the Industrial Revolution in Prussia 1740–1870*, Liverpool University Press, 1958, chapter 8.

28 Henderson, *The Rise of German Industrial Power*, pp. 176–7.

29 J. Hirschmeier and T. Yui, *The Development of Japanese Business 1600–1980*, Allen & Unwin, London, 1981, especially pp. 86–8; Takafusa Nakamura (trans. Robert A. Feldman), *Economic Growth in Prewar Japan*, Yale University Press, New Haven and London, 1983, pp. 59–76.

30 Seymour Martin Lipset, *The First New Nation: the United States in Historical and Comparative Perspective*, Heinemann, London, 1964, pp. 45–60.

31 Robert Lively, 'The American System: A Review Article', *The Business History Review* 29 (1955), p. 81, quoted in Lipset, op. cit., p. 54.

32 Ronald Dore, 'Industrial Policy and How the Japanese Do It', *Catalyst*, Spring 1986, pp. 45–58.

33 Chalmers Johnson, *MITI and the Japanese Miracle: The Growth of Industrial Policy, 1925–1975*, Stanford University Press, Stanford, California, 1982. For the 'economic general staff', see chapter 4.

34 Ira C. Magaziner and Thomas M. Hout, *Japanese Industrial Policy*, Policy Studies Institute, London, January 1980, p. 54.

35 Ibid., pp. 6–10.

36 Lawrence G. Franko, *The Threat of Japanese Multinationals – How the West Can Respond*, John Wiley & Sons, Chichester, 1983, pp. 18–22.

37 John Zysman, *Governments, Markets and Growth: Financial Systems and the Politics of Industrial Change*, Cornell University Press, Ithaca and London, 1983, pp. 234–51.

38 Chalmers Johnson, op. cit., p. 318.

39 Quoted in Richard F. Kuisel, *Capitalism and the state in modern France: Renovation and economic management in the twentieth century*, Cambridge University Press, 1981, p. 178.

40 This account of French post-war planning is based on Kuisel, op. cit., chapters 7–9; Shonfield, op. cit., especially chapters 5, 7 and 8; and Zysman, *Governments, Markets and Growth* (op. cit.), chapter 3.

41 Gøsta Esping-Andersen, *Politics Against Markets: The Social Democratic Road to Power*, Princeton University Press, New Jersey, 1985, pp. 229–35.

42 Karl Hardach, *The Political Economy of Germany in the Twentieth Century*, University of California Press, Berkeley, California, pp. 140–204; Shonfield, op. cit., chapters 11 and 12; Zysman, *Governments, Markets and Growth*, pp. 251–65.

43 Friedrich List, op. cit., pp. 108–260.

44 Zysman, *Governments, Markets and Growth*, p. 40.

45 For an illuminating discussion of this point see Lester Thurow. *The Zero-Sum Society: Distribution and the Possibilities for Economic Change*, Penguin Books, Harmondsworth, 1981.

46 Mancur Olson, *The Rise and Decline of Nations*, Yale University Press, New Haven and London, 1982.

47 This is the central thesis of F.A. Hayek, *The Mirage of Social Justice* (volume 2 of *Law, Legislation and Liberty*, op. cit.).

5 THE POLITICS OF ECONOMIC DECLINE

1 Quoted in G.C. Allen, *The British Disease*, Hobart Paper 67, Institute of Economic Affairs, 1979.

2 Martin J. Wiener, *English Culture and the Decline of the Industrial Spirit 1850–1980*, Cambridge University Press, 1981, pp. 167–70.

3 A.C. Floud, 'Britain 1860–1914: a survey' in Ronald Floud and Donald McCloskey *The Economic History of Britain since 1700, vol. 2, 1860 to the 1970s*, Cambridge University Press, 1981.

4 Crouzet, op. cit., pp. 395–6; David Landes, *The Unbound Prometheus: Technological Change and Industrial Development in Western Europe from 1750 to the Present*, Cambridge University Press, 1969, p. 320.

5 Landes, loc. cit., p. 331.

6 Crouzet, op. cit., p. 378.

7   Peter Mathias, *The First Industrial Nation: An Economic History of Britain 1700–1914*, Methuen, New York, 1983, p. 393.

8   W.A. Lewis, *Growth and Fluctuations 1870–1913*, George Allen & Unwin, London, 1978, p. 123.

9   D.H. Aldcroft, 'Introduction' in D.H. Aldcroft (ed.), *The Development of British Industry and Foreign Competition 1875–1914*, University of Toronto Press, 1968, p. 21.

10 Lewis, op. cit., p. 129.

11 David Landes, op. cit., p. 323.

12 Alfred Maizels, *Growth and Trade*, Cambridge University Press, 1970, p. 192.

13 Aldcroft, op. cit., p. 23.

14 Lewis, op. cit., p. 120.

15 W.B. Walker, 'Britain's Industrial Performance 1850–1950: a failure to adjust', in Keith Pavitt (ed.), *Technical Innovation and British Economic Performance*, Macmillan, London, 1980, p. 27.

16 Maizels, op. cit., pp. 276–7.

17 Aldcroft, op. cit., pp. 23–4; Maizels, op. cit., pp. 196–7.

18 Maizels, op. cit., p. 295.

19 D.H. Aldcroft, 'The Mercantile Marine' in Aldcroft, op. cit., pp. 326–363.

20 M.W. Kirby, *The Decline of British Economic Power since 1870*, George Allen & Unwin, London, 1981, p. 138.

21 Crouzet, op. cit., pp. 359–70; Sidney Pollard, *The Development of the British Economy 1914–1980*, Edward Arnold, London, 1983, p. 10.

22 For the bicycle industry see S.B. Saul, 'The Engineering Industry' in Aldcroft, op. cit., pp. 213–6; Mathias, op. cit., p. 356.

23 See in particular Donald McCloskey, *Enterprise and Trade in Victorian Britain: essays in Victorian economics*, George Allen & Unwin, London, 1981.

24 My account of the way in which they did so is based on Elie Halevy, *A history of the English People in the Nineteenth Century*, Vol. V, *Imperialism and the Rise of Labour*, Ernest Benn, London, second edition, 1951; Richard Jay, *Joseph Chamberlain: A Political Study*, Clarendon Press, Oxford, 1981; G.R. Searle, *The Quest for National Efficiency: A Study in British Politics and Political Thought*, Basil Blackwell, Oxford, 1971 and Bernard Semmel, *Imperialism and Social Reform: English Social-Imperial Thought 1895–1914*, Allen & Unwin, London, 1960. I have also learned a lot from Andrew Gamble, *Britain in Decline* (op. cit.), pp. 166–74.

25 Quoted in Bernard Semmel, op. cit., pp. 62–3.

26 For the free-trade empire see Bernard Semmel, *The Rise of Free Trade Imperialism: Classical Political Economy, the Empire of Free Trade and Imperialism*, Cambridge University Press, 1970.

27 Quoted in Jay, op. cit., p. 260.

28 For the Social Liberals see Peter Clarke, *Liberals and Social Democrats*, (op. cit.); Michael Freeden, *The New Liberalism: An Ideology of Social Reform*, Clarendon Press, Oxford, 1978; and L.T. Hobhouse, *Liberalism*, Home University Library, London, 1911.

29 Freeden, op. cit., especially pp. 128–34.

30 Leopold Amery, quoted in Jay, op. cit., pp. 271–2.

31 Ibid., p. 311.

32 Sidney Pollard, op. cit., p. 2.

33 Semmel, *Imperialism and Social Reform*, pp. 57–82.

34 B.W. Alford, 'British Industry Between the Wars' in Floud and McCloskey, op. cit., pp. 308–31.

35 Ibid.

36 The chief proponent of this view is H.W. Richardson in 'The Basis of Economic Recovery in the Nineteen-Thirties: a review and a new interpretation', *Economic History Review*, 2nd Series, vol. 15, 1962–63, pp. 344–63.

37 Alford, op. cit.

38 Wayne Lewchuk, 'The Motor Vehicle Industry', in Bernard Elbaum and William Lazonick (eds), *The Decline of the British Economy*, Clarendon Press, Oxford, 1986.

39 Neil K. Buxton, 'Introduction' in Neil K. Buxton and Derek H. Aldcroft (eds), *British Industry Between the Wars: instability and industrial development 1919–1939*, Scolar Press, London, paperback edition, 1983, pp. 9–23.

40 Ibid., p. 21.

41 Middlemas, *Politics in Industrial Society*, (op. cit.), pp. 229–30.

42 *The Economic Consequences of Mr Churchill* (op. cit.).

43 Keith Middlemas and John Barnes, *Baldwin: A Biography*, Weidenfeld & Nicolson, London, 1969, especially chapter 12, pp. 278–316.

44 For the details see R.J. Skidelsky, *Politicians and the Slump: the Labour Government of 1929–1931*, Macmillan, London, 1967.

45 W.H. Janeway, 'The Economic Policy of the Second Labour Government 1929–1931', Cambridge University Ph.D. thesis, p. 93.

46 The details are to be found in David Marquand, *Ramsay MacDonald*, Jonathan Cape, London, 1977, chapters 23 and 24.

6 A STATE OF PERFECT FREEDOM

1 Quoted in Lawrence Stone, 'The Results of the English Revolutions of the Seventeenth Century', in J.G.A. Pocock (ed.), *The Three British Revolutions: 1641, 1688, 1776*, Princeton University Press, New Jersey, 1980, p. 35.

2 Matthew Arnold, *Culture and Anarchy*, ed. J. Dover Wilson, Cambridge University Press, 1966, p. 75.

3 Speech to the TUC September, 1956. Quoted in Geoffrey Goodman, *The Awkward Warrior Frank Cousins: His Life and Times*, Spokesman, Nottingham, 1979, p. 134.

4 See, in particular, Martin J. Wiener, *English Culture and the Decline of the Industrial Spirit 1850–1980*, Cambridge University Press, 1981.

5 For this view see Olson, op. cit.

6   For characteristic expressions of this view, see Corelli Barnett, *The Collapse of British Power*, Alan Sutton, Gloucester, 1984 and *The Audit of War: the illusion and reality of Britain as a great nation*, Macmillan, London, 1986.

7   Robert Reich, *The Next American Frontier: a provocative program for economic renewal*, Penguin Books, New York, 1984.

8   Alexander Gerschenkron, 'Economic Backwardness in Historical Perspective' in A. Gerschenkron (ed.), *Economic Backwardness in Historical Perspective*, Harvard University Press, Cambridge, Mass., 1966, pp. 5–30.

9   Andrew Shonfield, *Modern Capitalism*, pp. 93–4.

10 W.H. Greenleaf, *The British Political Tradition*, vol. 1, p. 63. Barnett, *The Audit of War*, tries to show that Britain's wartime economy was less efficient than had hitherto been supposed, but his examples seem to me to reveal inefficiency in the *peacetime* economy, not in the wartime one.

11 Alan Cawson, op. cit., p. 67.

12 For the differences between British and continental attitudes to the state see Kenneth Dyson, *The State Tradition in Western Europe: A Study of an Idea and an Institution*, Martin Robertson, Oxford, 1980.

13 For 'patrimonial' power see Max Weber, *The Theory of Social and Economic Organisation*, ed. with an introduction by Talcott Parsons, The Free Press, New York, 1947, pp. 346–58.

14 John G. Gagliardo, *Enlightened Despotism*, Thomas Y. Crowell, New York, 1967. See also Charles Tilley, 'Reflections on the History of European State-making' in (ed.) *The Formation of National States in Western Europe*, Princeton University Press, New Jersey, 1975.

15 Christopher Hill, *The Century of Revolutions 1603–1714*, Thomas Nelson, Edinburgh, 1961, pp. 111–92.

16 The term is, of course, borrowed from C.B. Macpherson, *The Political Theory of Possessive Individualism, Hobbes to Locke*, Oxford University Press, paperback edition 1985.

17 James Bulpitt, *Territory and power in the United Kingdom: an interpretation*, Manchester University Press, 1983.

18 Olson, op. cit.

19 Colin Leys, *Politics in Britain: An Introduction*, Heinemann Educational, London, 1983, pp. 41.

20 Colin Crouch, 'Conditions for Trade Union Wage Restraint' in Lindberg and Maier, op. cit., pp. 105–39.

21 Wolfgang Streeck, *Industrial Relations in West Germany: A Case Study of the Car Industry*, Heinemann, London, 1984, especially chapter 8.

22 Gerhard Lehmbruch, 'Consociational Democracy, Class Conflict and the New Corporatism' in Philippe C. Schmitter and Gerhard Lehmbruch (eds), *Trends Towards Corporatist Intermediation*, Sage Publications, London and Beverly Hills, 1979, pp. 55–8 and 'Introduction: Neo-Corporatism in Comparative Perspective' in Philippe C. Schmitter and Gerhard Lehmbruch (eds), *Patterns of Corporatist Policy Making*, Sage Publications, London and Beverly Hills, 1982, pp. 16–19; Bernd Marin,

'Austria – The Paradigm Case of Liberal Corporatism?' in Wyn Grant (ed.), *The Political Economy of Corporatism*, Macmillan, London, 1985, pp. 89–125.

23 Streeck, op. cit., pp. 141–2.

24 For neo-corporatism see, in particular, Suzanne Berger, *Organising Interests in Western Europe: pluralism, corporatism and the transformation of politics*, Cambridge University Press, 1981; Alan Cawson, op. cit., John H. Goldthorpe (ed.), *Order and Conflict in Contemporary Capitalism*, Clarendon Press, Oxford, 1984; Wyn Grant, op. cit.; Ghita Ionescu, *Centripetal Politics: Government and the New Centres of Power*, Hart-Davis MacGibbon, London, 1975; Philippe C. Schmitter and Gerhard Lehmbruch (eds), *Trends Towards Corporatist Intermediation*, Sage Publications, London and Beverly Hills, 1979 and *Patterns of Corporatist Policy Making*, Sage Publications, London and Beverly Hills, 1982; Andrew Shonfield (ed. Zuzanna Shonfield), *In Defence of the Mixed Economy*, Oxford University Press, 1984, pp. 127–56; Wolfgang Streeck and Philippe C. Schmitter (eds), *Private Interest Government: Beyond Market and State*, Sage Publications, London, 1985.

25 Philippe C. Schmitter, 'Neo-Corporatism and the State' in Wyn Grant, op. cit., p. 37.

26 The term comes from Keith Middlemas, *Politics in Industrial Society* (op. cit.).

27 Bernd Marin, op. cit.

28 Andrew Martin, 'Wages, Profits and Investment in Sweden', in Lindberg and Maier, op. cit., pp. 403–66; Ramon Mishra, *The Welfare State in Crisis: Social Thought and Social Change*, Wheatsheaf, Brighton, 1984, pp. 115–9.

29 Wyn Grant and David Marsh, *The Confederation of British Industry*, Hodder & Stoughton, London, 1977.

30 Alan Fox, *History and Heritage: The Social Origins of the British Industrial Relations System*, Allen & Unwin, London, 1985, chapters 1–4.

31 Robert Currie, *Industrial Politics*, Oxford University Press, 1979, p. 31.

32 Martin J. Wiener, op. cit.

33 Harold Perkin, *The Origins of Modern English Society* (op. cit.), chapters VII and VIII.

34 Ibid., p. 436.

35 David S. Landes, op. cit., p. 354.

36 For a characteristic expression of this view see Harold Lever and George Edwards, 'Banking on Britain' in David Coates and John Hillyard (eds), *The Economic Decline of Modern Britain: The Debate Between Left and Right*, Wheatsheaf, Brighton, 1986, pp. 180–6.

37 Alistair Mant, *The Rise and Fall of the British Manager*, Pan Books, London, 1979, p. 98.

38 For an interesting expression of this view see John H. Goldthorpe, 'The Current Inflation: Towards a Sociological Account' in Fred Hirsch and John H. Goldthorpe (eds), *The Political Economy of Inflation*, Martin Robertson, London, 1978, pp. 204–10.

39 For an illuminating comparison between the 'outputs' in Sweden and in Britain see Richard Scase, *Social Democracy in Capitalist Society: Working-Class Politics in Britain and Sweden*, Croom Helm, London, 1977.

40 Ronald Dore, 'The Confucian Recipe for Industrial Success', *Government and Opposition*, volume 20, no. 2, spring 1985, pp. 213–4.

41 Ronald Dore, *British Factory – Japanese Factory: The Origins of National Diversity in Industrial Relations*, University of California Press, Berkeley and Los Angeles, 1973.

7 CLUB GOVERNMENT IN DISARRAY

1 A.V. Dicey, *Introduction to the Study of the Law of the Constitution*, Macmillan, London, 1950 edition, pp. 68–70.

2 For the Benthamite views of representation see Jack Lively and John Rees, *Utilitarian Logic and Politics*, Clarendon Press, Oxford, 1978, pp. 34–51. For Bentham's view of sovereignty see H.L.A. Hart, *Essays on Bentham, Studies in Jurisprudence and Political Theory*, Clarendon Press, Oxford, 1982, especially chapter IX.

3 Dicey, op. cit., p. 145.

4 Anthony Lester, 'Fundamental Rights in the United Kingdom' (op. cit.).

5 Dicey, op. cit., p. 199.

6 Ibid., p. 83.

7 J.P. Mackintosh, *The Government and Politics of Britain*, Hutchinson, London, 1977 edition, pp. 160–5 and 174–5.

8 Ibid., pp. 89–92 and 104–6; Samuel H. Beer, *Modern British Politics: Parties and Pressure Groups in the Collectivist Age*, Faber & Faber, London, 1982 edition, chapter XII, pp. 318–51.

9 J.J. Richardson and A.G. Jordan, *Governing Under Pressure: The Policy Process in a Post-Parliamentary Democracy*, Martin Robertson, Oxford, 1979.

10 Quoted in John Morley, *The Life of William Ewart Gladstone*, Macmillan, London, 1905 edition, vol. I, p. 760.

11 Beer, *Modern British Politics* (op. cit.), pp. 86–102.

12 An NOP survey carried out for Granada Television in the early 1970s asked which was the most important institution in law making. 63 per cent said Parliament, 24 per cent said the political parties and 23 per cent said the Cabinet. Nearly half those questioned said they would go to their MP if they wished to change the laws against crime or to increase old age pensions, while only around one quarter said they would go to the government department concerned. *The State of the Nation – Parliament*, Granada Television, London, 1973, pp. 197–203.

13 Daniel Bell, *The Radical Right: The New American Right Expanded and Updated*, Doubleday, New York, 1964.

14 Gabriel A. Almond and Sidney Verba, *The Civic Culture: Political Attitudes*

and Democracy in Five Nations, Princeton University Press, New Jersey, 1963, pp. 108 and 185.

15 Ibid., for the view that Britain and the United States approximated most closely to a 'civic culture' see p. 493. For arguments implying that Britain was even closer to it than the United States see especially pp. 32 and 222–3.

16 There is a substantial literature on these changes. Useful brief accounts are to be found in Gavin Drewry, 'Select Committees and Backbench Power' in Jeffrey Jowell and Dawn Oliver (eds), *The Changing Constitution*, Clarendon Press, Oxford, 1985, pp. 127–48; Janet P. Morgan, *The House of Lords and the Labour Government*, Clarendon Press, Oxford, 1975, chapters 7 and 8, pp. 169–220; Douglas Ashford, 'At the Pleasure of Parliament: the Politics of Local Reform in Britain' in Donley T. Studlar and Jerold L. Waltman, *Dilemmas of Change in British Politics*, Macmillan, London, 1984, pp. 102–25; Vernon Bogdanor, *Devolution*, Oxford University Press, 1979; and Harry Lazer, 'The Referendum and the British Constitution' in Studlar and Waltman, op. cit., pp. 155–83.

17 M. Goldsmith and K. Newton, 'Central-Local Relations: The Irresistible Rise of Centralised Power', in H. Berrington (ed.), *Change in British Politics*, Cass, London, 1984, pp. 216–33; Douglas Ashford, 'At the Pleasure of Parliament', op. cit.

18 For the technocratic strand in the policies of the 1960s and 1970s see Beer, *Britain Against Itself*, pp. 120–6.

19 Lord Hailsham, *The Dilemma of Democracy*, Collins, London, 1978; Sir Leslie Scarman, *English Law: the New Dimension*, Stevens & Sons, London, 1975; S.E. Finer (ed.), *Adversary Politics and Electoral Reform*, Anthony Wigram, London, 1975; Lord Crowther-Hunt and Professor A.T. Peacock, Royal Commission on the Constitution 1968–1973, vol. II, *Memorandum of Dissent*, HMSO, London, October 1973, Cmnd. 5460–1.

20 Philip Norton, *Dissension in the House of Commons 1974–1979*, Clarendon Press, Oxford, 1980; *Conservative Dissidents*, Temple Smith, London, 1978.

21 Sir John Hoskyns, 'Conservatism is Not Enough', *The Political Quarterly*, volume 55, no. 1, January–March 1984, pp. 3–16; Brian Sedgemore, *The Secret Constitution: An Analysis of the Political Establishment*, Hodder & Stoughton, London, 1980.

22 Ivor Crewe *et al.*, 'Partisan Dealignment in Britain', *British Journal of Political Science*, vol. 7, 1977, pp. 129–90.

23 Dick Leonard, 'Paying for Party Politics', (PEP broadsheet no. 555), Political and Economic Planning, London, 1975.

24 For a useful discussion of the reasons see Ian Budge, David McKay *et al.*, *The New British Political System*, Longman, London, 1983, pp. 178–89.

25 Quoted in Denis Kavanagh, 'Political Culture in Great Britain: the Decline of the Civic Culture', in Gabriel A. Almond and Sidney Verba, *The Civic Culture Revisited*, Little Brown, Boston, 1980, p. 149.

26 Royal Commission on the Constitution, *Minority Report*, (op. cit.), p. 14.

27 Vivien Hart, *Distrust and Democracy: Political Distrust in Britain and America*, Cambridge University Press, 1978, pp. 38–43.

28 Alan Marsh, *Protest and Political Consciousness*, Sage Publications, London and Beverly Hills, 1977, pp. 45, 118 and 221–34.

29 Kavanagh, op. cit., p. 153.

30 For the relationship between 'righteous indignation' and protest potential, see Marsh, op. cit., pp. 101–3.

31 Ibid., p. 227.

32 Hart, op. cit., p. 28.

33 Ibid., p. 29.

34 John P. Mackintosh, 'The declining respect for the law' in David Marquand (ed.), *John P. Mackintosh on Parliament and Social Democracy*, Longmans, London, 1982, pp. 143–4.

35 Scarman, op. cit.

36 Kavanagh, op. cit., p. 170.

37 Ronald Inglehart, *The Silent Revolution: Changing Values and Political Styles Among Western Publics*, Princeton University Press, New Jersey, 1977.

38 Beer, *Britain Against Itself*, chapters IV and V, pp. 107–208.

39 Inglehart, op. cit., pp. 36–7 and 49.

40 Beer, *Britain Against Itself*, p. 128.

41 Michael J. Piore and Charles Sabel, *The Second Industrial Divide: Possibilities for Prosperity*, Basic Books, New York, 1984, especially pp. 189–92 and 205–20.

42 Denis Kavanagh, 'The Deferential English: A Comparative Critique', *Government and Opposition*, vol. 6, 1971, pp. 333–60.

43 Richard Hoggart, *The Uses of Literacy*, Chatto & Windus, London, 1957, p. 62.

44 Henry Pelling, *Popular Politics and Society in Late-Victorian Britain*, Macmillan, London 1968, especially pp. 2–18.

45 James Bulpitt, op. cit., chapters 6 and 7, pp. 164–223.

8 THE PUBLIC REALM

1 Aristotle, *Politics*, book I, ii. trans. B. Jowett, Clarendon Press, 1885, pp. 4–5.

2 Konrad Lorenz (trans. Marjorie Latzke), *On Aggression*, Methuen, London, 1979, p. 212.

3 Edmund Burke, *Reflections on the Revolution in France*, Penguin edition, Harmondsworth, 1982, p. 135.

4 Donald Schon, *Beyond the Stable State*, Temple Smith, London, 1971, chapter 2.

5 Jeremy Bentham, *An Introduction to the Principles of Morals and Legislation*, ed. J.H. Burns and H.L.A. Hart, Athlone Press, University of London, 1970, p. 12, quoted in Daniel Bell, *The Cultural Contradictions of Capitalism*, Heinemann, London, second edition, 1979, p. 257.

6 In different ways, John Stuart Mill and F.A. Hayek both seem to me to be prime examples.

7   Alasdair Macintyre, *After Virtue: a study in moral theory*, Duckworth, London, second edition, 1985, pp. 228–9.

8   Quoted in David Collard, *Altruism and Economy: A Study in Non-Selfish Economics*, Martin Robertson, Oxford, 1978, p. 176.

9   For Smith's views on what are now called public goods and on the Sovereign's duty to provide them see *The Wealth of Nations*, book V, chapter I, part III. (Chicago University Press edition vol. 2, p. 244–5).

10 Daniel Bell, *Cultural Contradictions of Capitalism*, p. 252.

11 For man as a learning animal see H.A. Simon, *The Sciences of the Artificial*, M.I.T. Press, 1969. For a summary of the findings of modern psychologists see Judith Marquand, *The Sources of Economic Growth*, Wheatsheaf, Brighton (forthcoming), chapter 4.

12 Mary Midgley, *Beast and Man: The Roots of Human Nature*, Methuen, London, 1980, especially part 4.

13 Ibid., p. 47.

14 For the way in which institutions and roles transmit values see Peter Berger and Thomas Luchman, *The Social Construction of Reality: A Treatise in the Sociology of Knowledge*, Penguin Books, Harmondsworth, reprinted 1985.

15 Colin Turnbull, *The Mountain People*, Triad/Paladin edition, London, 1984.

16 For trust as a public good see Kenneth Arrow, *The Limits of Organization*, W.W. Norton, London and New York, 1974, pp. 23–6.

17 MacIntyre, op. cit., p. 263.

18 Bell, op. cit., p. 245.

19 Ghita Ionescu, *Politics and the Pursuit of Happiness: an inquiry into the involvement of human beings in the politics of industrial society*, Longman, London, 1984, p. 43.

20 E.P. Thompson, 'The Moral Economy of the English Crowd in the Eighteenth Century', *Past and Present*, no. 50, 1971, pp. 76–136.

21 Noel W. Thompson, *The People's Science: the popular political economy of exploitation and crisis 1816–34*, Cambridge University Press, 1984.

22 Perkin, *The Origins of Modern English Society* (op. cit.), pp. 237–52.

23 Gertrude Himmelfarb, *The Idea of Poverty: England in the Early Industrial Age*, Faber & Faber, London, 1984, especially chapters VIII, IX, XVI and XIX.

24 For a useful discussion of some of these see Stefan Collini, 'Hobhouse, Bosanquet and the State', *Past and Present*, no. 72, August, 1976, pp. 86–111.

25 Karl Polanyi, *Origins of Our Time: The Great Transformation*, Victor Gollancz, London, 1945.

26 For a classic contemporary view of the growth of 'Collectivism' see A.V. Dicey, *Lectures on the Relation Between Law and Opinion in England during the Nineteenth Century*, Macmillan, London, reprinted 1963, especially chapters IV to IX, pp. 62–310.

27 David Owen, *Social Market & Social Justice*, Tawney Society, London, 1987.

28 Anthony Heath, Roger Jowell and John Curtice, *How Britain Votes*, Pergamon, Oxford, 1985, chapters 9 and 10.

29 John Rawls, *A Theory of Justice*, Clarendon Press, Oxford, 1972.

30 Ibid., pp. 105–6.

31 For 'preceptoral' relations see Lindblom, op. cit., especially chapters 4 and 21.

32 C. Argyris and D. Schon, *Organizational Learning*, Addison-Wellesley, Reading, Mass., 1978.

33 In an interview with the author.

34 Crowley, op. cit., p. 14.

35 G. Moyser, G. Parry and Neil Day, 'Political Participation in Britain: National and Local Patterns'; A.P.S.A. meeting paper, 1986, Washington D C.

36 Piore and Sabel, op. cit., pp. 303–6.

37 John Stuart Mill, *Essays on Politics and Culture*, (ed. G. Himmelfarb), New York, 1963, p. 186, quoted in Carole Pateman, *Participation and Democratic Theory*, Cambridge University Press, 1970, p. 31.

38 John Stuart Mill, *Principles of Political Economy*, Routledge & Sons, London, 1903 edition, p. 607.

39 Bruno Bettelheim, *The Informed Heart*, Penguin, Harmondsworth, 1986.

40 Robert E. Goodin, 'Laundering Preferences' in Jon Elster and Aanund Hylland (eds), *Foundations of Social Choice Theory*, Cambridge University Press, 1986, pp. 75–101.

41 Arend Lijphart, *Democracy in Plural Societies: A Comparative Exploration*, Yale University Press, New Haven and London, second printing, 1980.

42 For John Mackintosh's views on this see J.P. Mackintosh, 'Political Institutions' (op. cit.); for Sir Ian Gilmour's, *Britain Can Work*, Martin Robertson, Oxford, 1983, pp. 186–220. For a useful summary of other proposals on the same lines see David Coombes, *Representative Government and Economic Power*, Heinemann Educational, London, 1982, pp. 128–47.

43 Michael Stewart, op. cit., pp. 97–9.

Bibliography

Paul Addison, *The Road to 1945: British Politics and the Second World War*, Quartet Books, London, 1977.

D.H. Aldcroft (ed.), *The Development of British Industry and Foreign Competition 1875–1914*, University of Toronto Press, 1968.

G.C. Allen, *The British Disease*, Hobart Paper 67, Institute of Economic Affairs, London, 1979.

Gabriel A. Almond and Sidney Verba, *The Civic Culture: Political Attitudes and Democracy in Five Nations*, Princeton University Press, New Jersey, 1963.

Gabriel A. Almond and Sidney Verba, *The Civic Culture Revisited*, Little Brown, Boston, 1980.

James E. Alt, *The Politics of Economic Decline: Economic Management and Political Behaviour in Britain since 1964*, Cambridge University Press, 1979

James E. Alt and K. Alec Chrystal, *Political Economics*, Wheatsheaf Books, Brighton, 1983.

C. Argyris and D. Schon, *Organizational Learning*, Addison-Wellesley, Reading, Mass., 1978.

Kenneth Arrow, *The Limits of Organization*, W.W. Norton, London and New York, 1974.

Douglas E. Ashford, *The Emergence of the Welfare States*, Basil Blackwell, Oxford, 1986.

Denis Barnes and Eileen Reid, *Governments and Trade Unions: The British Experience 1964–79*, Heinemann Educational, London, 1980.

Corelli Barnett, *The Collapse of British Power*, Alan Sutton, Gloucester, 1984.

Corelli Barnett, *The Audit of War: the illusion and reality of Britain as a great nation*, Macmillan, London, 1986.

Brian Barry, *The Liberal Theory of Justice*, Clarendon Press, Oxford, 1973.

Samuel H. Beer, *Modern British Politics: Parties and Pressure Groups in the Collectivist Age*, Faber & Faber, London, 1982.

Samuel H. Beer, *Britain Against Itself: the political contradictions of collectivism*, Faber & Faber, London, 1982.

Daniel Bell, *The Cultural Contradictions of Capitalism*, Heinemann, London, second edition, 1979.

Tony Benn, *Parliament, People and Power: Agenda for a Free Society*, Interviews with *New Left Review*, Verso Editions and NLB, London, 1982.

Peter Berger and Thomas Luchman, *The Social Construction of Reality: A Treatise in the Sociology of Knowledge*, Penguin Books, Harmondsworth, reprinted 1985.

Suzanne Berger, *Organising Interests in Western Europe: Pluralism, Corporatism and the Transformation of Politics*, Cambridge University Press, 1981.

Bruno Bettelheim, *The Informed Heart*, Penguin Books, Harmondsworth, 1986.

William Beveridge, *Full Employment in a Free Society*, George Allen & Unwin, London, 1944.

A.H. Birch, *Representative and Responsible Government: An Essay on the British Constitution*, George Allen & Unwin, London, seventh impression, 1979.

F.T. Blackaby (ed.), *British Economic Policy 1960–74*, Cambridge University Press, 1978.

F.T. Blackaby (ed.), *De-Industrialisation*, Heinemann Educational, London, 1978.

F.T. Blackaby, 'Deindustrialisation', paper presented to Manchester Statistical Society, 13 January 1981.

Vernon Bogdanor, *Devolution*, Oxford University Press, 1979.

Vernon Bogdanor, *The People and the Party System: the referendum and electoral reform in British politics*, Cambridge University Press, 1981.

Robert Boothby *et al.*, *Industry and the State: A Conservative View*, Macmillan, London, 1927.

Nick Bosanquet, *After The New Right*, Heinemann Educational, London, 1983.

Samuel Brittan, *Steering the Economy*, Secker & Warburg, London, 1969.

Samuel Brittan, 'The Economic Contradictions of Democracy', *British Journal of Political Science*, vol. 5, April 1975.

Samuel Brittan, *The Economic Consequences of Democracy*, Temple Smith, London, 1977.

Samuel Brittan, *The Role and Limits of Government: essays in political economy*, Temple Smith, London, 1983.

J.M. Buchanan, John Burton and R.E. Wagner, *The Consequences of Mr Keynes*, Hobart paper 78, Institute of Economic Affairs, London, 1978.

Ian Budge, David McKay *et al.*, *The New British Political System*, Longman, London, 1983.

Alan Bullock, *The Life and Times of Ernest Bevin, Vol. I, Trade Union Leader, 1881-1940*, Heinemann, London, 1960.

Jim Bulpitt, *Territory and Power in the United Kingdom: An Interpretation*, Manchester University Press, 1983.

John Burton, *Picking Losers ..? The Political Economy of Industrial Policy*, Hobart Paper 99, Institute of Economic Affairs, London, 1983.

David Butler and Donald Stokes, *Political Change in Britain*, Macmillan, London, 1969.

David Butler and Denis Kavanagh, *The British General Election of 1979*, Macmillan, 1980.

Neil K. Buxton and Derek H. Aldcroft (eds.), *British Industry Between the Wars: instability and industrial development 1919-1939*, Scolar Press, London, paperback edition, 1983.

Alec Cairncross, *Years of Recovery: British Economic Policy*, Methuen, London, 1985.

Angus Calder, *The People's War: Britain 1939-45*, Jonathan Cape, London, 1969.

Richard E. Caves *et al.*, *Britain's Economic Prospects*, George Allen & Unwin, London, 1968.

Richard E. Caves and Lawrence B. Krause (eds), *Britain's Economic Performance*, The Brookings Institution, Washington DC., 1980.

Alan Cawson, *Corporatism and Welfare: Social Policy and State Intervention in Britain*, Heinemann Educational, London, 1982.

Alan Cawson, 'Functional representation and democratic politics: towards a corporatist democracy?' in Graeme Duncan (ed.), *Democratic Theory and Practice*, Cambridge University Press, 1983.

A.D. Chandler, *The Visible Hand: The Managerial Revolution in American Business*, Harvard University Press, Cambridge, Mass., 1977.

Carlo M. Cipolla (ed.), *The Fontana Economic History of Europe: The Twentieth Century: Part Two*, Collins/Fontana Books, London, 1976.

Peter Clarke, *Liberals and Social Democrats*, Cambridge University Press, 1978.

Hugh Clegg, *How to Run an Incomes Policy and Why We Made such a Mess of the Last One*, Heinemann, London, 1971.

G.D.H. Cole, *Guild Socialism Re-stated*, Leonard Parsons, London, 1920.

Stefan Collini, 'Hobhouse, Bosanquet and the State', *Past and Present*, no. 72, August 1976.

Commission of the European Communities, *Eurofutures: the challenges of innovation*, (the FAST report) Butterworths, London, 1984.

David Coombes, *Representative Government and Economic Power*, Heinemann Educational, London, 1982.

Ivor Crewe *et al.*, 'Partisan Dealignment in Britain', *British Journal of Political Science*, vol. 7, 1977.

C.A.R. Crosland, *The Future of Socialism*, Jonathan Cape, London, 1956.

Colin Crouch (ed.), *State and Economy in Contemporary Capitalism*, Croom Helm, London, 1979.

Brian Lee Crowley, 'The Limitations of Liberalism: the Self, the Individual and the Community in Modern British Political Thought with special reference to F.A. Hayek and Sidney and Beatrice Webb', London University Ph.D., 1985.

Michel Crozier *et al.*, *The Crisis of Democracy: report on the governability of democracies to the Trilateral Commission*, New York University Press, 1975.

Robert Currie, *Industrial Politics*, Oxford University Press, 1979.

A.V. Dicey, *Introduction to the Study of the Law of the Constitution*, Macmillan, London, 1950 edition.

A.V. Dicey, *Lectures on the Relation Between Law and Opinion in England during the Nineteenth Century*, Macmillan, London, reprinted 1963.

A.W. Dilnot, J.A. Kay and C.N. Morris, *The Reform of Social Security*, Clarendon Press, Oxford, 1984.

Ronald Dore, *British Factory – Japanese Factory: The Origins of National Diversity in Industrial Relations*, University of California Press, Berkeley and Los Angeles, 1973.

Ronald Dore, 'The Confucian Recipe for Industrial Success', *Government and Opposition*, vol. 20, no. 2, spring 1985.

Ronald Dore, 'Industrial Policy and How the Japanese Do It', *Catalyst*, spring 1986.

James Douglas, 'The Overloaded Crown', *British Journal of Political Science*, vol. 6.

Christopher Dow, *The Management of the British Economy 1945–1960*, Cambridge University Press, 1964.

Elizabeth Durbin, *New Jerusalems: The Labour Party and the Economics of Democratic Socialism*, Routledge & Kegan Paul, London, 1985.

Evan Durbin, *The Politics of Democratic Socialism: An Essay on Social Policy*, Routledge & Kegan Paul, London, 1957 impression.

Kenneth Dyson, *The State Tradition in Western Europe: A Study of an Idea and an Institution*, Martin Robertson, Oxford, 1980.

Bernard Elbaum and William Lazonick (eds), *The Decline of the British Economy*, Clarendon Press, Oxford, 1986.

Jon Elster and Aanund Hylland (eds), *Foundations of Social Choice Theory*, Cambridge University Press, 1986.

Gøsta Esping-Andersen, *Politics Against Markets: The Social Democratic Road to Power*, Princeton University Press, New Jersey, 1985.

S.E. Finer (ed.), *Adversary Politics and Electoral Reform*, Anthony Wigram, London, 1975.

R. J. Flanagan, David Soskice and Lloyd Ulman, *Unionism, Economic Stabilisation and Incomes Policies: European Experience*, The Brookings Institution, Washington DC., 1983.

Peter Flora and Arnold J. Heidenheimer, *The Development of Welfare States in Europe and America*, Transaction Books, New Brunswick, New Jersey, paperback edition, 1982.

Roderick Floud and Donald McCloskey (eds), *The Economic History of Britain since 1700, Vol. 2, 1860 to the 1970s*, Cambridge University Press, 1981.

Alan Fox, *History and Heritage: The Social Origins of the British Industrial Relations System*, Allen & Unwin, London, 1985.

Lawrence G. Franko, *The Threat of Japanese Multinationals – How the West Can Respond*, John Wiley & Sons, Chichester, 1983.

Derek Fraser, *Evolution of the British Welfare State*, Macmillan, London, 1973.

Michael Freeden, *The New Liberalism: An Ideology of Social Reform*, Clarendon Press, Oxford, 1978.

C. Freeman and L. Soete, *Information Technology and Employment: An Assessment*, Science Policy Research Unit, University of Sussex, 1985.

Milton Friedman, *Capitalism and Freedom*, University of Chicago Press, reissued 1982.

John G. Gagliardo, *Enlightened Despotism*, Thomas Y. Crowell, New York, 1967.

Andrew Gamble, *Britain in Decline: Economic Policy, Political Strategy and the British State*, Papermac, London, 1981.

Andrew Gamble, 'The Free Economy and the Strong State' in Ralph Miliband and John Savile (eds), *The Socialist Register 1979*, Merlin Press, London, 1979.

A. Gershenkron (ed.), *Economic Backwardness in Historical Perspective*, Harvard University Press, Cambridge, Mass., 1966.

Ian Gilmour, *Britain Can Work*, Martin Robertson, Oxford, 1983.

M. Goldsmith and K. Newton, 'Central-Local Relations: The Irresistible Rise of Centralised Power', in H. Berrington (ed.), *Change in British Politics*, Cass, London, 1984.

John H. Goldthorpe (ed.), *Order and Conflict in Contemporary Capitalism*, Clarendon Press, Oxford, 1984.

Geoffrey Goodman, *The Awkward Warrior Frank Cousins: His Life and Times*, Spokesman, Nottingham, 1979.

Ian Gough, *The Political Economy of the Welfare State*, Macmillan, 1979.

Wyn Grant and David Marsh, *The Confederation of British Industry*, Hodder & Stoughton, London, 1977.

Wyn Grant (ed.), *The Political Economy of Corporatism*, Macmillan, London, 1985.

W.H. Greenleaf, *The British Political Tradition* (two volumes), Methuen, London, 1983.

Lord Hailsham, *The Dilemma of Democracy*, Collins, London, 1978.

Elie Halevy, *A history of the English People in the Nineteenth Century, Vol. V, Imperialism and the Rise of Labour*, Ernest Benn, London, second edition, 1951.

W.K. Hancock and M.M. Gowing, *The British War Economy*, HMSO, London, 1949.

Leslie Hannah, *The Rise of the Corporate Economy*, Methuen, London, second edition, 1983.

Karl Hardach, *The Political Economy of Germany in the Twentieth Century*, University of California Press, Berkeley, California, 1980.

José Harris, *William Beveridge: A Biography*, Clarendon Press, Oxford, 1977

Vivien Hart, *Distrust and Democracy: Political Distrust in Britain and America*, Cambridge University Press, 1978.

F.A. Hayek, *The Road to Serfdom*, republished by University of Chicago Press, 1976.

F.A. Hayek, *The Constitution of Liberty*, Routledge & Kegan Paul, London, reprinted 1976.

F.A. Hayek, *Law, Legislation and Liberty* (three volumes), Routledge & Kegan Paul, London, 1979.

F.A. Hayek, *1980s Unemployment and the Unions: The Distortion of Relative Prices by Monopoly in the Labour Market*, Hobart Paper 87, Institute of Economic Affairs, London, second edition 1984.

David Heald, *Public Expenditure*, Martin Robertson, Oxford, 1983.

Anthony Heath, Roger Jowell and John Curtice, *How Britain Votes*, Pergamon, Oxford, 1985.

Hugh Heclo and Aaron Wildavsky, *The Private Government of Public Money: Community and Policy inside British Politics*, Macmillan, second edition, London, 1981.

W.O. Henderson, *The State and the Industrial Revolution in Prussia 1740–1870*, Liverpool University Press.

W.O. Henderson, *The Rise of German Industrial Power 1834–1914*, Temple Smith, London, 1975.

Christopher Hill, *The Century of Revolutions 1603–1714*, Thomas Nelson, Edinburgh, 1961.

Gertrude Himmelfarb, *The Idea of Poverty: England in the Early Industrial Age*, Faber & Faber, London, 1984.

Fred Hirsch and John H. Goldthorpe (eds), *The Political Economy of Inflation*, Martin Robertson, London, 1978.

Albert O. Hirschman, *The Passions and the Interests: Political Arguments for Capitalism before Its Triumph*, Princeton University Press, 1977.

J. Hirschmeier and T. Yui, *The Development of Japanese Business 1600–1980*, Allen & Unwin, London, 1981.

L.T. Hobhouse, *Liberalism*, Home University Library, London, 1911.

Richard Hoggart, *The Uses of Literacy*, Chatto & Windus, London, 1957.

Stuart Holland, *The Socialist Challenge*, Quartet Books, London, 1975.

Martin Holmes, *The Labour Government, 1974–79: Political Aims and Economic Reality*, Macmillan, London, 1985.

Sir John Hoskyns, 'Conservatism is Not Enough', *The Political Quarterly*, vol. 55, no. 1, January–March 1984.

House of Lords, Session 1984–85, Report from the Select Committee on Overseas Trade, (the 'Aldington Report') vol. 1, *Report*, HMSO, London, 30 July 1985.

Ronald Inglehart, *The Silent Revolution: Changing Values and Political Styles Among Western Publics*, Princeton University Press, New Jersey, 1977.

Institute of Economic Affairs, *The Taming of Government*, IEA Readings 21, Institute of Economic Affairs, London, 1979.

Ghita Ionescu, *Centripetal Politics: Government and the New Centres of Power*, Hart-Davis MacGibbon, London, 1975.

Ghita Ionescu, *Politics and the Pursuit of Happiness: An inquiry into the involvement of human beings in the politics of industrial society*, Longmans, London, 1984.

W.H. Janeway, 'The Economic Policy of the Second Labour Government 1929–1931', Cambridge University Ph.D. thesis, n.d.

Douglas Jay, *The Socialist Case*, Faber & Faber, London, 1937.

Richard Jay, *Joseph Chamberlain: A Political Study*, Clarendon Press, Oxford, 1981.

Chalmers Johnson, *MITI and the Japanese Miracle: The Growth of Industrial Policy, 1925–1975*, Stanford University Press, Stanford, California, 1982.

Aubrey Jones, *The New Inflation: the politics of prices and incomes*, Penguin Books, Harmondsworth, 1973.

Sir Keith Joseph, *Reversing the Trend – a Critical Re-appraisal of Conservative Economic and Social Policies*, Barry Rose, Chichester and London, 1975.

Sir Keith Joseph, *Stranded on the Middle Ground*, Centre for Policy Studies, London, 1976.

Jeffrey Jowell and Dawn Oliver (eds), *The Changing Constitution*, Clarendon Press, Oxford, 1985.

Denis Kavanagh, 'The Deferential English: A Comparative Critique', *Government and Opposition*, vol. 6, 1971.

William Keegan, *Mrs Thatcher's Economic Experiment*, Penguin Books, Harmondsworth, 1984.

John Maynard Keynes, *The Economic Consequences of Mr Churchill*, Hogarth Press, London, 1925.

John Maynard Keynes, *The General Theory of Employment, Interest and Money*, Macmillan, London, 1954.

Anthony King, 'Overload: Problems of Governing in the 1970s', *Political Studies*, vol. 23, 1975.

M.W. Kirby, *The Decline of British Economic Power since 1870*, George Allen & Unwin, London, 1981.

Richard F. Kuisel, *Capitalism and the State in Modern France: renovation and economic management in the twentieth century*, Cambridge University Press, 1981.

David Landes, *The Unbound Prometheus: Technological Change and Industrial Development in Western Europe from 1750 to the Present*, Cambridge University Press, 1969.

Dick Leonard, 'Paying for Party Politics', (PEP broadsheet no. 555), Political and Economic Planning, London, 1975.

Jacques Leruez, *Economic Planning and Politics in Britain*, (trans. Martin Harrison), Martin Robertson, London, 1975.

Anthony Lester, 'Fundamental Rights in the United Kingdom: the Law and the British Constitution', *University of Pennsylvania Law Review*, vol. 125, no. 2, December 1976.

W.A. Lewis, *Growth and Fluctuations 1870–1913*, George Allen & Unwin, 1978.

Colin Leys, *Politics in Britain: An Introduction*, Heinemann Educational, London, 1983.

Liberal Party, *Britain's Industrial Future: being the report of the Liberal Industrial Inquiry of 1928*, Ernest Benn, London, second impression 1977.

Arend Lijphart, *Democracy in Plural Societies: A Comparative Exploration*, Yale University Press, New Haven and London, second printing, 1980.

Leon N. Lindberg and Charles S. Maier (eds), *The Politics of Inflation and Economic Stagnation*, The Brookings Institution, Washington D C., 1985.

Charles E. Lindblom, *Politics and Markets: The World's Political-Economic Systems*, Basic Books, New York, 1977.

Seymour Martin Lipset, *The First New Nation: the United States in Historical and Comparative Perspective*, Heinemann, London, 1964.

Friedrich List, *The National System of Political Economy* (trans. Sampson S. Lloyd), Longmans Green, London, 1909.

Konrad Lorenz (trans. Marjorie Latzke), *On Aggression*, Methuen, London, 1979.

F.S.L. Lyons, *Ireland Since the Famine*, Fontana, London, 1973.

J.P. Mackintosh, *The Government and Politics of Britain*, Hutchinson, London, 1977 edition.

Alasdair Macintyre, *After Virtue: a study in moral theory*, Duckworth, London, second edition, 1985.

Harold Macmillan, *The Middle Way: A Study of the Problem of Economic and Social Progress in a Free and Democratic Society*, Macmillan, London, 1938, reissued 1966.

C.B. Macpherson, *The Political Theory of Possessive Individualism: Hobbes to Locke*, Oxford University Press, paperback edition, 1985.

Angus Maddison, *Phases of Capitalist Development*, Oxford University Press, New York, 1982.

Ira C. Magaziner and Thomas M. Hout, *Japanese Industrial Policy*, Policy Studies Institute, London, January, 1980.

Alfred Maizels, *Growth and Trade*, Cambridge University Press, 1970.

Alistair Mant, *The Rise and Fall of the British Manager*, Pan Books, London, 1979.

David Marquand, *Ramsay MacDonald*, Jonathan Cape, London, 1977.

David Marquand (ed.), *John P. Mackintosh on Parliament and Social Democracy*, Longman, London, 1982.

Judith Marquand, *The Sources of Economic Growth: Learning and Change in the Information Age*, Wheatsheaf, Brighton (forthcoming).

Alan Marsh, *Protest and Political Consciousness*, Sage Publications, London and Beverly Hills, 1977.

T.H. Marshall, *Citizenship and Social Class and other Essays*, Cambridge University Press, 1950.

Peter Mathias, *The First Industrial Nation: An Economic History of Britain*, Methuen, New York, 1983.

Arthur Marwick, 'Middle Opinion in the Thirties: Planning, Progress and Political "Agreement"', *English Historical Review*, vol. lxxix, 1964.

Michael Meacher, *Socialism with a Human Face: the political economy of Britain in the 1980s*, George Allen & Unwin, London, 1982.

Keith Middlemas and John Barnes, *Baldwin: A Biography*, Weidenfeld & Nicolson, London, 1969.

Keith Middlemas, *Politics in Industrial Society: The Experience of the British System since 1911*, André Deutsch, London, 1979.

Keith Middlemas, *Industry, Unions and Government: Twenty-One Years of NEDC*, Macmillan, London, 1983.

Mary Midgley, *Beast and Man: The Roots of Human Nature*, Methuen, London, 1980.

John Stuart Mill, *Principles of Political Economy*, Routledge & Sons, London, 1903 edition.

Ramon Mishra, *The Welfare State in Crisis: Social Thought and Social Change*, Wheatsheaf, Brighton, 1984.

Joan Mitchell, *Groundwork to Economic Planning*, Secker & Warburg, London, 1966.

Janet P. Morgan, *The House of Lords and the Labour Government*, Clarendon Press, Oxford, 1975.

Kenneth Morgan, *Labour in Power 1945–51*, Clarendon Press, Oxford, 1984.

Takafusa ·Nakamura (trans. Robert A. Feldman), *Economic Growth in Prewar Japan*, Yale University Press, New Haven and London, 1983.

National Economic Development Council, *Information Technology*, NEDC (84) 40, 22 May 1984.

Philip Norton, *Conservative Dissidents*, Temple Smith, London, 1978.

Philip Norton, *Dissension in the House of Commons 1974–1979*, Clarendon Press, Oxford, 1980.

Claus Offe, *Contradictions of the Welfare State*, (ed. John Keane), Hutchinson, London, 1984.

James O'Connor, *The Fiscal Crisis of the State*, St Martin's Press, New York, 1975.

Mancur Olson, *The Rise and Decline of Nations*, Yale University Press, New Haven and London, 1982.

Peter Oppenheimer, 'Muddling Through: the Economy 1951–64' in V.Bogdanor and R.J. Skidelsky (eds), *The Age of Affluence*, Macmillan, London, 1970.

Carole Pateman, *Participation and Democratic Theory*, Cambridge University Press, 1970.

Keith Pavitt (ed.), *Technical Innovation and British Economic Performance*, Macmillan, London, 1980.

Alan T. Peacock and Jack Wiseman, *The Growth of Public Expenditure in the United Kingdom*, Oxford University Press, London, 1961.

Henry Pelling, *Popular Politics and Society in Late-Victorian Britain*, Macmillan, London, 1968.

Eustace Percy, first Baron Percy of Newcastle, *Democracy on Trial: a preface to an industrial policy*, John Lane, The Bodley Head, London, 1931.

Harold Perkin, *The Origins of Modern English Society 1780–1880*, Routledge & Kegan Paul, paperback edition, London, 1972.

Harold Perkin, 'The State and Economic Growth: an International Perspective', lecture delivered at Salford University, 15 September 1983.

Henry Phelps Brown, *The Origins of Trade Union Power*, Oxford University Press, 1986.

Michael J. Piore and Charles Sabel, *The Second Industrial Divide: Possibilities for Prosperity*, Basic Books, New York, 1984.

Leo Pliatzky, *Getting and Spending: Public Expenditure, Employment and Inflation*, Basil Blackwell, Oxford, revised edition, 1984.

J.G.A. Pocock (ed.), *The Three British Revolutions: 1641, 1688, 1776*, Princeton University Press, Princeton, New Jersey, 1980.

Karl Polanyi, *Origins of Our Time: The Great Transformation*, Victor Gollancz, London, 1945.

Sidney Pollard, *The Development of the British Economy 1914–1980*, Edward Arnold, London, 1983.

John Rawls, *A Theory of Justice*, Clarendon Press, Oxford, 1972.

Robert Reich, *The Next American Frontier: a provocative program for economic renewal*, Penguin Books, New York, 1984.

H.W. Richardson, 'The basis of economic recovery in the nineteen-thirties: a review and a new interpretation', *Economic History Review*, 2nd Series, vol. 15, 1962–3.

J.J. Richardson and A.G. Jordan, *Governing Under Pressure: The Policy Process in a Post-Parliamentary Democracy*, Martin Robertson, Oxford, 1979.

Richard Rose and Guy Peters, *Can Government Go Bankrupt?* Macmillan, London, 1979.

Richard Rose, 'Ungovernability: is there fire behind the smoke?', *Political Studies*, vol. 27, 1979.

Royal Commission on the Constitution 1968–1973, (the Kilbrandon Commission) vols I and II, HMSO, London, October 1973, Cmnd. 5460 and 5460–I.

Sir Leslie Scarman, *English Law: the New Dimension*, Stevens & Sons, London, 1975.

Richard Scase, *Social Democracy in Capitalist Society: Working-Class Politics in Britain and Sweden*, Croom Helm, London, 1977.

Philippe C. Schmitter and Gerhard Lehmbruch (eds), *Trends Towards*

Corporatist Intermediation, Sage Publications, London and Beverly Hills, 1979.

Philippe C. Schmitter and Gerhard Lehmbruch (eds), *Patterns of Corporatist Policy Making*, Sage Publications, London and Beverly Hills, 1982.

Donald Schon, *Beyond the Stable State*, Temple Smith, London, 1971.

Joseph Schumpeter, *Capitalism, Socialism and Democracy*, George Allen & Unwin, London, 1979 impression.

G.R. Searle, *The Quest for National Efficiency: A Study in British Politics and Political Thought*, Basil Blackwell, Oxford, 1971.

Brian Sedgemore, *The Secret Constitution: An Analysis of the Political Establishment*, Hodder & Stoughton, London, 1980.

Bernard Semmel, *Imperialism and Social Reform: English Social-Imperial Thought 1895–1914*, Allen & Unwin, London, 1960.

Bernard Semmel, *The Rise of Free Trade Imperialism: Classical Political Economy, The Empire of Free Trade and Imperialism*, Cambridge University Press, 1970.

Margaret Sharp, Geoffrey Shepherd and David Marsden, 'Structural Adjustment in the United Kingdom Manufacturing Industry', World Employment Programme research working paper, ILO, Geneva, 1983.

Andrew Shonfield, *Modern Capitalism: The Changing Balance of Public and Private Power*, Oxford University Press, London, 1965.

Andrew Shonfield (ed. Zuzanna Shonfield), *The Use of Public Power*, Oxford University Press, 1982.

Andrew Shonfield (ed. Zuzanna Shonfield), *In Defence of the Mixed Economy*, Oxford University Press, 1984.

H.A. Simon, *The Sciences of the Artificial*, M.I.T. Press, Cambridge, Mass., 1969.

R.J. Skidelsky, *Politicians and the Slump: the Labour Government of 1929–1931*, Macmillan, London, 1967.

Adam Smith, *An Inquiry into the Nature and Causes of the Wealth of Nations*, ed. with an introduction by Edwin Cannan, University of Chicago Press, 1976.

Trevor Smith, *The Politics of the Corporate Economy*, Martin Robertson, Oxford, 1979.

Michael Stewart, *The Jekyll and Hyde Years, Politics and Economic Policy since 1964*, J.M. Dent, London, 1977.

Michael Stewart, *Controlling the Economic Future: Policy Dilemmas in a Shrinking World*, Wheatsheaf, Brighton, 1983.

Wolfgang Streeck, *Industrial Relations in West Germany: A Case Study of the Car Industry*, Heinemann, London, 1984.

Wolfgang Streeck and Philippe C. Schmitter (eds), *Private Interest Government: Beyond Market and State*, Sage Publications, London, 1985.

Donley T. Studlar and Jerold L. Waltman, *Dilemmas of Change in British Politics*, Macmillan, London, 1984.

R.H. Tawney, *The Acquisitive Society*, G. Bell & Sons, London, 1922.

E.P. Thompson, 'The Moral Economy of the English Crowd in the Eighteenth Century', *Past and Present*, no. 50, 1971.

Noel W. Thompson, *The People's Science: the popular political economy of exploitation and crisis 1816–34*, Cambridge University Press, 1984.

Lester Thurow, *The Zero-Sum Society: Distribution and the Possibilities for Economic Change*, Penguin Books, Harmondsworth, 1981.

Lester Thurow, *Dangerous Currents: The State of Economics*, Vintage Books, New York, 1984.

Charles Tilley (ed.), *The Formation of National States in Western Europe*, Princeton University Press, New Jersey, 1975.

Gordon Tullock, *The Vote Motive*, Hobart paperback 9, Institute of Economic Affairs, London, 1976.

Colin Turnbull, *The Mountain People*, Triad/Paladin edition, London, 1984.

Sidney and Beatrice Webb, *A Constitution for the Socialist Commonwealth of Great Britain*, Longmans Green, London, 1920.

Max Weber, *The Theory of Social and Economic Organisation*, ed. with an introduction by Talcott Parsons, The Free Press, New York, 1947.

Martin J. Wiener, *English Culture and the Decline of the Industrial Spirit 1850–1980*, Cambridge University Press, 1981.

G.D.N. Worswick and P. Ady (eds), *The British Economy in the Nineteen-Fifties*, Clarendon Press, Oxford, 1962.

Barbara Wootton, *Freedom Under Planning*, George Allen & Unwin, London, 1945.

John Zysman, *Governments, Markets and Growth: Financial Systems and the Politics of Industrial Change*, Cornell University Press, Ithaca and London, 1983.

Index

NOTE: References in bold indicate a chapter on the subject